MAGIC
POWER
LANGUAGE
SYMBOL

About the Author

Patrick Dunn has studied witchcraft, the Qabalah, chaos magic, and anything else he can get his hands on. In addition to obtaining his PhD in literature, he has studied linguistics and stylistics. He lives in Illinois, where he teaches English literature. Dunn is also the author of *Postmodern Magic: The Art of Magic in the Information Age*.

To Write to the Author

If you wish to contact the author or would like more information about this book, please write to the author in care of Llewellyn Worldwide and we will forward your request. Both the author and publisher appreciate hearing from you and learning of your enjoyment of this book and how it has helped you. Llewellyn Worldwide cannot guarantee that every letter written to the author can be answered, but all will be forwarded. Please write to:

Patrick Dunn
⅟ Llewellyn Worldwide
2143 Wooddale Drive, Dept. 978-0-7387-1360-1
Woodbury, MN 55125-2989, U.S.A.
Please enclose a self-addressed stamped envelope for reply,
or $1.00 to cover costs. If outside the U.S.A., enclose
an international postal reply coupon.

Many of Llewellyn's authors have websites with additional information and resources. For more information, please visit our website at http://www.llewellyn.com.

MAGIC
POWER
LANGUAGE
SYMBOL

A MAGICIAN'S
EXPLORATION OF
LINGUISTICS

Llewellyn Publications
Woodbury, Minnesota

First Edition
First Printing, 2008

Book design by Steffani Sawyer
Editing by Brett Fechheimer
Cover art © 2008 by Brand X
Cover design by Gavin Dayton Duffy
Interior illustrations by the Llewellyn Art Department
Llewellyn is a registered trademark of Llewellyn Worldwide, Ltd.

The Library of Congress Cataloging-in-Publication Data for *Magic, Power, Language, Symbol: A Magician's Exploration of Linguistics* is pending.
    ISBN-13: 978-0-7387-1360-1

Llewellyn Publications
A Division of Llewellyn Worldwide, Ltd.
2143 Wooddale Drive, Dept. 978-0-7387-1360-1
Woodbury, Minnesota 55125-2989, U.S.A.
www.llewellyn.com

Printed in the United States of America

For Eric

Acknowledgments

People write books for many reasons: desire for fame, desire for money, desire to fill a gap in knowledge, desire to see their name in print, temporary insanity, divine command . . .

But people help other people write books for one reason: they care. Thank you:

Mom: for everything, from morel hunting to tarot cards to last week's phone call.

Chris: for reading the manuscript and offering your suggestions. I can say with certainty that they improved the book tremendously.

Eric: for evenings of coffee, books, and philosophical arguments. Your comments about the semiotic web and reductive materialism gave me the impetus to write this book. And you turned me on to Buber, as well.

Ed: for years of good debates about magic, religion, and rationality, good suggestions about music and reading material, as well as the computer program that saved me hours of work on this particular book.

Peter: for your friendship and suggestions. Thanks especially for listening politely when I go on about irregular Hebrew verbs and the like.

Betty: for margaritas and conversations, not to mention suggesting half of the linguistics articles and books that appear in this one's works cited.

Richard: for making my life beautiful, giving me faith in myself, and loving me as I love you—with a love that holds the stars in place.

Also thank you to various spirits whom I will not name here, as well as gods, daemons, angels, ascended masters, and what all else I have no idea exists, but may: in other words, however the undifferentiated substance of infinite qualities manifests to my little dual mind: thanks.

I'm also one of those people who writes with a soundtrack. Therefore, thanks to the following musicians, who didn't know that they helped me write this book, but did:

The Adicts
Apocalypse Hoboken
Atmosphere
Cake
Cramps
Dropkick Murphys
Eddie and the Hot Rods
The Faint
Guttermouth
Jets to Brazil
mc chris
Motion City Soundtrack
Mouthwash
Nirvana
Operation Ivy
Pitchshifter
The Pogues
The Ramones
Rancid
Randy
Soul Coughing
The Streets
The Strokes

Contents

Introduction

If you're looking for magical words, you really can't do better than *abracadabra!* No one really knows what abracadabra means, if it ever meant anything. Its earliest mention is in a recipe for an amulet. Why this word—out of countless words engraved on charms, talismans, and tablets from the ancient world—survived is a mystery as well. Why do stage magicians not shout, for example, "Abrasax!" or "Abalatha!" Why abracadabra?

I fantasize that perhaps the word itself ensured its survival and popularity. Perhaps it serves as a reminder that real magic, no matter what stage magicians do with their trickery, still exists. Abracadabra could provide the key to magic.

One possible origin for the word is an Aramaic phrase: *avra kedabra.* This sentence means "I create as I speak." Aramaic is a language closely related to Hebrew; Jesus, when he spoke to friends and relatives and God, spoke Aramaic. The verb *avra,* "I create," in Aramaic is cognate with the verb *evra* in Hebrew. But Hebrew makes a distinction between different types of creation: if you make something from nothing, you say "evra," but if you make something from something else, you say "etzor."

So abracadabra is saying, "I create something from nothing when I speak, just as my words come from nothing." Yet in the relevant cosmologies, only God can create out of nothing. *Evra* is a verb for God to use, not humans. Therefore, to say *abracadabra* is to speak an incantation of apotheosis.

I don't care much about apotheosis. But I do care about language and magic. There are six thousand languages on Earth, give or take, and every healthy child will learn at least one of them. Children learn language effortlessly, without study or memorization, and while they sometimes make amusing mistakes, they make far fewer than any adult learning a new language would. The speed with which children learn language is evidence that there's something about it that's ingrained in our makeup as humans.

Magic is not as universal as language, but it comes close. Most cultures have some concept of magic, and the majority of people on Earth believe in it to a greater or lesser degree. Some materialists might deplore that state of affairs as evidence of regrettable ignorance. But clearly, just as there is something inborn in humans that compels us to learn language, there's also something inherent in humans that encourages us to learn magic.

My goal in this book is to explore the ways in which magic and language interact with each other. Attitudes toward language not only shape magic in the past and present, but the sciences of linguistics and semiotics illuminate the study of magic in interesting ways. After my first book, many people wrote to me expressing a desire for a more scholarly treatment. Yet I did not want to write a book of mere scholarship; I wanted to write something practical as well as edifying. My first book contained many exercises and rituals; this book contains few. My first book contained techniques; this one contains theories. Yet the magician seeking practical techniques or even spells won't come away empty-handed. On the contrary, this book contains information on the structure of incantations, glossolalia, evocation and invocation, mantras, and meditation. For those who want techniques, this book explores them in greater depth than would a book of mere step-by-step instructions.

In the first chapter I discuss how the theories of linguistics and semiotics shed light on the practice of magic in surprising ways. Here I introduce the idea of the semiotic web, and how to use it for more effective magic. I also offer a theory of magic that involves re-creating our semiotic codes, by which we interpret reality, every time we do magic.

The second chapter continues the first by explaining the way in which language bridges the world of matter and the world of mind. Again, I provide some summary of the theory of phonetics to explore the nature of magical sounds.

The third chapter covers incantations. Here, I explore traditional incantations from various sources, ranging from traditional Irish and Scottish musical charms to Old English and Vedic charms. I analyze their structure and the surprisingly significant things they have in common, despite their far-flung origins. The reader seeking tips on creating spoken magical charms might find this chapter useful.

The next chapter, chapter 4, explores the flip side of incantations: written magical signs and sigils. In my last book I discussed the *defixio*, a very simple form of magic; here I go into greater depth, showing what a postmodern defixio working can look like.

In the fifth chapter, "From Babel to Enochian: The Search for the Primal Language," I explore attempts to arrive at an original language, both scientific and magical. I provide some tips for composing in Enochian, and a method for expanding Enochian vocabulary through basic linguistic principles of compounding and derivation.

In the sixth chapter I talk about another way of arriving at a primal language: *glossolalia*, or speaking in tongues. I discuss the use of this undervalued technique in various magical operations.

In the seventh chapter, "The Qabalah: The Grammar of Number," I explain the basic operations of gematria. I also discuss the existence of an English Qabalah. Appendix 1 contains an English qabalistic dictionary.

In the eighth chapter I explain the traditional and more contemporary uses of the mantra or formula of power. Linguists rarely study mantras, but certain linguistic phenomena, including semantic satiation, help explain how mantras—and perhaps much magic—work. I discuss how to arrive at and create new mantras and formulas, and how to employ them in magic.

Chapter 9 discusses the structure of ritual as a type of myth or narrative. The study of narrative and myth, as well as contemporary thought on metaphor, helps explain how we view the world, and how we can go about changing it.

The final chapter explains how the stories we tell ourselves, inwardly, sometimes hold us back from effective magic. I end by discussing how language seems to bar us from the infinite, but can also be used to open doorways into mystery.

In opening that door, I'm hoping this book can act not as a key but perhaps as a key ring. Everyone's key to enlightenment is different, but one thing we share in common, no matter how much we differ, is language. We all create as we speak. May you find your magical word, your *abracadabra*.

ONE

The Theory of Symbols: The Practice of Magic

Every art distinguishes between theory and practice. One may practice an art without studying its theory, and one may study its theory without practicing the art. Ideally, however, theory informs practice and practice tests theory. In magic, some people are interested only in the practical side; these are people who, when faced with a problem, find a spell to solve it and go on with their lives. That approach isn't wrong. I, however, enjoy speculating about theories of magic. Sometimes people dismiss theory as useless, and if it never leads to practice, it can be. But theory provides the foundation stones out of which we can build our own ideas of magic.

The role of magical theory, and its differences from scientific theory, is the focus of Ramsey Dukes's *S.S.O.T.B.M.E.*, and since a new edition of that book has recently been published, I won't repeat its material here.[1] I will mention, however, that Dukes explores some differences between

---

1. Ramsey Dukes, *S.S.O.T.B.M.E. Revised: An Essay on Magic.* London: The Mouse That Spins, 2002 (third revised edition).

scientific theory and magical theory that might be useful in a study of the role of language in magic. Dukes points out that for a scientific theory to be useful, it needs to be falsifiable. In other words, it needs to contain predictions that can be proven wrong through observation. For example, part of Newton's physics is that time is a constant. Einstein theorized that time is not a constant but varies according to one's viewpoint in relation to the speed of light. According to Einstein, if two twins were separated and one was sent on a trip at a significant fraction of the speed of light, when that twin returned he would find his stay-at-home brother had aged much more than he had. This prediction, while it looks unlikely, can be tested. We can separate two carefully calibrated clocks, for example, and accelerate one to a considerable speed (not to the speed of light as that's well beyond our capabilities), and then compare them. In fact, this experiment has been done and has falsified Newton's physics and endorsed Einstein's.[2]

Science's approach to theory is falsification, but magic's approach is relation. Counterintuitively, all scientific theories strive to be proven wrong, and the failure to do so over time makes them stronger and stronger. Dukes argues that magical theories are not falsifiable in the same way. Instead, rather than making predictions that can be falsified, they describe experiences that a magician can try to relate to. Rather than seeking the flaw in a magical theory, a magician seeks something that's true in it. What this means is that magicians have multiple, conflicting, and sometimes even silly theories about magic, all of which have personal value. Obviously, what I value in a theory you may not, and vice versa. But once we find some truth in a magical theory we can use it, not to make predictions in the scientific sense but to structure magical operations. For example, if I believe in spirits, and I find some truth in a magical theory that describes spirits, I can try to summon and communicate with them. Only a fool would argue that we should abolish the scientific approach to falsifiability; in reality, we need both approaches to truly understand reality.

---

2.   J. C. Hafele and R. E. Keating used an aircraft and a set of carefully calibrated clocks. Their experimental write-up can be found in "Around-the-World Atomic Clocks: Predicted Relativistic Time Gains." *Science* 177 (1972), 166–177.

My goal in this book is to provide some interesting new theories about magic, as well as explore the role of language in magic from a practical standpoint. There won't, however, be any spells per se in this book. Spells grow out of theory. If your theory is that a magical energy exists and is responsible for magic, then obviously your spell will look different from someone's who believes that there are spirits responsible for magic. I will include discussions of how people in various magical and religious traditions have used language in interesting and unique ways, what the science of linguistics and specifically the field of semiotics[3] has to say about such things, and some exercises and experiments you can try—not to falsify the theories I suggest, but to see if you can find something in them that resonates for you.

Before we get to the meat of magic, let's have a couple scoops of mundane dressing. Any intelligent conversation about the role of language in magic is going to require an understanding of the role of language in more ordinary settings. Science approaches language in two ways: linguistics and semiotics. Linguistics studies three branches of language: semantics (the meaning of individual words), syntax (how words fit together to make sentences), and pragmatics (how language is used in real life). I will refer to various theories of linguistics from time to time in this book, but I want to point out that this book is making no linguistic claims, only magical ones. Semiotics, the second way of studying language, is the formal study of symbols and signs. This study includes more, obviously, than mere language—it also includes graphics, visual rhetoric (the way, for example, advertisements are laid out), and body language. Semiotics is almost untapped as a field for elucidating and creating magical theory. My goal is to present it, and linguistic theory, in such a way that you will, if so inclined, be able to make your own personally appealing magical theories out of the material.

---

3. The formal study of symbols.

Semiotics: The Science of Signs

Symbols are important to magicians—from the qabalist meditating on the shapes and meanings of the Hebrew letters, to the Hoodoo worker dressing her lodestone, to the chaos magician meditating on a sigil. All of these are symbols, objects that represent something other than what they inherently are. Semiotics is the formal study of such things. This definition might seem straightforward, except that a century of formal study of symbols has revealed that there's nothing straightforward about symbols. For example, we tend to think that there is a class of things that are symbols, and a class of things that aren't symbols. We see the word *tree* and think, "Ah, that's a symbol representing an object in the real world," which is actually one commonly accepted theory of the structure of a symbol. A symbol, says that theory, consists of three parts: the sign, which is the visual or verbal (or sensory in some way) physical object that makes up the symbol; the signified, which is its meaning in the world of ideas; and the physical object to which that idea applies. The problem, as postmodern semioticians such as Jacques Derrida have pointed out, is that there is not a clear distinction between a sign and its signified. A signified may itself be another sign pointing to another signified, and the physical object to which an idea applies is, itself, merely another symbol.

It's difficult to identify what, exactly, any given sign points to. Take the example of *tree*—the word seems to point to an idea in the real world, but show me the actual "tree" to which the word refers. Is it an elm? A poplar? The tree outside your window? The tree outside my window? A tree I used to climb as a child? You might say, "Sure, be a sophist, but everyone knows what I mean when I say 'tree': I mean a class of objects that shares similarities." What are those similarities, however? At what exact height does a shrub, for example, become a tree? The category "tree" that we claim is an actual physical thing is just a collection of experiences we have labeled together. In some languages there is no equivalent word for *tree*—instead, you must name the exact type of tree you're speaking of. The class of "tree" is just as arbitrary as any other idea we might point to with symbols. This arbitrary nature of symbols becomes apparent when you compare different languages. For example, in English we have two words for pig: when it's alive, it's a pig, and when it's dead, it's pork. But other languages have just one word for these same things. So which of us is right? Both. In reality, there are only arbitrary distinctions to be made.[4]

According to postmodernists, everything is a symbol. I've sometimes seen the criticism, "If everything is just symbolic, then we can act any way we want and hurt anyone we want!" It's difficult to get one's mind around what postmodernists are saying about reality. They are not saying, "Everything is just a symbol," because that word *just* implies that there's something that isn't a symbol, something more real than the symbol. There isn't. *Symbol* doesn't mean non-real to the postmodernist; it means really real. There's no other way to be real than symbolically. So if we hurt something, we really hurt them, even if they are symbols and our actions are symbols—they're still symbols that hurt. The advantage of recognizing the symbolic nature of reality is that we can make choices about the way that we interpret it, which could make us less vulnerable to being hurt. We can also be more conscious that what we observe is not necessarily what we interpret. If we see someone cut us off in traffic, being aware of the symbolic nature of reality we don't need to automatically assume that they are a jerk. That act could symbolize that they are in a rush to take someone to the hospital, or that they are late for an important appointment, or that they are just having a bad day.

Postmodernists are also, mostly, not denying the existence of reality or, necessarily, the existence of a reality beyond the symbol. Perhaps there's a reality that isn't symbolic, but we, as symbolic creatures, can never experience that reality. And even if we could experience it, we couldn't actually talk about it. Interestingly, one of the characteristics of many religious experiences is an inability to talk about them or describe them in symbols. Anything we can talk about is, by definition, symbolic, because anything we talk about is something we have translated into symbols (i.e., words).

---

4.   I can imagine a reader saying, "It's not so arbitrary for the poor pig!" and that's true. Some of these arbitrary distinctions break down along fairly reasonable lines; the difference between a dead pig and a living pig is a pretty obvious difference. But other arbitrary distinctions are less salient. For example, we have separate names for people with certain skin colors, but not for people who can and cannot wiggle their ears or roll their tongues.

We cannot experience something without experiencing it as a symbol, and we develop ways of dealing with symbols, called "codes." Codes are simply frameworks into which we place our symbols. Language itself is a code, but many codes are not so formal. If you're watching a movie and the director chooses to tilt the camera slightly (a "Dutch angle"), that's a code that you're supposed to read the main character as confused or disoriented.[5] When a novel begins "Ted got out of his Ford Focus and stretched," we know that Ted is likely to be the main character. But if someone said that sentence to you in conversation, you would be compelled to ask, "Who's Ted?" In a novel, treating the main character as if the reader already has some knowledge of him or her is a code. We rarely think about the codes we use to interpret symbols; we learn most of them so early and so effortlessly that we rarely need to. But codes, like the symbols they interpret, are mostly arbitrary. Movies in the 1930s and '40s often showed people walking from one location to another—from the car to a front door, for example; now we use an arbitrary code, a jump cut, to indicate the same sort of motion. We have such codes in language, too. When you ask your friend, "Can you pass the salt?" he or she knows the code that, when you ask an irrelevant question about ability, you're actually making a request.

Some codes are particularly relevant to magic. These aren't artistic or linguistic codes, but codes that frame the way we experience reality. Try an experiment: go for a short walk, perhaps around the house, but fix your eyes as straight-ahead and unmovingly as you can. Pay attention especially to the edge of your vision; you will notice that, with each step, your vision bounces and jerks. In fact, such bouncing and jerking is going on constantly as we move, but we have a code that filters it out so we have the experience of smooth fields of vision without bouncing around. If you hold a video camera up on your shoulder and walk around in the same way, you'll notice that the film is also jerky and wobbly. Some people, watching such poorly shot videos, complain that the

---

5.   Sometimes such codes backfire, especially when they become obvious. Many of the negative reviews for the movie *Battlefield Earth*, for example, mentioned the overuse of this particular code.

motion makes them seasick, but they experience the same sort of jerky visual field every time they walk somewhere. They just compensate with eye motion and psychological codes that cancel it out. Another way to experience a code that changes the way we experience reality is to stare at a single point ahead of you until your depth perception goes away. We have the illusion of depth not just because of our binocular vision, but because we expect to. It is part of the code by which we perceive reality.

These codes are probably at least somewhat ingrained in us from birth. After all, there's an evolutionary advantage to a smooth field of vision, and the illusion of depth provides us with plenty of advantages. But there's some historical evidence that even these codes, which seem so natural and biological, change over time. For example, some argue that pre-Renaissance paintings have no concept of depth perception, but a closer examination shows that there is merely a different code employed. For example, objects higher in the painting are often farther away. On the other hand, our current codes for depicting depth perception in two-dimensional paintings involve a complex mathematical relationship between size and foreshortening. However, both such codes are merely illusions of depth perception, a two-dimensional depicting of the way that we perceive the world. While the later code is perhaps a bit closer to our own perceptual code, it is still a perceptual code and not an objective part of reality.

We also have codes that have nothing to do with the way that we interact with matter. For instance, we have codes about our attitudes toward sex.[6] When you strip sex of all its codes, it is the rubbing together of certain mucous membranes in order to cause a reaction in nerve cells that leads to muscle spasms in certain parts of the body, which we interpret as pleasurable. And to the materialist[7] that's all that sex is. But in reality, we have so many codes around this act that my description above reads as bizarre—it is not even clinical; it is alien. Some people regard sex as a way to connect emotionally with another person. Others regard it as a means of dealing with issues of power and submission. Still others regard it merely

---

6. I could have used almost anything here, of course, such as money, time, or love.

7. By "materialist" here and elsewhere, I mean the philosophy that holds that only matter exists. The big, boring enemy of magic.

as physical exercise. But notice that even regarding sex as mere physical exercise is not the same as regarding it without codes—after all, physical exercise is an idea. We have notions about exercise; in other words, we have codes that interpret an act as exercise, or as pleasure, or as romance. For many people, our codes are even strong enough to override our own desires. One may *want* to regard sex as a spiritual connection between two people, and instead have a code interpreting it as an affirmation of self-worth or a compulsion. We are not always in complete control of our codes.

What do these codes have to do with magic, then? Magic gives us a way to control our codes, which can change our attitudes about sex, money, and so forth. In that respect, magic is a form of psychology. On the other hand, I'm willing to claim that magic can make objective changes in the real world. Since I've already argued that the real world is ultimately symbolic, it's a small step to argue that changing our codes about reality changes reality. I want to explore how this theory works out in practice.

To begin, let me state the theory as clearly as I can: reality is, at some very deep level, a set of interrelated and self-referencing symbols. We interpret these symbols, and therefore explore reality, according to a set of codes, not all of them conscious. Some codes have a stronger claim than others. We interpret gravity according to a set of formal codes, for example, that clearly and reliably predict its behavior. Many other codes, especially those connected to our day-to-day lives, are less reliable. Some are even detrimental. Changing those codes makes it more likely that we will get what we desire, not just because we will see things in a new and more productive way, but also because reality itself will be affected by our changed codes, bringing new symbols in contact with us. One way of conceiving of codes is as structures in a *semiotic web,* an interlocking set of symbols that reference each other. Later, I will describe how to draw out a model of your semiotic webs so you can make direct changes to it. I want to show how this magical theory works out in practice and then milk it for suggestions for further magical experimentation.

Semiotics and Magic

Let's begin with the simplest, most bare-bones magic: the use of sigils. In brief,[8] a sigil is a monogram in which a desire, spelled out in English, is made into a single symbol by combining letters. Sigils were popular as a magical technology in the 1980s, but have probably existed as a magical device since people could scratch symbols on rocks. The method for employing them, however, is fairly new. It begins with the work of A. O. Spare but has been refined by the chaos magicians of the last twenty years. The magician activates the sigil by achieving gnosis, a state in which one's conscious mind shuts down briefly. One common means of achieving gnosis is orgasm, but others—such as meditation, intense excitement or pain, or self-suffocation—also work. After achieving gnosis while contemplating the sigil, the magician is supposed to forget the operation.

From the semiotic perspective, the activation of a sigil is a restructuring of the codes that we interpret as reality. First of all, the magician turns a desire into a symbol that will not immediately recall the desire. By thinking actively about the desire, a magician is likely to strengthen the preexisting codes that prevent its manifestation. Contemplating a sigil that doesn't immediately invoke those codes provides an opportunity to restructure them. But to restructure the codes, we must first destroy the old ones. The only way to do so is to shut down our perception of reality, or our conscious minds. Doing so wipes away the codes. Usually when we do so—when we enter a driving trance or have an orgasm—we come back and immediately restructure our old codes. But the sigil acts as a seed, just as a speck of dust acts as a nucleus for a snowflake to form around. The first thing we see when our conscious mind returns is the sigil, and we use that as the framework for rebuilding our codes. Inevitably, then, our new codes include the idea hidden in our sigil. We forget the operation because

---

8. For a fuller discussion, see my book *Postmodern Magic: The Art of Magic in the Information Age*. Woodbury, MN: Llewellyn, 2005.

otherwise we might be tempted to rebuild our old codes again. If we fall back into our old habits, we fall back into our old codes.

Magic, at least from this perspective, is both a destructive and a creative act. We actually dismantle reality (or, at least, our own perceptions of reality, which amounts to much the same thing), and then rebuild it "nearer the heart's desire." From the semiotic perspective, reality is deconstructed and our symbolic codes are dismantled in the state of gnosis. Suspecting this, we can widen our understanding of gnosis or the altered states of consciousness that can be useful for magic. We can use any state of consciousness in which our symbolic web becomes fluid. For example, you can use the hypnogogic state just before sleep or just after sleep to create a sigil. If you place a sigil in a location where it's the last thing you see at night and the first thing you see as you awaken, the symbolic desire it represents will shape your day's experiences.

We have the codes we do for a reason. Our old codes must have served some purpose. Our codes about the world, our expectations and beliefs, offer us an advantage. For example, seeing yourself as perpetually single offers the advantage of never having to deal with the stress of meeting people. Obviously, this advantage isn't a particularly pleasant one, but if a magician wishes to change this code he or she needs to address the advantage as well as the desire. The desire, in this case, is to meet someone. Before beginning an act of magic, it's wise to contemplate and introspect on what advantages our current lifestyle offers us. A magician may even decide he or she likes being single and doesn't need to do the magic at all. Or one may decide that part of the statement of desire needs to include a low-stress relationship. The semiotic view of magic recognizes that we do not come to desires out of a vacuum, nor do they come to manifestation in a vacuum.

Semiotics also offers an alternative to merely forgetting one's spell after doing it. It's natural to worry and fantasize about our desire, but doing so can prevent manifestation. Not that worry and fantasy are necessarily bad things, just that they tend to yank at the new semiotic web while it's still pretty tender. Putting the desire out of your mind is one way to let that part of the web form around the desire, but there are others that have both historical precedence and, according to our semiotic theory of magic, should work as well. Three other alternatives exist.

The first is A. O. Spare's attitude of "need not be/does not matter."[9] In this method, one cultivates an attitude of fatalistic indifference. Magic is a lark, and no desire is serious enough—according to this attitude—to obsess over when so much other fun is available. Obviously, this attitude can be a difficult one to cultivate. I advise meditation practice with strongly held, even biological, desires: for example, fast for a day and tell yourself that food need not be and does not matter. Or become aroused and then shift your mind suddenly away from the idea of sex.

The second means of preventing interference with our new semiotic web (which is exactly what forgetting a spell does) is the substitution of desire. Instead of thinking "need not be/does not matter," when a desire arises substitute it with another desire. So if you're looking for a job and you keep fantasizing about the money you'll make if your magic works, substitute that fantasy with another one, perhaps becoming a famous rock star or writing a best-selling book.

The third method is, like the first, nothing new: it's been called "acting in accord." In this method, the magician pretends the spell has already worked, perhaps offering thanks to the gods for it and behaving as if it's all "in the bag." Donald Michael Kraig tells a story about the early twentieth century magician Aleister Crowley, who performed a spell for money and then went out and spent his last few dollars on ice cream.[10] My only caveat here is to avoid acting in accord in such a way that it reminds you of the desire specifically. It becomes too easy to slide into worry and fantasy from there. For example, if enchanting for a job, do not write your letter of resignation for your old one. That may seem like a good way of acting in accord, but it is likely to make you compare your old job and your new one in ways that will lead to obsessive worry and fantasy.

---

9. A. O. Spare, *The Book of Pleasure (Self-Love): The Psychology of Ecstasy.* Oxford, UK: I-H-O Books, 2005.

10. Donald Michael Kraig, *Modern Magick: Eleven Lessons in the High Magickal Arts.* St. Paul, MN: Llewellyn, 1988, 292–293.

The goal of all three methods is to prevent us from "picking at it." Worry is the great enemy of magic. I classify "fantasy" along with worry. Many fantasies that we indulge are just thinly disguised worry. Often, we slip into a fantasy in order to reassure ourselves that our worry is groundless, but the worry is still there. In fact, I believe that we could simply eliminate worry and think about our desire all we like, and still achieve the desired effect; acting in accord is just such a method. Interestingly, the word *worry* comes from an Old English verb that originally meant "to chew on" (and *worry* still retains this meaning in some contexts—we talk of dogs worrying bones, for example).[11] Obviously, if you're trying to spin a delicate structure of symbols, the last thing you want to do is chew on it! So how do you eliminate worrying about the results of your spell so that it can work, at least according to the semiotic model?

Worry, just like any other emotion, is nothing more than a collection of symbols.[12] So to change that emotion, we just need to change the symbols. In college I took many psychology classes, and in one of them we learned that most of our strong emotions are largely interpretations we apply to physiological stimulation. The increased heartbeat and muscle spasms in our abdomen that we call "butterflies in the stomach" when we're nervous, a "pounding heart" when we're afraid, and a "breaking heart" when we're sad are all the same physical thing given manifold symbolic interpretations. And a little personal experiment[13] proved my professors correct; the next time I felt nervous before a test, I forced myself to think about a person I found attractive, and felt myself interpreting the exact same physical sensations as fondness. It is moderately easier to take an exam when in love than when in anxiety. This insight is the base of the technique of switching desires, but we can also get to the very root

---

11. Originally it was the idea that chewed on the worrier, not the other way around, but such things have a way of swapping around in language.

12. A friend objected to this theory, arguing that surely "love" isn't just a symbol. I pointed out that there's no "just": everything is a symbol. And saying "love" is a symbol is saying love is real, not "just" a chemical reaction!

13. In science, experiments are always public with occasional personal application. In magic, experiments are always personal with occasional public appreciation.

of worry and eliminate it (or at least reduce it), which will improve our magic and our lives.

Being symbolic, we can use our symbolic technology to dig into worry or any other emotion. Our greatest symbolic technology is, of course, language. So take out a pen and paper. Go on, do it. This assignment is worth 40 percent of your grade! We're going to draw a model of the semiotic web we've constructed around the worry, so that we can snip the strands holding it in place and let it drop into oblivion.

Drawing a Semiotic Web

Choose something you're worrying about, perhaps something you might try to do magic concerning. Write that thing in the middle of the page. Draw a circle around it and sit back. Look at it and pay attention to the feeling in the area just above your stomach. Now think about it in your usual way, which I presume is a worrying way. When you feel a clenching in your stomach, identify the thought you're having right then and write it down, joining it to the main idea with a line. There may be multiple related thoughts—link them together. Others may be addressing different worries. When you finish, you'll have a more or less complex map of the part of the semiotic web connected to your worry.

Next, get a clean sheet of paper and write the subject of your worry again in its center. You're going to make some deliberate changes to that part of the semiotic web. It'll have roughly the same shape as the original (give or take a few extra filaments and nodes you may doodle in), but it will have different content. For every idea that caused you a clenching in your stomach, replace it with a rational response. It may help to focus, this time, not on your belly but on your forehead, about an inch to two inches inward. For example, if the worry-causing thought was "If my car breaks down, I'll lose my job!" replace it with something more rational: "If my car breaks down, I'll have to have it fixed and find transportation to work. That may involve calling on some favors from friends." You may have created a further worry: "If I lose my job, I'll end up homeless!" You could replace that with what sort of rational idea? Maybe, "If I lose my job, I'll have to find another one. I can get unemployment until that happens."

So now you have two competing maps, an old one and a brand-new one. The advantage of this method is that it mimics the structure, to some degree, of the old part of the web you wish to get rid of. So it addresses all your basic needs but more consciously and rationally, and from the head rather than the belly. The belly is handy at telling us that the rustling in the underbrush is likely to want to eat us; it's less good at planning proper car maintenance.

Take the old map and symbolically mark it as no longer valid. You might draw a big X across it, or lock it up in a certain place. You could also, of course, destroy it, but I like to keep records of my changing thoughts. The new map should now be placed somewhere it can take effect, perhaps in a place where you come and go several times a day, or you might just take it out before you go to bed and look at it briefly, not necessarily read it, but contemplate its structure. Of course, you may find none of this ritual action necessary; sometimes (often) just the act of making the new map shifts us away from our old habits.[14]

You may find a variation of this exercise more useful, depending on whether you respond best to immediate feedback or not. If you do prefer immediate feedback, you may want to respond directly on the old web with new rational thoughts. If you do so, you might find it productive to use various colors or some other symbol indicating the importance and primacy of the new thought over the old. You can also modify this exercise as your ingenuity guides you; for instance, if you know something about cognitive therapy or general semantics, you may want to mark cognitive distortions with some sort of code.

You may also find drawing the semiotic web around an idea useful in creative endeavors, to understand the hidden links between symbols.

---

14.   This method is related to cognitive behavioral therapy (for which see Judith Beck, *Cognitive Therapy: Basics and Beyond.* New York: Guilford Press, 1995), and mind mapping, a method of taking notes that I've found useful because it mimics the semiotic web in which we think. For more on mind mapping, see Tony Buzan, *The Mind Map Book: How to Use Radiant Thinking to Maximize Your Brain's Untapped Potential.* (New York: Plume, 1996). Obviously, I suspect neither the practitioners of cognitive behavioral therapy nor mind mapping would heartily approve of my application of this method for magical purposes.

You can do so to create what I call a *sigil mandala*. A mandala is a circular diagram that represents the universe in various Indian spiritual practices. They are sometimes used as magical circles or as objects of meditation. You can create a semiotic sigil mandala by entering a receptive state and doodling sigils around a central sigil, or by planning out certain sigils to put in certain places. The sigil mandala can help break down internal resistance to very complex ideas and unify your will toward change. If you want extra money, you may have unknown and deep-seated notions about wealth that interfere with your manifesting that desire. A sigil mandala can head off such obstacles.

The Sigil Mandala

I've created a particular kind of sigil mandala, the three-part sigil mandala, that is particularly useful in causing difficult changes to which we may have unconscious resistance. As I said before, the semiotic theory of magic implies that our current semiotic codes have some interpretive advantage, which is why we have them. To change them requires recognizing their advantages and addressing them, either by providing for them in some other way or by recognizing them as true disadvantages. The three-part sigil mandala addresses three things I've found important in motivating people: desire, feeling, and need. The center of the mandala is used to express, through sigils or some other symbolic means, one's desire. The middle ring represents the positive feelings the fulfillment of that desire will cause, and the outer ring represents the need that desire fulfills (see figure 1). It's important to remember to focus on positive feelings and personal needs. For example, if I enchant for wealth, I may predict that getting money will make me worry about how to invest it. Worry isn't a positive emotion, but excitement at new opportunities is. I sigilize excitement or opportunity in place of "worry." I also recognize that wealth will fulfill my needs for security, respect, and freedom. It might also fulfill needs to take

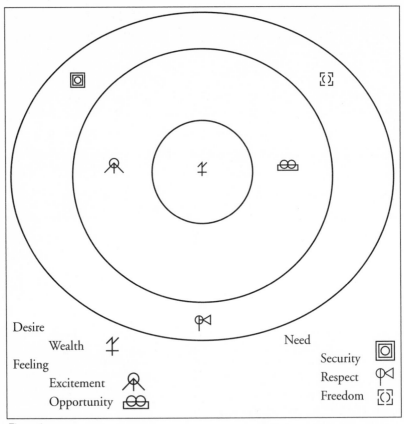

Figure 1

care of, for example, my family—but those are needs of other people, and it is my own consciousness I'm working on.[15]

One uses this mandala much like a sigil, although I prefer slow, steady gnosis over a period of time to quick, abrupt gnosis. I particularly like the hypnogogic or near-sleep gnosis. In this gnosis, one drifts in and out of sleep, looking at the sigil or mandala while awake and then letting oneself slowly drift toward sleep. As you fall off, force yourself awake. You may find it difficult to do this without practice, but there are methods. Apparently, Thomas Edison frequently used the hypnogogic gnosis in order to get new ideas; he would rest in a chair with his hands hanging over

---

15. I don't mean to imply that one can't do magic to affect other people, only that the goal of overcoming inner resistance to change must, of course, focus on oneself.

the sides. In each hand, he'd hold a weight, and below the weight he'd rest a pie tin, so when he fell into a deep enough sleep for his fingers to relax, the weights would clang against the pie plates, waking him up to record his ideas. Ron Hale-Evans modifies this technique, instead holding his arm up so its falling will wake him just as he enters the hypnogogic trance.[16] While Hale-Evans doesn't use this gnosis for magical work, there's no reason we couldn't. The advantage of this technique from our theoretical perspective is that sleep is the place in which our semiotic web loosens and rearranges anyway. We wake up to a new reality every morning (surely you have had dreams that have changed your entire mood for the coming day?); we might as well take some control of that restructuring of reality.

Another use of the semiotic web is as a divination device. If you're like me, you often find yourself dissatisfied with traditional tarot card spreads because they sometimes seem irrelevant. If I'm asking about love I don't care about "financial status," and if I'm asking about a specific course of action I don't need "past" explained to me. Yet when you choose a tarot spread, you're locked into a certain semiotic web. That can be useful if you're reading professionally for others, since they often don't know what their question really is or whether to trust you. Telling them something they already know about the past can be useful. But when reading for myself, I like a more nuanced reading that's more relevant to my concerns. To that end, I draw a semiotic web around my problem. For example, if I'm concerned about money I might put "money" in the center, and then draw filament connecting to ideas such as "safety and security" and "health care." I might make the filament connecting to safety and security a bit thicker, because that's a very fundamental need. I might also make a place for "fun." I might create a node for "possible sources," from which radiate several options. And so on. Finally, I draw a single card, or if I want more detail, three cards, for each of the nodes. I might want the forecast on health care to know if I need to save up some money for any impending medical needs. Or I might lay out several cards for "possible sources."

16. Ron Hale-Evans, *Mind Performance Hacks: Tips & Tools for Overclocking Your Brain.* Sebastopol, CA: O'Reilly, 2006.

I can even keep records of the reading on the map itself, by darkening filaments that the cards say are more important than I thought, or creating new nodes explaining old ones.

Semiotic Theory in Evocation

Sigils and divination are not the only magical operations. For example, what about evocation, the contacting of spiritual beings? What new practices can the semiotic theory lead to on that front? In evocation, one calls a spirit outside oneself to communicate with it, usually in a triangle, crystal, or other such object. The goal of evocation is communication, and communication is the trading of symbols.

One model of communication is that, instead of transferring information back and forth, we actually just build up similar models in our minds. The closer our symbolic models match, the better we've been said to communicate. If you say to me, "Pass me the salt," you are assuming I will have the same semiotic ideas of motion, salt, and so forth that you do. In that case, you're likely to be in luck. In other kinds of communication, we can't assume that someone has the same semiotic relationships in his or her mind. If I say, "We need to fight for freedom," I'm assuming you know what I mean by "fight" (physical violence? political action?) and "freedom" (a word used by many a tyrant to justify tyranny throughout history). I've given you a crude blueprint of my idea, and I hope that you can construct it. I may be wrong, and if so I need to try something new.[17]

The wise communicator comes to expect miscommunication and prepares by carefully planning ahead. Similarly, the magician plans ahead to communicate with noncorporeal entities.

And in fact, all the items traditionally associated with evocation are geared toward making it easier for you to construct a symbolic map that matches the spirit's. The magician surrounds herself with symbols of that

---

17. This idea is most eloquently and convincingly explicated by M. J. Reddy in "The Conduit Metaphor—A Case of Frame Conflict in Our Language about Language." In *Metaphor and Thought*. A. Ortony, ed. Cambridge: Cambridge University Press, 1979, 284–297.

spirit in the form of its name, seal, special incenses, and so on. She takes careful precautions to separate herself from the spirit—there's the danger of making your mind so much like the spirit's that you become it. Then she recites a traditional litany—or one she makes up herself—to justify her authority to the spirit and also to encourage communication. She addresses the spirit by name, invokes particular divine names and historical or mythical events, and charges the spirit with certain actions. All of this serves to create a semiotic code that more and more closely matches the spirit's, so that the magician can perceive and communicate with it. We are used to a crude form of communication that uses the vibrations of air or graphic symbols on paper to poke at our semiotic web and rearrange it. In this case, the magician must rely on a sort of spooky action at a distance. Magicians have to hope that a nonphysical entity will modify our semiotic web to match its own enough to communicate.

Put that way, the dangers of evocation become obvious: we may become too much like the spirit to come back to being ourselves. But that's why we have the circles, magic rings, and so on—symbolic anchors to bring us back to our sense of ourselves if the whole process works *too* well. In any event, the question isn't whether one should do evocations, but how does the semiotic theory of magic improve our approach to evocation? For one, it lets us know what sort of precautions we should take. We need to secure our own mind and consciousness by having a firm sense of our own morality, likes, dislikes, and preconceptions. After that, it also tells us how to prepare for the evocation. While we wouldn't want to completely identify with a spirit, it helps to understand a spirit by playing a game I like to call "What Would Buer Do?" Buer is simply a spirit listed in the *Lesser Key of Solomon*. In place of Buer,[18] you could put any other spirit's name. In WWBD, you observe situations and ask "WWBD?" For example, if watching a sitcom, you might ask "WWBD?" According to the grimoire,[19] Buer heals all distempers. Which characters in that sitcom are distempered and how might Buer heal them? If playing a computer

---

18. I use Buer partially because he did me a favor, and also because he's probably the most innocuous of all the Goetic demons.

19. In this case, the *Goetia*. There are other, better grimoires.

war game, you might ask, "How would Buer solve this problem?" Buer appears as a centaur with a bow and arrow, so he might rush around the edges and shoot from a distance. I'd advise against applying the WWBD game to serious issues in your life—that brings you too close to invocation and full identification with the spirit. But inconsequential, entertaining things will give you a chance to create a framework for communication with Buer when you evoke him.

We can also use the gimmick of drawing a semiotic web for Buer, which over time might become quite complicated. The magician makes a space in his consciousness for Buer to communicate with. Again, this requires being willing to connect a bit with this spirit—one reason I encourage people not to try evocation of dangerous or possibly dangerous entities. In drawing a semiotic web for Buer, we start with his name and then draw out filaments to obvious characteristics from the grimoires. After this, we fill in new circles with insights. For example, "heals all distempers" might grow filaments, as you begin to understand the spirit, that say "through fire" and "not always completely." Or perhaps you'll understand the spirit differently. Learning the correspondences of a spirit in this graphical form, which mimics the way our mind actually stores information, can help clear a space in the mind for the spirit to write on.

We can also use the semiotic theory to understand and modify our verbal litany. Each evocation includes an invocation of divine forces, an address to the spirit, and a charge. The invocation should obviously be to an aspect of the divine you actually feel some attraction toward. If you don't particularly believe in the divine, you need to find something else that serves the purpose of (a) elevating your sense of self and (b) granting you the authority to call and command (or at least, request) spirits. The address can include the information you've gleaned through preparatory introspection and contemplation. Third, the charge can be couched in terms the spirit is more likely to accept and understand; in other words, you can aim your request to create an appropriate symbolic reaction. For example, if you wish to be healed, you might couch your illness in medieval terms rather than contemporary medical terms. Alternatively, or in addition, you can sigilize your charge and offer it to the spirit as a graphic representation of your symbolic desire.

If a magician approaches magic from the framework of a semiotic theory, his or her operations may look no different from someone else's, using another theory. But that doesn't mean they aren't different. If the theory appeals to a magician, it's more likely to lead to new insights. And while two magicians might both call on Adonai during a ritual, the traditional magician just sees it as a name meaning "my Lord" while the semiotic magician sees it as a signifier that fits in a certain way into his or her semiotic web. I might see it as a name for the underlying substance of infinite qualities, while you might see it as a conscious, anthropomorphic entity with a specific role in our shared cultural history. Both of us, however, might still understand the name as a symbol that calls upon a set of signifieds useful for the operation we are doing. In fact, magicians conscious of semiotic theory might even do things "wrong" deliberately, because they are aware that their semiotic webs are idiosyncratic and personal. My magical elemental tools, for example, are a branch of a thornbush, a geode, an arrowhead, and a clay cup. From the standpoint of ceremonial magic, the kind of magic I do most often, they ought to be inscribed with magical symbols and names, and be a wand, a disk, a dagger, and a stemmed cup. But these tools mean something more to me, symbolically, than the traditional tools ever could.

One universal magical tool is subject to infinite variation: language. Every magical operation involves some use of language, even if it is just to conceptualize and define the desire. And language is a strange and mysterious thing: it bridges mind and matter, it comes from we-know-not-where, and it has a complex reciprocal relationship with our thoughts. No wonder it's such a ready tool for magic. In the next chapter I will explain how linguistics can shed some light on the magical use of language, both theoretically and practically.

TWO

Language:
The Bridge of Mind and Matter

Language bridges the mind and the body, consciousness and matter. We can think our thoughts in silent language, or we can speak them aloud, creating a change in matter (vibration of air) that encodes our meaning. If we speak certain languages, we can even encode our ideas in marks on paper, impressions in clay, or magnetic particles on a computer in order to decode them later. Imagine a book in a library, a book that has fallen behind the shelf and lies there, dusty and forgotten. It is the last copy of its printing, and there are no others in the world. If no one finds that book and opens it, does it still contain the ideas written in it? In one sense, certainly not—without a mind to perceive it, those words are just particles of ink on paper. But in another sense, the book exists and at any moment a mind could find it, open it, read it, and recover those words from oblivion, and out of those words build ideas. The book needs hands to hold it, eyes to engage it, a mind to translate its symbols into language; however, at the same time, the book and its ideas exist . . . somewhere . . . separate from any body.

Humans are indeed unique among animals because, like no other animal, we are built for language, and language is built for magic. Language comes from the body, propagates through matter, and leads to changes in the mind—both our individual minds and the universal Mind. Before we can understand the magical role of language, it's productive to understand how language works in both the physical and mental sense.

The Physicality of Sound

Start with your fleshy lips. Stick them out as if giving an exaggerated kiss. Stretch them wide in a great teeth-showing grin. Purse them and make a tiny round hole as if sucking through a straw. Flap them together. Press them tight and puff out your cheeks: your lips create an airtight seal. Finally, run your tongue between your teeth and upper lip and notice how much space there is. We have incredibly flexible lips, much more than we need to keep food in our mouth. Apes also have such flexible lips, but few other mammals do. Look at a dog's lips, if one can call them that. A dog can bare its teeth, but it cannot purse its lips, flap them and trill them, or make kissing noises. With our lips we can make /p/ and /b/ sounds, as in *bridge* and *poker*. We can also make /w/ sounds, like *whist*. We can purse our lips for vowel sounds like /o/ and /u/ in *truco*.

Take a short step back from your lips to your teeth. We have, if we're healthy, thirty-two teeth (or a couple more, depending, and some genetic variation exists), the same number of teeth as the Qabalah has paths of wisdom. In the back we have flower-shaped molars, which crush our food, while in the front we have a portcullis of flat cutting teeth, or incisors. If we use our incisors and lips together, and let them cooperate, we can make the /f/ sound in *football* and the /v/ sound in *volleyball*. You might train a dog to play volleyball, but you could never train him to say it, even if the dog were a genius. He simply can't rest his lip on his front teeth as we can.

Our back teeth, our molars, can press against our tongue to make, if we happen to be speaking Gaelic, the {ll}[20] sound that appears in words such as . . . well, *Llewellyn*, for one. In English, we use our amazing tongue for other sounds, however. Few animals have a tongue so flexible, and those that do (such as the anteater) use it exclusively to maneuver food. We use our tongue for that, too, but if that were its only purpose, we'd hardly need it to be so flexible and sensitive. If you tap that ridge of hard flesh just behind your upper front teeth, called the alveolar ridge, you can make /t/ and /d/ sounds, such as those in *tennis* and *dodgeball*. If you just hold the tip of the tongue close to that ridge and hiss through it, you can make /s/ and /z/ sounds in *soccer* and *zanga*. But that's not all: the back of the tongue can curl up to touch the place where the hard palate and soft palate join, called the velum, and make the sounds of /k/ and /g/ in *canasta* and *golf*. You can even bounce rapidly between /t/ and /k/; no other animal's tongue is so flexible and versatile.

If you go even farther, you can touch the very back of your tongue to the fleshy bit that dangles in the back of your throat, the uvula. You can trill the uvula against the tongue to make the French /r/, or you can close off your throat there and make the /q/ sound of the Hebrew letter *qoph*. In English, we do not use either of those sounds, but we can still make them. In fact, with a bit of training and practice, you can make every sound in every language, no matter how strange, including things like clicks and whistles in some of the world's most exotic languages.

Farther back yet, we find two flaps of thin muscle that can close when we're eating. In fact, they do close, in order to prevent us from inhaling our food. But what in most animals is automatic, humans can control, which means we're much more likely to accidentally inhale our food and choke. Why would we find an evolutionary advantage in being able to choke? Because controlling this valve, the glottis, allows us to make even more sounds. We can close it off entirely and make the *glottal stop* in "Uh-oh," but we can also choose to vibrate the two thin flaps of muscle and

---

20. By convention, linguists use slanting lines, such as /kot/, to indicate sounds, and curly brackets, such as {coat}, to indicate the spelling of those sounds in a language's orthography.

differentiate between /p/ in *poker* and /b/ in *bridge*. This vibration is also what differentiates /z/ and /s/, /f/ and /v/, and many other sounds. When the glottis vibrates, linguists call a sound *voiced*. When it doesn't, they call the sound *unvoiced*. The sound /p/ is unvoiced; /b/ is voiced.

Waltzing back a step into the mouth, we find a tube that leads up to our sinuses. Mostly, this tube is for drainage and breathing, but we can also stop up the air in our mouth and cause it to come out the nose, changing the quality of the sound and producing /m/ and /n/, as in *new market*. In all, the area from the glottis to the front of the lips can make a wide variety of sounds, hundreds in total, although in English we only use about forty to forty-five, depending on our accent. Computers can encode entire libraries of information using only two distinctions, 1 and 0, so it's easy to see that forty speech sounds are enough to express a great quantity of information very efficiently.

One final organ proves useful to the noisemaking capability of humans, and that is the lungs. In order to make any of these noises, we must generate a column of air and push it through the complex machine of our throat, mouth, and nose. Fortunately, our lungs are quite efficient at moving air, and they already have the task of separating oxygen from nitrogen, and exhaling the result mixed with carbon dioxide from our bodies. By using that exhaust system, we can communicate ideas.

Physically speaking, human beings are machines for making noises. Our vocal capabilities are so varied that we can imitate other animals accurately, but more importantly we can encode information and pass it on in a way that no other animal can. Dolphins have a complex system of calls, and some apes have been taught rudimentary sign language, but none of them can manage the complexity that human beings can. In fact, every nonpathological human being, exposed to language from birth, develops the ability to speak and understand his or her native language effortlessly. If exposed to another language before the age of about thirteen, a child will also learn that language effortlessly, and even compartmentalize the two languages, recognizing that they are different means of communicating. Even children who cannot physically speak or hear develop sign language if exposed to it, and sign language is not simply English translated into gestures. It has its own grammar and is a language in its own right.

The body, then, has this role in spoken language: it's a machine for making vibrations in the air and (although I did not discuss the ear) deciphering them. The body, the part of us made of matter, must be understood and explored fully if we're to understand and explore language and use it as a gateway to consciousness. I'd like to offer some exercises, which you can take or leave, although I do encourage you to become aware of your body through these exercises, since they make other, more rarefied experiments easier to manage. I begin with the lungs, because breath is the center of language for most people, and because breath has been linked in magic and religion to the idea of life itself. The word *spirit* is from the Latin *spiritus*, meaning "breath," and in Hebrew *ruach*, "soul," comes from the same root as the Hebrew words for "air" and "breath," while *nefesh*, the word for the animal soul, comes from the same root as the verb meaning "to breathe."

The Breath

Our heartbeats, unless we train ourselves, are mostly outside our conscious control, but our breath is both within our conscious control and automatic. To understand the boundaries of our control, and also to understand the vital role breath plays in determining our state of consciousness, try the following experiment. *Warning:* if you suffer from a heart condition, a respiratory problem, or another medical condition that could lead you to harm yourself through these exercises, you should simply read and consider them, and not actually do them.

Begin by breathing slowly and deeply, feeling the air fill your lungs and your lungs expand. Your lungs are driven by a sheet of muscle, the diaphragm, right under your rib cage. It pulls down to fill your lungs and relaxes to empty them. Feel the strength of that muscle. Note that when you consciously think about it, you can control it, but when your mind wanders, it effortlessly shifts over to automatic. Try to detect the exact moment this shift occurs.

Now, between exhaling and inhaling, without taking an extremely large breath, stop your diaphragm. Let your breathing cease. Feel the pain building up? This pain comes from a mixture of carbon dioxide and an increase in lactic acid, but mostly it is your body starving for oxygen. Continue to hold your breath; you may have to block your nose. Notice the pain in your head, the pressure behind your eyes, and the muscle twitches in your jaw and throat. Your mouth wants to open. Notice that your vision dims slightly; if you continue your vision will eventually blacken into a tunnel and go out as you lose consciousness. Once you lose consciousness (which I don't recommend), your diaphragm will start up again and your lungs will work to reoxygenate your blood. Do not hold your breath to the point of passing out, but do hold it to the point of unbearable pressure. When you finally do inhale, pay close attention to your consciousness: what are you thinking about? Probably nothing at all—for a moment your mind has blanked, as your brain, conserving oxygen, shuts down your rational functions and leaves you with an animal mind striving for its next breath. Speaking of which, that first breath after holding your breath feels pretty good, doesn't it?

The influx of oxygen can clarify the mind and improve the mood. There is another way to increase the amount of oxygen in your blood: controlled hyperventilation. This exercise should be done some time after the first, perhaps on a different day. It involves the opposite—instead of using your control of the diaphragm to stop your breath, you can use your control of the diaphragm to deliberately hyperventilate, filling your blood with excess oxygen. If you have a medical problem, or an anxiety problem, this exercise can be dangerous, so you may not want to do it.

Lie down and put your arms above your head, folded behind it in a triangle, hands on the back of your head. Inhale deeply and then use your diaphragm to shove the air out of your lungs with as much force as you can muster. Your diaphragm will naturally rebound and pull air into your lungs. Let it, and again push that air out quickly. You want to take deep, deep breaths—much deeper than normal—and expel much more air than you normally do. Try filling your lungs from the bottom up.

You are overloading your blood with oxygen, and soon you will feel a tingling in your extremities. At this point, you can stop and let your breath return to normal, although you may notice a tendency to breathe shallowly, or not at all. You won't feel any of the discomfort of suffocation, however, because your body is not starving for oxygen.

Notice, if you can, your state of mind. You probably feel a bit dizzy and perhaps slightly euphoric. You might feel some of the effects of oxygen intoxication, which can involve hallucinations of bright lights, strong feelings of peace and well-being, and sometimes insight into problems that might have stumped you. You may also feel, as you come down, a sour stomach or other symptoms of gastrointestinal stress, as the extra load of oxygen pushes your body to work faster.

Both of these exercises demonstrate the clear link between our breath and our state of mind. No wonder, then, that in culture after culture, language after language, people chose to form the word for *spirit* from the word for *breath*. Obviously, both of these techniques are extreme, and neither is particularly versatile in ritual. If you hold your breath until you pass out in a ritual, for example, you might very well hurt yourself as you fall on your candles! And if you try to hyperventilate during a ritual, you might find it difficult to recite your incantations. Fortunately, the link between consciousness and the breath also works subtly. We can control our state of mind by the rough method of suffocating ourselves or hyperventilating ourselves (and sometimes we might want to do so, for a particular magical or mystical purpose), but we can also control our state of mind by making smaller, less dramatic changes to our breath. For example, in the next exercise you will learn to use rhythmic breathing to relax into a state of mind essential to the practice of magic.

The Fourfold Breath

Begin by getting comfortable in a sitting or standing position (this exercise will also work lying down, but I recommend learning it sitting and standing so that you don't confuse the state of relaxation with sleepiness—especially since we pass through this state on our way to sleep). If sitting, put your palms on your thighs; this posture is known in ceremonial magic as the God posture, because many Egyptian gods have been depicted in it. If standing, hold your hands at your sides with your palms facing behind you; relax your shoulders so that your arms dangle and aren't held rigidly. This posture is sometimes referred to as the Wand posture, because one stands as straight as a wand. In both positions your back should be straight or, rather, naturally erect—which means curved slightly but not slumping. If you have trouble straightening your back, imagine that a string attached to the top of your head is gently pulling your head up. Also, bend your knees slightly if standing; doing so will help you align your lower back. If sitting, you may want to put a small pillow against your lower back and not rest on the chair's backrest.

Once in position, notice but do not direct your breath. Focus attention on your breath, telling yourself silently "Now I'm breathing in" and "Now I'm breathing out." This practice alone is a powerful meditation in its own right, and I recommend it for clearing the mind. But our aim is not psychological but magical, so we can take it further.

Once you get a sense of how your breath feels and an awareness for how much your lungs can hold in one breath, begin to count to four as you inhale. When your lungs are about 60 to 70 percent full, hold your breath for an equivalent count of four, then exhale for a count of four, and hold for a count of four before inhaling, again for a count of four. This process is known as the fourfold breath. Like hyperventilating, it increases the oxygen content of your blood, although without the detrimental effects or strain. It also slows the breath and simultaneously relaxes the mind. If you find yourself struggling or uncomfortable, speed up or slow down the counts of four, until you can maintain a more or less even rhythm without strain or discomfort.

You may wish to relax your muscles consciously as you breathe, working your way up from the feet to the head. But even without conscious intervention, focusing on your breathing will unknot your muscles. If you feel small twinges of pain from your muscles as they relax, do not worry. They will go away quickly; it just means that you're under a lot of stress. You may also feel some strong emotions come and go. Do not hold onto any of them particularly, but just let them pass without judgment. Eventually, your body will feel relaxed enough that although you could move your arm, you don't want to. You will also probably feel warm and comfortable. You might feel sleepy—in reality, you are quite

alert (unless you're sleep-starved, which many people are and don't realize), but we're used to associating this deep state of relaxation with sleep.

The greatest advantage of this state is that your critical faculties become blunted. You become open to suggestion. This fact is the origin
of the famous posthypnotic suggestion. Some people go to hypnotists in
order to be put into a hypnotic trance in which the hypnotist suggests that
the client stops smoking or develops healthier eating habits. Some hypnotists rely on the suggestive state of mind (and people's desire to please their
friends and be the center of attention) to convince people to do ridiculous
things as entertainment. Magicians use this state of mind, however, for
more rarefied—or, in another light, more practical—purposes. We relax to
release all the obstacles to our will that our everyday consciousness erects.

When you do a spell for money, what thoughts do you have? Desire
for material things? Guilt about that desire? You probably don't have just
one opinion about money or, for that matter, about anything else. It is
difficult to do magic unless your will is unified toward a single desire,
without distraction. You may want money, but do you want to want it?
Deep relaxation helps unify the will, because it rids us of the doubt and
distractions of our waking consciousness and replaces them with relaxed
self-confidence and self-trust.

Using the breath to relax is particularly appropriate in the magical use
of language, because almost every human language begins with the breath.
And like language, which connects the world of matter to the world of
ideas, breath connects the world of our body to the world of our mind.
Many magicians ignore the body, ultimately to their detriment. Matter is
surely the foam that floats on the ocean of consciousness, but it is still part
of that ocean and not to be ignored. We build a mystery with our minds
but explore it with our bodies, and we should not forget that. Just as the
body is connected to the mind, there is a connection between the parts of
the mouth and the sounds we make with them. The study of this connection is the science of phonology. Phonology can give us a vocabulary to
discuss possible correspondences between sound and magical symbols.

The Sounds of Language

As already mentioned, the number of possible speech sounds is enormous. The International Phonetic Alphabet, an alphabet of speech sounds suitable for describing the pronunciation of any word in any language, has seventy-four basic consonants and twenty-five basic vowels. But to give you an idea how many sounds are really possible, each of those twenty-five basic vowels can be voiced, whispered (unvoiced), or semi-voiced (creaky voice), yielding 25 x 3 = 75 possible vowels, each of which can be nasalized or not, leading to 150 possible vowels, each of which can be expressed long, short, or semi-long, giving us 450 possible vowels, each of which could also, in some languages, receive one of any number of tones (Cantonese has nine tones, for example), which might yield . . . a heck of a lot of possible vowels. And even more consonants! (And I didn't even count extremely rare sounds, clicks, and whistles.) Fortunately for our sanity, we're only obligated to train our mouths to make a few such sounds depending on the language—forty or so in English. In this book, because time and space have limits, I'll focus on the sounds of English (and sometimes Hebrew, because I can't help it).

Phonology is the science of language sounds, and it's one of the few things in linguistics we actually understand pretty well. We know, for example, that our mouths are trained to make certain sounds very early, before we even manage to learn language itself. Therefore, it is difficult to learn a second language in adulthood without an accent, which is simply the habits of our mouth applied to another language. For example, in English we make a /t/ sound by putting our tongue against the bony ridge behind the upper front teeth. Spanish speakers make a /t/ sound by putting the tip of the tongue just on the outside of that ridge. It's a difference of a millimeter, but we can detect the difference in the Spanish /t/ even if we're not able, at first, to make it. Our ears are precisely tuned to hear the subtle variations in the dance of our tongue, lips, and teeth.

From a magical perspective, very little has ever been written on the magical use of speech sounds divorced from meaning. The earliest and most comprehensive writing on the topic is probably the fragments of spells from the Greek Magical Papyri. These spells, mostly theurgic in nature (i.e., dealing with gods), contain long strings of vowels. Somewhere around the middle of the first century B.C.E., Philo Judaeus (whose name clearly connects him with the Qabalah as well as Greek theurgy) links the seven Greek vowels to the seven visible planets.[21] It is important to note, however, that the vowels that Philo Judaeus uses are not the phonetic vowels—the vowels as they are actually sounded in the mouth—but the orthographic vowels—the vowels as written. To illustrate, in English we have only five orthographic vowels (or six, if you wish to count {y}). But we have twelve (or so, depending on dialect and accent) phonetic vowels. In fact, the most common vowel sound in English, the *uh* sound at the end of the word *sofa*, has no orthographic sign of its own in the English alphabet. Called a *schwa*, this sound is represented in the International Phonetic Alphabet as an upside-down *e*, {ə}, but in English spelling may be represented by any of the five orthographic vowel signs. It can be like the {a} in *sofa* or the first {e} in *receipt*,[22] and so on, but it is always the same sound. No language has an orthography (a way of writing) that is perfectly representative of its phonology (the actual sounds).[23] The work of Judaeus, therefore, focuses on the Greek letters rather than the sounds those letters represent.

Magical exploration of speech sound, rather than orthography, is rare. Part of the problem is that we didn't really recognize the difference between phonology and orthography until relatively recently. Linguistics, after all, is largely a twentieth-century science. Aleister Crowley makes a rather clumsy but clever stab at determining a magical significance for the sounds, at least, of Hebrew:

---

21. Kieren Barry, *The Greek Qabalah: Alphabetic Mysticism and Numerology in the Ancient World.* York Beach, ME: Samuel Weiser, 1999, 38. Et passim for a full treatment of the topic.

22. If you say this word slowly or emphasize it, you may say it "ree-seet" rather than "ruh-seet." This peculiarity of pronunciation is why English has no letter for schwa; schwa is really an unstressed vowel's tendency to drop into the middle of the mouth. But the original vowel sound often lurks in the schwa, coming out when the sound is stressed, such as the stressed and unstressed versions of *the*.

23. Some languages, however, come very close: Korean, Cherokee, Italian, and some others.

> I put to myself this question: when I pronounce the letter so-
> and-so, what thought or class of thought tends to arise in my
> mind? (If you practice this in public, people may wonder!)
> . . . . We'll call it D-Day and drop our paratroops. *D* is a
> sharp, sudden, forceful, explosive sound, cut off smartly.
> Now I can't tell whether you will connect this with ejacula-
> tion, with the idea of paternity. In any event, a vast number
> of people did so in the dawn of speech. Even today children
> seem instinctively to say "dad" for "father," though no allow-
> ance can be made for cases of mistaken identity . . . [24]

Crowley goes on to analyze the sounds /n/, /l/, /s/, /m/, and /r/. His method consists of a mixture of introspection and historical linguistics. Unfortunately, in Crowley's time historical linguistics was quite imperfect, and so he unknowingly relies on suppositions that we now know are rather absurd (such as the theory that Sanskrit is the farthest back we can trace language, while we now have reconstructed Proto-Indo-European, the language from which Sanskrit, Proto-Germanic, Proto-Latin, and Proto-Greek all came). Crowley also relies heavily on the physical sensation of the sound of the letters, pointing out for example that producing an /s/ sound requires one to bare one's teeth—an observation that doesn't hold true in my dialect of English but is still interesting. Yet I think that Crowley was largely on the right track. Focusing on the physical sensation and the change in consciousness that flows from it can help us understand the symbolic place of the sounds of our language in our own symbolic universe.

Such a project, however, provokes the question, why bother? What good does it do to understand the symbolic place of a given speech sound? Several possibilities occur to me, and you may be able to think of others. First, knowing the symbolic meaning of speech sounds can help us interpret words and names; if we meet a spirit in a dream and he says his name is "Tak," we can ask ourselves what those three sounds /t/, /a/, and

---

24. Aleister Crowley, *Magick Without Tears*. Scottsdale, AZ: New Falcon, 1991, 408 and 411.

/k/ mean together. Doing so might reveal what message Tak is trying to tell us, or even if we should listen to him at all. Second, like the Hellenic Greeks, we can use sounds divorced from meaning in our incantations if we have linked those sounds to a symbolic significance. For example, if we identify /t/ with Mercury, and /a/ with inspiration, we can use the syllable /ta/ as a mantra to invoke Mercury. Of course, the danger of such an approach is its mechanical nature; we might be tempted to tabulate all sounds into a single, great one-for-one correspondence chart. Doing so can take some of the fun out of magic and language.

Still, it is worthwhile to recognize the iconic nature of some sounds, even if we are not to make an exhaustive correspondence list of all sounds. Perhaps surprisingly, some linguists have already begun our work for us, identifying sounds that, across languages, seem to represent certain ideas. For example, a large number of words in unrelated languages referring to the nose or nostrils have a nasal sound, /n/ or /ng/, in them. That makes a certain amount of sense, because the nose is involved in pronouncing nasals. Also, most babies' first words for their parents have a bilabial sound /p/ or /m/ in them, probably because we develop motor control of our lips before we master the movements of the tongue. Words meaning *tiny* in many languages have an /i/ or /I/ sound, and words meaning *large* often have an /o/ or /a/ (notice, though, that English is perverse, with our *small* /smal/ and *big* /bIg/). A class of words in every language is identified as onomatopoeic, or "sounding like the thing they reference." Examples of onomatopoeia in English include *crash, whine, boom,* and *meow.*

Some linguists have speculated, although without much hard evidence, that language may have begun as onomatopoeia—pointing at a bird and saying "twee" may have led to the word "twee" representing a bird, and so on. Over time, as sounds changed and meanings shifted, we might have lost what originally made the word onomatopoeic, and just remembered it as an arbitrary symbol for "bird." The only large flaw in this theory is its lack of evidence, and the fact that what is onomatopoeic in one language isn't necessarily onomatopoeic in another. For example, in English we say a dog makes the sound "arf arf," while in Spanish a dog says "guau guau." My favorite is what a rooster says in Italian—not "cock-a-doodle-doo" but "cocorico"! Other linguists,[25] a relatively small number of them, argue that language is still onomatopoeic, but that we are unconscious of it unless it is pointed out.

Magic is the realm of the subjective, not the objective, so what convinces linguists or fails to convince linguists is not so much a concern of ours. We might not arrive at the absolute objective truth about the iconic nature of speech sounds with the methods of magic, but we can expect to arrive at personal, subjective truths. There are, as in most magical endeavors, two ways to approach uncovering the iconic meaning of our speech sounds. The first is analytic—it identifies the features of speech sounds and links them up with common magical models in order to make a handy table of correspondences. The other is intuitive and relies on our imaginations to make such links. I'll provide an example of each, starting with the analytic, which requires another dip into the cold pool of linguistic theory.

The field of phonology, the study of speech sounds, already divides up the features of phonemes (individual speech sounds) for us, so all it remains for us to do is to link them to common magical models and discover their correspondences. Simplifying slightly, we can classify sounds according to three dimensions. First, where the flow of air is restricted in the mouth. In English we restrict this flow in six possible places: the lips, the alveolar ridge (the ridge of cartilage just behind your upper teeth), near or on the teeth, the palate (the roof of the mouth), the velum (the spot where the roof of your mouth goes from being hard to soft as you run your tongue backwards along it), and the glottis (your vocal cords). These are designated with the traditional adjectives *labial* (lips), *alveolar* (alveolar ridge), *dental* (teeth), *velar* (velum), and *glottal* (glottis).

---

25. Margaret Magnus, "Magical Letter Page." Online at http://www.conknet .com/~mmagnus/ (accessed 29 April 2008). She actually has a dictionary listing all the iconic meanings for the sounds of English, a task I do here only in embryonic fashion. Despite the name of the page, Magnus is not a magician (as far as I know) and her page is straight, albeit rather fringe, linguistics. (N. B.: Linguistics, being a rather new science, is still often a bit fringy even in the center, so being a fringe linguist isn't as career-destroying as being, say, a fringe physicist. Fortunately for me.)

The second dimension linguistics identify is how much the air stream is closed off. A completely closed off air stream is a *stop*, while one open just enough to let air through is a *fricative* (which is fun to yell when you stub your toe!), and a closure in which air is hardly impeded at all is an *approximant*. The final dimension isn't a dimension at all, but an on-off switch; if you vibrate your vocal cords while you say the sound, the sound is voiced, and if you do not, it is unvoiced.[26]

To provide some concrete examples for these abstract terms, the sound /p/ as in *pizza* is an unvoiced bilabial stop (unvoiced, because your vocal cords don't vibrate, bilabial because it involves both lips, and a stop because you completely stop the airflow when you say it, albeit briefly). Its brother /b/ for *brioche* is a voiced bilabial stop. If you put your hand over your throat, touching your Adam's apple, you'll feel it vibrate when you say "buh buh" and not "puh puh." We don't have a bilabial fricative in English, but we do have a labiodental fricative. If you say /f/ as in *fillet* you'll be making an unvoiced labiodental fricative by pushing a hissing stream of air between your lip (labio) and teeth (dental), while not vibrating your vocal cords. If you start vibrating your vocal cords, suddenly your /f/ will transform into /v/ for *veal*.

Any speech sound can be described by combining these terms. In fact, we can describe sounds that don't exist in English—for example, we don't have a voiced bilabial fricative, but we can imagine one if we make a /b/ and then let our lips relax just enough to let air through. But for our purposes, trying to discover the magical significance (or a magical significance) of the phonemes of English, we only need the terms we have, and some variations. Here is a short list of sounds of English, example words, and how they're described in my slightly simplified terminology:

---

26. This explanation is simplified. The actual dimensions are a little fuzzier than this and more complex, but for our purposes this will suffice. If you actually find yourself interested in how speech sounds are produced, I recommend J. C. Catford, *A Practical Introduction to Phonetics*. Oxford, UK: Claredon Press, 1998. Catford actually describes how to produce every known speech sound in any human language (including those clicks you hear on TV). It's grand fun to work through the exercises in this book, especially in a public place.

Unvoiced	Voiced			
/p/	/b/	bilabial	stop	**p**epper, **b**ean
/t/	/d/	alveolar	stop	**t**ent, **d**oor
/k/	/g/	velar	stop	**k**ing, **g**ift
/s/	/z/	alveolar	fricative	**s**auce, **z**oom
/f/	/v/	labiodental	fricative	**f**airy, **v**at
/th/	/dh/	interdental	fricative	**th**istle, **th**at*
/w/		bilabial	approximant	**w**izard
/y/		palatal	approximant	**y**ahoo
/r/		palatal	approximant	**r**oar**
/l/		alveolar	approximant	**l**ove
/h/		glottal	fricative	**h**air***
/sh/	/zh/	palatal	fricative	**sh**oe, plea**s**ure
/n/		alveolar	nasal	**n**ose
/m/		bilabial	nasal	**m**other
/N/		velar	nasal	thi**ng**

*   A strange and rare sound, actually. It's interdental because you actually stick out your tongue between your teeth to make it.

**   Another rare sound. This palatal approximant is usually designated with an extra adjective, *retroflex*, which means the tongue is curled back.

***   /h/ has no voiced counterpart because it's made in the glottis, and the glottis can't really vibrate and constrict the airflow enough to make a fricative at the same time. (This explanation is also simplified—but it's approximately correct.)

Notice that these sounds don't necessarily have much connection to our system of writing. For example, the word *cough* is pronounced /kawf/ even though it has no {f} in it. Also notice that these sounds might be realized slightly differently by people speaking different dialects, or even different accents, of English. Ask a Cockney to say *bottle*, for example, and you'll hear a glottal stop rather than a /t/. And you might never hear the /r/ in *car* if you ask someone in Bawston to say the word for you! (And if you're from Boston, you might wonder where all those extra /r/s come from in Iowa's version of *wash*.)

Magically speaking, we can identify the six locations of constriction with the planets and the degree of constriction with the elements. One scheme for doing so is as follows: I associate the alveolars /t/, /d/, /s/, /z/,

/n/, and /l/ with Mercury, because the tongue moves fluidly and quickly in producing them. With Venus I associate the labials /p/, /b/, /m/, and /w/, since the lips are sexual (or at least sensual) organs as well as vocal organs. Mars is associated with the dentals, because the teeth are hard and destructive, like Mars: /th/, /dh/, /f/, and /v/ (note that /f/ and /v/ are also labial, and therefore associated with Venus—which might explain why the English word denoting both sex and violent disgust begins with an /f/). Because of their association with tasting and enjoying, I associate Jupiter with the palate and velum—so /y/, /k/, and /g/. And finally I associate Saturn with the glottis, as being the deepest, most secret part of the throat, and the only place of articulations that isn't visible if you open your mouth, which gives Saturn the sound /h/ and the glottal stop /'/, which occurs in English only in words beginning with a vowel and is never depicted in writing.[27] But what about the sun and the moon? I've already mentioned that some sounds are differentiated by whether or not the vocal cord is vibrating—whether they're voiced or not. Voiced sounds, because they contain the vibrations of life, can be related to the sun, and unvoiced sounds, the moon.

The degree of constriction of a sound, whether the airflow is completely stopped or partially stopped, can be associated with the elements, so that earth is the solid stops (/p/ /b/ /t/ /d/ /k/ /g/), fire is the hissing fricatives (/f/ /v/ /s/ /z/ /h/), water is the gentle approximants (/w/ /y/ /l/), and nasals then fall under air (/n/ /m/ /N/). Each sound therefore has two associations—a planetary association and an elemental association. For those sounds that can be voiced or unvoiced, they also have a solar or lunar association.

I certainly wouldn't want to build a whole Qabalah off of this system, but it could be used to create, for example, an invocation or chant. If you wanted to invoke the sun, you might make sure to include many voiced sounds, while if you wanted an invocation to Earth, you might want to fill the incantation with stops like /b/ and /k/. Also, in creating words of

---

27. This is true for dialects of English spoken in America and some dialects of British English. Other dialects make free use of the glottal stop in words—Cockney, for example, often uses the glottal stop in place of /t/ in the middle of words.

power, such a system could make meaningless words that nonetheless correspond to elements and planets.

Notice that in the above I have left the vowels unmentioned. Part of the problem with vowels is that English has an extremely complex vowel system, and linguists use a completely different set of terms to describe vowels. Vowels are described according to the height of the jaw and the location of the tongue, which may be retracted into the mouth or pushed forward. We therefore speak of "front" vowels—where the tongue is very far forward—and "back" vowels—where the tongue is very far back. We also speak of "high" vowels and "low" vowels, depending upon whether the jaw is held up or dropped down. Because of a quirk of terminology, "high" vowels also tend to be of a higher frequency than "low" vowels, since the size of the resonating chamber (the mouth) is larger for low vowels than for high vowels. (Think of the frequency of sound as you blow into bottles—those mostly filled with water have a high pitch, while those mostly empty have a low pitch. The same process occurs in the mouth, except it is the tongue, and not water, that fills the mouth's "bottle.") In English we have eleven or twelve vowels, depending on dialect, and the description of how to make them is often opaque to nonlinguists. In fact, while one can learn the terminology and create a consonant just from following directions as to how to place the tongue, most linguists just memorize the vowels and the terms that describe them.

To simplify my discussion of vowels, I am just going to talk about the five cardinal vowels identified by linguists. If a language has only five vowels, these are the vowels that language will have. The first three are /i/ as in *bean*, /a/ as in *father*, and /u/ as in *tuba*. If a language has only three vowels (like classical Arabic), most likely it has these three vowels (although in the case of Arabic, /i/ can sometimes sound like /e/ to us, and /u/ like /o/, but a native speaker identifies them as variations of the same vowel). The other two are the /e/ sound spelled "ai" in the word *bait* and the /o/ in *boat*.[28]

An excellent way to understand the role of the vowels in magic, and by far the best way to understand the experiential method of gaining magical knowledge about them, rather than the analytic method of correspondence listed above, is to intone or sing them. Vowels, unlike most consonants, can be sung. Start with /a/ as in *father*—"aaaahhhh"—and hold it on a comfortable tone. Hold it for an entire lungful of air, and don't be afraid to annoy the neighbors. If you're very relaxed, you may notice a part of your body vibrating along with your voice; notice where this is, and then jump up to /i/ as in *see*—"eeeeeee."

Where does /i/ seem to vibrate? If you're like me, /i/ will vibrate the bones and muscles of your face, whereas you will feel /a/ closer to your solar plexus. Of course, you may not be like me, which is exactly why the experiential method is so rewarding; you discover what you're like. Try dropping all the way down to a low rumbling /u/. It may help speakers of British English to imagine a silent {r} at the end of that /u/ to get rid of the usual off-glide; American English speakers can just imagine saying "Betty Booooooooooooooooo(p)." Let your lips pooch out in a big round kiss; this rounding of the lips is the reason /u/ and /o/ are called "round" vowels. Where does /u/ vibrate? For me, it vibrates in my hipbones, the wall of muscle behind my navel, and at the bottom of my spine, and if I drop it down low enough I can even feel it in my thighs.

It's useful and pleasant to combine certain vowels and see how they operate in combination. /iau/ is pretty close to the Gnostic name of God, IAO, and takes us from the top of our vowel frequency to the depth. Going in the order /i e a o u/ is also interesting, because it seems to run right down the body for some people.[29] But try other combinations as

---

28. Again, I am simplifying for the layperson. In reality, the cardinal vowels almost never appear in their "pure" form in English—the /o/ in "boat" is really more of an /ow/ and our /u/ is almost always /yu/. But one really needn't be concerned unless interested in a more in-depth study of linguistics.

29. This effect is used in the Gnostic Ritual of the Pentagrams, a ritual invented by Peter Carroll and published in *Liber Kaos* (York Beach, ME: Weiser, 1992).

well. Try to get a feel for what each of the vowels may be used for—for me, /i/ feels aggressive, /e/ feels communicative, /a/ feels creative, /o/ feels defensive, and /u/ feels sensual, at least at the moment.

You might also experiment with the other English vowels, listed below with example words:

- /I/ *pit, bit*
- /E/ *pet, bet*
- /ae/ *pat, bat*
- /O/ *bought* (in the Midwestern dialect of English; in other dialects, this sound collapses into /a/)
- /U/ *put*
- /ə/ *uh, sofa* (the final {a})

In all your experiments, realize that language rides on a column of air that runs down the middle of your body. You might try breathing consciously while standing or sitting upright, feeling the diaphragm muscle behind your navel pull the breath into your lungs, and then let it out in a vowel sound, feeling how it vibrates the column of air that extends from the root of your body up to your head. Where consonants cut off this column of air in one way or another, vowels modulate it to create a variety of frequencies and timbres. While doing this meditation, you might introspect on metaphorical questions such as "What color is this vowel? What planet or planets is it like? What elements is it like? How does it taste? How does it smell?"

One interesting experiment is to acquire the instrument known as a jew's-harp[30] and shape your mouth for the vowels while plucking it. This instrument, a metal frame with a tongue that vibrates when plucked, uses the skull as a resonating chamber. It is often regarded as a child's toy, like the kazoo, but in fact it has a long history in magic. Siberian shamans

---

30.   No one is quite sure where the name *jew's-harp* comes from, but it probably does not have a racist origin—it may be a corruption of a French word meaning "play." In English, it is often turned into "juice harp," which is, while evocative and descriptive of what happens during extended play, probably not the original version of the name.

still use it in healing rituals. The frame is placed against, not between, the teeth, and the tongue of the instrument is plucked outward. The shape of the mouth picks out overtones in the instrument's drone note—when not pressed against teeth, the instrument sounds like a faint plucking in one note, but when placed against the teeth, the player can select which overtones to emphasize by shaping the mouth. One way of doing so is to form the mouth for vowels but not voice them. This practice clearly emphasizes the frequency of certain vowels; an enlightening experiment is to take a piece of metrical poetry, such as Edgar Allan Poe's "The Raven," and form only the vowels of the poem while plucking the harp. Doing so reveals a melody hidden in the frequencies of the vowels in many poems.

My goal in the above is to give you an idea of how to explore possible meanings of sounds without explaining definitively what they might mean. Other languages, of course, have other sound systems, and even languages with similar phonologies often make tiny variations in phonemes that can have large psychological and magical effects. Think about the crisp sound of Spanish dental consonants, for example—a crispness that results in advancing the tongue just a couple of millimeters forward.

If you speak another language besides English, or use Hebrew or some similar language in your magic, you may want to explore the sounds of that language as well. The Hebrew Qabalah, in fact, describes meditative practices that involve permuting letters and pronouncing them aloud, so that, for example, all possible letters of a certain class are paired with all other letters of that class. If you wish to try this, you might begin with the "mother letters," which consist of the glottal stop as in *uh-oh* (represented by the letter *alef*), the sound /sh/ (represented by the letter *shin*), and the sound /m/ (represented by the letter *mem*). One interesting and instructive way to do this combines the meditation on vowels and these three consonants, by reciting or intoning the following:

> 'im 'ish mi' mish shi' shim
> 'em 'esh me' mesh she' shem
> 'am 'ash ma' mash sha' sham
> 'om 'osh mo' mosh sho' shom
> 'um 'ush mu' mush shu' shum

Obviously, such a method only works if you permute a relatively small number of consonants, but it is a good way to understand the relationships between sounds—we could, for example, permute the stops /p/ /t/, and /k/ with the three vowels /i/ (as in *see*), /a/ (as in *father*), and /u/ (as in *boot*) to try to gain a better understanding of the magical power of their sounds:

pit pik tip tik kip kit
pat pak tap tak kap kat
put puk tup tuk kup kut

If you introspect in a quiet, relaxed state while you permute the sounds, you may get an inkling of their uses: an image, a color, an emotion. For example, while reciting "pi pe po pa pu" I feel a sense of hovering over some airy abyss from a great height. The word *precipice* comes to mind. I might decide, therefore, if that's the consistent reaction I get from that sound, that for me /p/ symbolizes the precipitous potential of peril. It's important to conduct such an experiment in calm and relaxed surroundings. Mere reading cannot give a full understanding of the power and poetry of sound, unless you use the reading as an opportunity to experiment.

The above information is enough to explore sound yourself, experientially and analytically, and arrive at some uses of pure sound that might be valuable for your own individual Great Work. The important thing to keep in mind is that in one respect sound is the medium of language and therefore of much of our thought, and sound is physical. A strong grounding in the physical world is necessary to understand the role of language in magic, but language at the same time is nonphysical as well. Language bridges the physical and the nonphysical. In one sense we can point to language as marks in clay or on paper, stone, or wood, or we can hear someone agitate the air with vibrations of his or her vocal apparatus and say, "That's language," but so is the silent thought that runs through our mind without ever moving any part of our body. And so is the word of power we construct from meaningful sounds for a ritual, even though that word itself has no definition in any language, no semantic meaning. Such a word takes an abstract idea from our mind and turns it into a concrete vibration of air in the physical world; such a vibration of air heard by our ear then is translated back into the ideal world of our mind. Perhaps it is language that the Emerald Tablet of Hermes describes when it says, "It ascends from ye earth to ye heaven & again it descends to ye earth and receives ye force of things superior & inferior."[31]

---

31.   "Emerald Tablet of Hermes," translation by Isaac Newton (c. 1680). Internet Sacred Texts Archives. http://www.sacred-texts.com/alc/emerald.htm (accessed 18 April 2008).

THREE

Incantation:
The Poetry of Power

Every culture in the world, from villages of a few hundred people in the Amazon to global empires, has poetry, even cultures that do not have writing. Most cultures regard their poetry, whether written or oral, to be sacred and magical. Poetry designed to produce a magical effect is called an incantation, from Latin roots meaning "inner" and "sing." People use incantations to produce effects, often practical ones such as removing an eyelash from an eye.[32] Even in our culture, we use some magical incantations without necessarily realizing it, although we may not take them too seriously. For example:

> Star light, star bright:
> First star I see tonight.
> Wish I may, wish I might
> Have this wish I wish tonight.

32. Alexander Carmichael, *Carmina Gadelica: Hymns and Incantations Collected in the Highlands and Islands of Scotland in the Last Century*. Edinburgh, UK: Floris, 1992.

Few children who make such wishes expect them to come true (although I did, and many of the less impossible ones did come true), but many people still say the incantation. Incantations are so common, cross-culturally, that it's often hard to tell where incantation ends and poetry begins. In this chapter I will look closely at several traditions of incantation, with an eye toward analyzing their structure and forms, and how we might use those structures and forms to create our own incantations.

Our lives are filled with spells and incantations. I remember marching in ceremonial robes, while bagpipes played, to a large hall in which the very Christian president of my very Christian university performed a spell by reciting an incantation. The spell was pretty powerful: it gave me the ability to put BA after my name. It also gave me the power to apply to graduate school, the power to get certain jobs, and a certain degree of social responsibility. I also once saw a judge perform a spell by reciting an incantation and doing a ritual action; by saying, "In light of the lack of proof that reducing speed could have prevented this accident, I rule the defendant not guilty" and banging his ritual hammer, he not only prevented me from paying a hefty fine, but he also solved the problems of which insurance company had to pay, who was responsible for paying for the guardrail, and other far-ranging effects on people he would probably never meet. Some people have had a spell performed that binds them to another person; in our country, we empower religious leaders and judges to perform such spells, and we hold the results sacred. Our days, then, are full of spells. But most people don't realize it, or don't recognize that these actions are spells.

Performatives

Linguists classify verbal acts like those above as *performative utterances*. A performative utterance is a phrase that does something, makes some change in the world, at the moment of its being said. "Open the window" makes a change in the world, but only if I get up and open the window. "I now pronounce you husband and wife" makes a change in the world at the moment the words pass the officiating person's lips. Performative utterances are therefore said to have *illocutionary*[33] *force*, which simply means that the power of the words is not in its interpretation or in its being carried out by another person, but in the words themselves. All other utterances, such as "Close the window, please" and "Nice day, isn't it?" may have a perlocutionary effect—an effect that occurs as a result of the utterance but not at the same time as the utterance—but they do not usually have illocutionary force. Spells are illocutionary and perlocutionary—when we say the words of the spell, we have done the spell. The effects are the results of that saying, but the spell is done the moment one finishes the utterance.

Linguists, in their search for how performative utterances work, tell us something about the way spells work as well. A performative utterance cannot be evaluated as true or false; instead, it either happens or does not happen. It is not a report of an event, but the event itself. So if I say, "I now pronounce you husband and wife," it is meaningless to ask, "Is it true that you pronounced them husband and wife?" The more important question is, "Did you really marry them?" If I did, then the performative utterance "came off," or was "felicitous." A infelicitous performative, one that doesn't work, fails because it doesn't fulfill one or more "felicity conditions." For example, some of the felicity conditions in marriage are:

- You must be eligible to be married (adults, unmarried, and in most places in the United States for the time being, of opposite sexes)
- The person uttering the performative must be empowered to do so (for example, a judge, minister, or priest)
- You must be willing to be married
- The other ritual conditions must be met (i.e., presence of witnesses, signed papers, and so forth)

Felicity conditions are neither stable nor uniform. For example, I understand that in California, marriage does not require an officiating person.

---

33.   From *in* + *locutio* ("saying")—hence, "in the saying of."

In that case, the signing of the marriage contract in the presence of the witnesses is the speech act itself.

Marriage is an interesting ritual from a performative standpoint for several reasons. For one, it illustrates how seriously people take their performative rituals. In the United States, an attempt to change one of the felicity conditions in order to allow gay people to marry has been met with considerable resistance. As of this writing, the U.S. Congress has decided not to amend the Constitution to prevent it, but there will likely be future attempts to do so. The debate is often cast in terms of "defending marriage," as if the single felicity condition is and embodies the whole institution. Marriage is also an interesting ritual from a pagan perspective, since many pagans have chosen to be married outside of the traditional felicity conditions, performing their own religious ceremonies and making a legal union by means of a justice of the peace. However, a judge is still necessary because the power of the performative act is so overwhelming that the ceremony itself, while it may have a spiritual effect, has no legal effect.

Spells and incantations are a particular kind of performative and, like other performatives, have their own felicity conditions. In an admittedly rather sketchy attempt to enumerate them, we can look at the common expectations of most (though not all) spells:

- The person doing the spell must be qualified to do it
- The spell must be constructed "correctly," with the proper words going with the proper materials
- The verbal part of the spell must be uttered in the appropriate manner

Let's look at each of these felicity conditions in turn, and see what they can reveal about the way magic works.

The person doing the spell must be qualified to do it. In different cultures this condition means different things. Rarely can someone simply recite a spell and get an effect (although one occasionally sees such things in folktales and legends). Usually, the person doing the spell must have some power. In the Songhai culture of Africa, one learns the praise songs that call upon the power of deities, but unless one has been initiated by "eating the *kusu*," or food of the gods, the songs are merely empty words.[34] Similarly, the ritual incantations in Hinduism must be performed by a particular priest, a person empowered to do them. In the Qabalah, there is the legend of the Ba'al Shem Tov, the Master of the Good Name, who by uttering the name of God can perform miracles. But he (or she if a Ba'ath Shem Tov) gains that power not by the mere utterance of the Name[35] but by initiation into the Qabalah and by righteous living. The magical incantation does not function in the world of cause and effect and scientific reasoning, in which anyone performing an experiment should have the same results.

Two things tie all of these cultural ideas about power together: the concept of initiation and what might be called ritual purity. The Songhai sorcerer eats the initiatory food and consumes his or her initiation as a meal. Thereafter, the sorcerer must perform certain ritual actions on a regular basis to maintain the power granted him or her. Similarly, a Ba'al Shem Tov, at least in traditional Jewish Qabalah, must maintain the Jewish laws of ritual purity, including keeping kosher and so forth. And the Hindu master of the magical Vedic hymns must be an initiated priest, but more importantly must maintain ritual purity; certain ablutions are performed before the ceremony, and so forth.

The way the magician (or sorcerer, shaman, or priest) comes by this initiation varies from culture and culture, and even within cultures. In Songhai culture, a *sorko*, or sorcerer who uses incantations, must learn them from a master sorcerer who also feeds him the kusu in a ritual meal. The sorko-in-training sits by his or her teacher's feet and learns the songs orally, as well as the use of ritual powders and preparation, all by memory. Shamans of many cultures gain power songs or incantations from spirits. Spirits come only after an initiation, which often involves a long and mysterious illness from which the shaman recovers by accepting his or her new role. Initiations in heavily incantatory magical systems involve

---

34. Paul Stoller and Cheryl Olkes, *In Sorcery's Shadow: A Memoir of Apprenticeship among the Songhay of Niger*. Chicago: University of Chicago Press, 1989.

35. In Hebrew, the Name is rendered יהוה, or YHVH in English. The vowels are unknown, and the issue is confused because Yud, Heh, and Vav, the three letters that make up the name, can each stand for vowels in certain situations.

acquiring, recovering, memorizing, or creating the required incantations. Celtic bards may have memorized an incredible amount of poetry before they considered their initiation complete. Similarly, a Greek Gnostic magician may seek secret "names of God" to use in his or her incantations.

To imagine that we are unqualified to do magic because we do not belong to one of these cultures, nor have access to their initiatory traditions, would be a disheartening mistake. In fact, we do have magical traditions in America in the twenty-first century, and we would do well to recognize and make use of that fact. Initiation in most of our magical systems, while often marked by rituals (such as a Wiccan ceremony involving hoodwinking and binding, or a ceremonial lodge initiation involving recitation, memorization, and oaths), is often assumed to be an internal rather than an external process. In the Western magical traditions, we do not consume knowledge as the Songhai do, but imagine that it grows within us like a plant. For this reason, new initiates in ceremonial magic are sometimes called neophytes, a word from the Greek meaning "new plant." Think about how you have grown since you began practicing magic, and express that growth in words—you may find yourself creating, or discovering, a power song of your own to claim your power.

The second felicity condition of magic, that *the spell must be constructed "correctly," with the proper words going with the proper materials*, is peculiar because it is so flexible. What it means differs a lot from culture to culture and spell to spell. Some spells require particular and difficult-to-acquire materials, while other spells involve everyday objects or nothing at all, but no matter what the spell involves, its words must be consistent with the materials used. For example, the Old English metrical charms, a series of spells recorded in the eighth century, contain instructions for a number of magical purposes, many of them involving some ritual actions. Often, those ritual actions are described in the spell itself, in the same meter as the incantation. For instance:

> I circle myself with this stick   And take succor in God's fealty
>   Against the sore stitch   And the sore blow

Against ferocious fear
Against mighty misfortune   which is hateful to everyone.[36]

In some rituals in the Greek Magical Papyri, there are formulas that directly address the material being used, such as "Wine, you are wine. Wine, you are not wine. You are the head of Athene."[37] Clearly, such an incantation can be efficacious only if one says it over a goblet or other container of wine. In the American folk tradition of Hoodoo, one might say a little rhyme while putting together a mojo bag, but here it is the objects themselves that have power and not necessarily the incantation. It's easy to imagine that words connect to objects in some solid way, although they do not from a linguistic or postmodern perspective. Words are arbitrary, by which I mean they are simply collections of sounds we have all agreed point to a certain object or idea, but are not that object or idea itself—except in magic. In magic, we make a link between the word and the idea.

Some people have argued that this basis of magical thinking is inherently irrational.[38] To identify the word with the thing it's meant to represent is to mistake the map for the territory, they claim, and I agree with this. In magic, however, we move beyond the ordinary use of words, what the linguists call "propositional," and into the performative use of language. In the performative sense, words *are* the things they signify. As J. L. Austin says, "When I say 'I do,' I am not reporting on a marriage. I am indulging in it."[39] The words "I sentence you to life" *are* the sentence that is handed down—those words point to nothing outside of themselves,

---

36. My translation of the first part of the metrical charm for a journey, in George P. Krapp and Elliot V. K. Dobbie, *The Exeter Book*. New York: Columbia University Press, 1936.

37. Hans Dieter Betz, *The Greek Magical Papyri in Translation*. Chicago: University of Chicago Press, 1997. A friend once recast this incantation as, "Diet soda, you are diet soda. Diet soda, you are not diet soda." It didn't have quite the same ring.

38. Among them, S. I. Hayakawa, whose book *Language in Thought and Action* (New York: Harcourt Brace, 1990 [1939]) is otherwise excellent and interesting reading for the magician interested in the way his or her world is shaped by words.

39. J. L. Austin, *How to Do Things with Words: Second Edition*. Cambridge, MA: Harvard University Press, 2005.

because they are a type of magical act, in which the utterance becomes fact by means of its being uttered. Therefore, if "magical thinking" in the sense of connecting words to the objects they represent is the root of superstition and irrationality, most of our ritual institutions—including marriage, the courts, and binding contracts—are superstitious and irrational.

One way to get used to the magical use of language is the exercise of talking to inanimate objects. I occasionally talk, out loud, to trees and rocks, and if I'm not somewhere where it can ruin my reputation or career (like, say, on campus—I'll wait until I get tenure for that), I'll do it in public. I'll admit that it's difficult to overcome the sense of embarrassment and social pressure, especially at first, but it's exactly those constraints that this exercise breaks down. It also links our words to the world in a way that we rarely do otherwise; we begin to confront the natural world, or our day-to-day world, not as a collection of *it*s, but as a collection of *you*s. To regard the world as a *you* rather than an *it* means to regard it not as a linguistic object that we are distant from, but as both the subject of discourse and its object. We are speaking to an object about that object, just as we may discuss our real feelings with a friend. Strangely, opening up to rocks and trees can also help us treat our friends, family, and even strangers as *you*s rather than *it*s.[40] Or maybe not so strangely; after all, magically speaking, what separates the spirit of a rock from the spirit of a tree, and what separates these spirits from the spirit of my friend, other than incidental appearances? Perhaps something: a rock might have other things to teach, and a friend lives faster and experiences more in a shorter time. But it might be foolish to ignore one and expect to be open to the other.

The final felicity condition for a magical spell is that *the verbal part of the spell must be uttered in the appropriate manner.* What this means depends on context. The magical book called the *Goetia* takes its name from the Greek word for "howl," perhaps implying a type of spell that is shouted or grumbled (although it may also imply that the demons listed within shout or howl). The Greek Magical Papyri frequently give

---

40.   Martin Buber, *I and Thou.* (Walter Kaufmann, trans.). New York: Simon & Schuster, 1970. Buber explores this idea in greater depth.

instructions for how to utter spells, suggesting that they be accompanied with "popping sounds" or "hisses." Classical Roman and Greek spells were often muttered inaudibly or whispered, which served both to protect the sacred words from the ears of the profane and create a sense of community between the magician and the forces he or she invoked. The linguistic evidence indicates that magical spells were sometimes sung—hence, *incantation*, containing the root *cantare*, "to sing." The Golden Dawn encouraged "vibration" of words of power, which amounts to a sort of sonorous plainchant. What this means for contemporary practical work is that we should not slog through long, dull recitations of magical incantations in a monotone if we expect to have an effect. Nor should we automatically adopt the pretentious "public ritual voice" that one hears so often (and some of us have even perpetrated on innocent attendees at public Samhain rituals, for instance). Instead, we should consider our choice in voice consciously and carefully.

Linguists label the way we say something, rather than what we say, as a type of "voice qualification." Voice qualifications include such things as whispering, "creaky voice," laughter, and so on. Such voice qualifications encode information about the attitude or mood of an utterance, rather than its strict meaning or propositional content. So if I whisper something to you, you can assume that I mean you to keep it a secret, and if I yell something, you can assume I am speaking to someone some distance away or want you to regard the information as urgent. Imagine an utterance like "Watch out." If I whisper, "Watch out," I'm probably warning you in a subtle way to be careful about something you're about to do or say, perhaps in a social situation. Maybe you're about to mention a sensitive topic in a social milieu where it would be inappropriate. If I yell, "Watch out," I'm warning you of an immediate, probably physical, danger. The propositional content is the same, but the thing it refers to in the world—its pragmatic meaning—is different.

Consider how we utter our incantations. To whisper an incantation might imply that we feel the addressee is close by; to shout it might imply distance, or an urgency bordering on the physical or hysterical. To use a broken voice, or a voice that "catches," might convey strong emotional needs. There may even be a place for the stentorian sing-song pretentious

voice of much ceremonial magic, especially in magic that relies on tradition and ceremony. Jan Fries argues that "an invocation, even if the
meaning is right, does not amount to much if it is voiced in a dull or
everyday modulation."[41] In many cases, the way we say things means
more to us than what we say. As an example of this, imagine one of those
conversations about running into "oh, so-and-so, you know, what's-her-
name's kid at the . . . oh, you know, *that* guy!" And suddenly, the face you
pull and the way you say *that* reveals exactly whom you're talking about,
without any need for further identification. I know that for me, some of
the most effective prayers I've ever uttered have been wordless growls of
frustration and need, with little or no semantic content at all.

Magicians seeking the primal language of the angels ignore a primal
language we speak every day. Humans have productive language with
syntax, while most primates have only an inherited system of calls, genetic
and instinctive, with which they are born. What many people don't realize is that we, being primates, are also born with a genetic and instinctive
system of calls—which is why a person from China, a person from Africa,
a person from Alaska, and a person from England all laugh essentially
the same, all cry the same, all sigh the same, and all make the same tonal
contour (whether by humming or saying *uh* or *eh*) when expressing surprise and curiosity. We can usually tell when foreigners are happy or angry
from the tone contour of their voices.[42]

Including the growls, hisses, moans, and yelps of our primate ancestors in magical incantation may, from a ceremonial perspective, seem
undignified and even silly, but even in the Western mystery tradition,
imitating the sounds of animals has a long pedigree. From a qabalistic
standpoint, this primate language is the language of our *nefesh*, our animal
soul, and therefore a wise thing to be aware of, since much power comes

---

41.   Jan Fries, *Visual Magic: A Manual of Freestyle Shamanism*. Oxford, UK: Mandrake,
      1992, 92.

42.   With some exceptions, of course. Some Americans believe that spoken Mandarin
      sounds angry because it's spoken at a slightly higher volume than American English
      and at greater speed, and because it is tonal, with wider swings in tone that American
      English speakers associate with strong emotion.

from that soul. From a shamanic perspective using the sounds of animals identifies us with the animal world, which is the primal world from which power comes. I suspect the dignified tones of much ceremonial magical incantation comes ultimately from the nineteenth-century British preoccupation with correctness and dignity. We have to ask ourselves if we are willing to abandon correctness and dignity, and embrace the entropy of ecstasy, if we are willing to sacrifice our shyness and self-consciousness on the altar of the temple. If we are, we might be able to reclaim the magic of our ancient, howling ancestors.

Characteristics of Incantation

From a literary standpoint, little work has been done on the shared characteristics of incantations. Incantations from different cultures display similarities that might be explained by the ancientness of the literary form, or by convergent evolution in the separate cultures in which they occur, or by the fact that incantations are constructed, used, and passed on for utilitarian reasons. In other words, incantations work and because they work, they are passed on in relatively stable forms from generation to generation, even in cultures that do not have writing. Moreover, because they work according to real principles, there are fundamental literary similarities among them, even in cultures as diverse as Indian Hinduism, eighth-century Anglo-Saxons, and Scottish Celts. The Hindu *Atharvaveda*, the Anglo-Saxon metrical charms, and the Scottish *Carmina Gadelica* (or "Gaelic Songs") are all collections of incantations and spells, some of them possibly stretching back, in the case of the *Atharvaveda*, to the Indo-European diaspora ten thousand years ago. Despite the difference in time and culture, these incantations all share structural similarities, including invocation of forces outside the charm, the use of an elaborate language of metaphor, and repetition and rhythm.

Invocation

Simply speaking, an invocation in the literary, not necessarily the magical, sense consists of an apostrophe, or direct address to a deity, angel, or other spiritual figure. This invocation can be in the third person (addressing the figure as "he" or "she") or in the second person (addressing the figure as "you"). One sometimes sees first-person invocations, as well, where the magician identifies himself or herself with the deity in question; the famous Bornless Ritual is a good example. In this ritual, the magician addresses the Bornless One in second-person language: "Thou didst produce the moist and the dry, and that which nourisheth all created life." Later, the magician also addresses the Bornless One in the third person: "This is He, Who having made Voice by his Commandment, is Lord of All Things; king, ruler, and helper." Finally, the magician identifies himself or herself with the Bornless One: "I am He! the Bornless Spirit! having sight in the feet: Strong, and the Immortal Fire!" The purpose of all of this invocation is to "make all Spirits subject unto Me."[43] In the *Atharvaveda*, we find a charm "for earthly and heavenly success" that begins with a surprisingly low-key invocation, simply stating as a fact that the gods will support the petitioner: "Upon this (person) the Vasus, Indra, Pushan, Varuna, Mitra, and Agni,[44] shall bestow goods." Shortly thereafter, however, the priest addresses the gods directly in a performative utterance: "Light, ye gods, shall be at his bidding."[45]

The *Carmina Gadelica* also makes use of invocation, of strikingly similar type. In fact, as the *Atharvaveda* shies from invoking the supreme godhead, similarly the *Carmina Gadelica* prefers to invoke angels, saints, Mary, and Jesus. However, the invocation of the supreme godhead is not unheard of, although it almost always occurs in company with a hierarchy of saints and other religious figures. For example, in a charm to invoke a blessing for ocean travel, the enchanter says:

> Mary, Bride, Michael, Paul,
> Peter, Gabriel, John of love,

---

43. David Godwin, *Light in Extension: Greek Magic from Homer to Modern Times*. St. Paul, MN: Llewellyn, 1992, 79–81.

44. Interestingly, these are very old Indic gods, the worship of which was popular thousands of years ago.

45. *Atharvaveda*. I, 9. Prayer for earthly and heavenly success. The Internet Sacred Text Archive, http://www.sacred-texts.com/hin/av/av140.htm (accessed 8 October 2005).

Pour ye down from above the dew
That would make our faith to grow . . . [46]

It is very common, in the *Carmina*, for the enchanter to recall a meta-phorical and pseudohistorical connection between the performative magical act he or she is performing at the moment, and an archetypal performative magical act performed by some important figure, usually Mary. For example, a *sain* (blessing) for sheep claims that it is "The sain placed by Mary/ Upon her flock of sheep" and a similar charm listed right after it claims to be "The charm placed of Brigit/ About her neat, about her kine."[47] These claims occur within the charms themselves, as part of what is uttered, and not as prefaces or notes to the charms. They are part of the text. The words "The sain placed by Mary/ Upon her flock of sheep" is not the title of the piece, but part of the incantation itself. For Mary to have placed this sain on her flock, therefore, she had to quote *herself* in the mythological past. The author of this charm separates the historical and the mythological Mary, so that the historical Mary can quote the mythological Mary. The speaker who identifies with the mythological past essentially says, "What I am saying now, this important figure said in the mythological past."

The appeal to a mythological past is a feature of what Huston Smith calls "primal religion." Huston Smith, in his discussion of Aboriginal Australian Dreamtime, explains that the Dreamtime is peopled by timeless figures who originated all the paradigmatic actions of daily life: hunting, cooking, traveling, and so on. Religion, for Aborigines, consists of identifying with these archetypal figures, so that when hunting one becomes the primal Hunter. Smith writes, "We are inclined to say that when the Arunta go hunting they mime the exploits of the first and archetypal hunter, but this distinguishes them from their archetype too sharply. It is better to say that they enter the mold of their archetype so completely that each *becomes* the First Hunter; no distinction remains. Similarly for

---

46. Alexander Carmichael, *Carmina Gadelica*. Edinburgh, UK: Floris, 1992, 120.

47. Ibid., 339.

other activities, from basket weaving to lovemaking."[48] Although the
Celtic charm-enchanters are Christian, and not members of what Smith
would call a "primal religion," nevertheless they seem to share this idea
that somewhere in our mythological past, there is an archetype that can
be tapped through invocation.

Metaphor

Calling upon an archetypal figure is a type of invocation, but many
charms also call upon archetypal relationships that can only be described
as metaphoric. Before analyzing the magical metaphor we find in charms,
it might be useful to briefly summarize literary, nonmagical metaphors,
at least insofar as any artistic utterance can be described as nonmagical.
Magical metaphors, such as those we find in the Old English charms
and in the *Carmina Gadelica*, differ slightly from the literary metaphor,
and both differ slightly from the overarching metaphors that sometimes
guide our thoughts, as I will discuss in chapter 9.

The literary metaphor can be divided into two parts: the target and
the source. The target is the item to which we apply some characteristic of
the source, so "he is a lion" is a metaphor in which "he" is the target and "a
lion" is the source, and we are to extrapolate some feature of the lion and
apply it to the target. In this case, perhaps its ferocity or courage. Usually,
most literary metaphors are multivalent but somewhat transparent. We
might find several characteristics that apply to the target, but reject other
characteristics. "Bill's a lion in the boardroom" probably means that he is
aggressive, fierce, and courageous. It probably doesn't mean that he eats
antelope raw in the boardroom, or has four feet, or roars loudly. What
we know about Bill—he's a human being, and probably a civilized one—
and what we know about lions—they are predatory animals—have both
points of similarity and points of difference. A "tight metaphor" is one in
which only one reasonable link between the target and source can be dis-
cerned: "Jennifer is a wizard with computers" can really only reasonably
mean that she is very skilled at computers. A "loose metaphor," on the

---

48. Huston Smith, *The World's Religions: Our Great Wisdom Traditions*. San Francisco:
     Harper Collins, 1991 [1958], 367. Original emphasis.

other hand, has many points of similarity: "Her voice was a symphony" could mean that her voice was pleasant. It could also mean that it was filled with emotion. Obviously, the tightness or looseness of metaphors is not absolute—some metaphors are very loose, and some are very tight. Some are so loose that it's almost impossible to discover a link between the target and source: "This book is the buffalo of the library" could mean so many things that we cannot be certain what, exactly, it does mean. Sometimes this uncertain relationship is known as an antimetaphor, but I prefer the term *paralogical metaphor*: it is beside logic, because it requires a fluid uncertainty in our thinking. Few literary metaphors are paralogical or extremely loose, but many magical metaphors are.

Some linguists and cognitive scientists believe that metaphor is fundamental to our thinking, a primary activity, and even the foundation of all of our linguistic activity. All language, some argue, is metaphorical.[49] I've already discussed the concept of the semiotic web, a model for the interaction between our categories of meaning, our symbols. Metaphor, from a magical standpoint, is the material of the strands of that web.

Some metaphors become so habitual that they ossify our thinking. For example, there's a common metaphor of "Education *is* war," and one hears things like "Teachers are the guardians at the gates" and "Teachers fight ignorance," and so on. This metaphor, if accepted unthinkingly and mindlessly, prevents us from recognizing the fact that ignorance is not the enemy of education but a *necessary condition* of education. If a student is not ignorant, that student requires no teaching! Furthermore, it is a short step from "Education *is* war" to "Students *are* enemies." And once teachers begin thinking that way, education becomes unlikely. Another example of ossified thinking due to metaphors is the common conception of love as insanity: "I'm mad about him; she's crazy over you; I'm smitten [i.e., struck, as by madness]." Many people come to expect the insanity of love,

---

49. For the most convincing discussion of the importance of metaphors, the various works of George Lakoff are worth reading in depth—especially George Lakoff and Mark Johnson, *Metaphors We Live By*. Chicago: Chicago University Press, 1980. The terms *target* and *source* were invented by Lakoff, although they are now in fairly common usage. For more on this approach to metaphor, see chapter 9.

without recognizing that love is actually a healthy and natural emotion, and one can feel it and be quite stable mentally. Being trapped in our old metaphors prevents us not only from living a richly mindful life but also from accessing our power. Many of our metaphors limit us to certain actions or roles—we imagine "I am a businessman" without recognizing that "businessman" is an abstraction. "I *am* a businessman" is a type of (rather boring) metaphor. When we say "I *am* a teacher" or "I *am* a writer" or "I *am* a student," we limit ourselves. Does a teacher like punk rock? Does a writer play football? Does an economics major open a gallery?

Paralogical metaphors are magical metaphors because they break us out of these thinking habits. In the Western magical tradition, there's an idea of passwords of various grades of initiation. These passwords have all been published for almost a century, so they cannot possibly serve the purpose of a password—i.e., identify members of a group or of a certain class. Instead, they may represent stand-ins for the metaphors learned at that level of initiation that break the chains of our own, unmindful metaphors. Similarly, the paralogical metaphors of some incantations may break us out of our habitual metaphors. For example, the great bard Taliesin demonstrates his freedom from all restrictive metaphors:

> I have been a blue salmon,
> I have been a dog, a stag, a roebuck on the mountain,
> A stock, a spade, an axe in the hand,
> A stallion, a bull, a buck, . . .
> I have been dead, I have been alive.
> I am Taliesin.[50]

With this incantation, whatever Taliesin's original goal, he reweaves the semiotic web around his identity and becomes something new. We can take advantage of this: select something in your environment and declare yourself that thing. Or create a list of random nouns and meditate on how they relate to you as a metaphor.

---

50.   Taliesin. "I Am Taliesin. I Sing Perfect Metre," Ifor Williams, trans., 1999. http://www.cs.rice.edu/~ssiyer/minstrels/poems/175.html (accessed 21 April 2008).

Repetition

The final characteristic of incantation I'd like to talk about is repetition. Repetition is not only common in incantation, but in oral poetry in general. In fact, it is one of the few features of poetry that appears in all cultures, whether it be repetition of sounds (rhyme), repetition of metrical units (rhythm/meter), or repetition of phrases. Repetition comforts listeners of mundane poetry because we are surrounded by rhythms and repetitions—the seasons, the days, our heartbeats, and so on. Repetition also serves the magical poet because it can help induce magical trance. The subconscious responds well to a rhythmic repetition.

Repetition of sound is called *rhyme*, and includes not just what we often think of as rhyme (called more precisely *end-rhyme*), such as cat/bat and food/mood, but also other sound repetitions. *Assonance* is the repetition of vowel sounds: "So round sounds roll on." *Consonance* is the repetition of consonant sounds, such as "The steam sounds, hisses, and spits." A special type of consonance and assonance is the repetition of initial sounds; this kind of repetition is called *alliteration*, and is common in poetry worldwide: "True will takes time." The earliest English poetry alliterated according to strict rules. Any of these sound effects can be used in incantation to emphasize important lines or to link together important ideas.

Repetition of metrical elements can include, as it does in English, the repetition of stressed and unstressed syllables in a strict pattern, so that the sentence "When shall we three meet again?" has a pleasing regularity. Different patterns of stressed and unstressed syllables tend to give a different impression to speakers of English, so that some rhythms seem mysterious, some conversational, and so on.

The final type of repetition is rather uncommon in written poetry, but almost ubiquitous in oral poetry and incantation. The repetition of entire lines or phrases is actually one of the earliest identified characteristics of oral poetry. Known as "formulas," these chunks of repeated poetry were woven together by oral poets to compose at speed without having to think about each word; they could focus instead on chunks of lines and string them together to fit the meter.[51] In incantations, there is some evidence of formulaic composition, as well as another type of repetition that fulfills some of the same functions as formulaic repetition. The repetition of entire lines not only emphasizes those lines to the deep mind that makes incantation work, but also gives the poet time to think of the next line. This method of repetition can help to improvise incantations.

A practice I find enjoyable is to create a formulaic structure and then weave it into an incantation based on the things that spring to mind extemporaneously. For example, I've started impromptu chants of gratitude to the gods with "blessed be the X" in which "X" is the first thing I see: so, while taking a walk, "Blessed be the trees, with their leaves changing. I give thanks, I give thanks." I continue, then, changing the blessed object to the next thing that occurs in my mind, building an eventual chain of associations that can be very long indeed:

> Blessed be the mountains, their tops capped with snow.
> I give thanks. I give thanks.
> Blessed be the rivers, flowing to the sea.
> I give thanks. I give thanks.
> Blessed by the wind, blowing from the west.
> I give thanks. I give thanks.

This type of spontaneous composition is both satisfying and sometimes enlightening. You may, for example, find yourself giving thanks for things you never imagined that you were thankful for. Other formula patterns you might use as starters (although you would probably have more fun making up your own) include:

- *I am X.*—In which X is anything you see or imagine. Don't worry about making much sense—just think in the logic of metaphor. It also helps to vary the tense: I have been X. I will be Y.

---

51.   Albert B. Lord, *The Singer of Tales.* Cambridge, MA: Harvard University Press, 2000.

- *I see you, Goddess, in X.*—Again, X is anything you see or imagine. Try throwing in the names of people you don't much care for after going on a bit; you may find yourself developing compassion for enemies. You can also replace "Goddess" with a more specific deity, and use it as an invocation or meditation on a deity's qualities.

- *X, you are not X, but you are Y.*—This is actually a common formula in ancient Greek magic, such as that recorded in the Leyden papyrus. It was often used to consecrate a poppet or other object for magical purposes, often in the form "Poppet, you are not wax, but you are my lover So-and-so." This formula is handy in sympathetic magic, in which you do to some symbolic object what you intend also to occur to the thing is symbolizes.

- *. . . who . . .* A handy word in invocations, *who* can precede any statement about any deity or spirit. The rhythm of the repetition can lull you into trance while reciting an entity's characteristics or myths. "I call you, Apollo, who slew the python and was purified, who traded his cattle for the lyre, who slew the man-slaying Achilles, who . . . "

- *. . . and . . .* This little word is often undervalued, but the repetition of conjunctions like *and*, *but*, and *or* is an important feature of spontaneous oral poetry. Parataxis, rather than subordination, is a common feature of oral language as well. Instead of worrying about the relationship between ideas, parataxis (the use of conjunctions like *and*, *but*, and *or*) allows us to pile up ideas in a way that overwhelms the conscious mind and resonates with the deep mind.

Our preference for written incantation, set ritual, and memorized chants might just be a side effect of our literate culture rather than an actual necessity of magic. Although there's some evidence that classical magic, at least, required carefully memorized prayers, there's also the fact that in primarily oral cultures (those that have not invented or been exposed to writing), the idea of what it means to memorize something is different from what we conceive of. We think that to memorize something "word for word" is to memorize each individual word, while in many oral cultures, to memorize something "word for word" is to memorize it idea for idea, while the individual semantic words are more or less inconsequential. In magical practice, re-embracing our ancient oral heritage not only changes our consciousness[52] but also opens up the possibility of the spontaneous joy that many people seem to miss in their magic.

In most of our language, words point to things. In incantation, words *are* things. Seeing magical language as performative not only helps explain the structure and stability of incantations; it also helps us to see that "magical thinking" is not as irrational as we might think. Words structure all our social institutions, from marriage to work. Moving from social reality to reality in general requires little effort, since the two are largely one. In the end, the difference between "star light, star bright" and "by the power vested in me," is vanishingly small.

---

52.   Walter Ong. *Orality and Literacy: The Technologizing of the Word.* New York: Routledge, 1982. Ong's book is somewhat outdated by more contemporary research, but he makes a good case for the important shift in consciousness that occurs when one learns to read.

FOUR

Sigils, Glyphs, and Characters: The Alphabets of Magic

In the last chapter, I mentioned that incantations show signs of our pre-literate history and that we might advantageously return to those roots or at least revisit them. In this chapter, however, I want to discuss the magical uses of humanity's most remarkable invention: writing. Language itself isn't an invention per se; we probably have some biological (or spiritual?) predisposition to the use of language. We're born ready to speak, and the fact that we learn our native language so quickly when we are otherwise incapable of abstract intellectual feats just serves as evidence of our inherent grammar. But we learn to write at a much later date, and writing is artificial where language is natural. Moreover, while we have no idea who first spoke or under what circumstances, we do have some concept of where writing was invented and by whom. Finally, if one makes communication difficult or impossible, new languages arise from the confusion,[53] but writing itself has been developed only a few times in human history.

Only three different writing systems have ever been invented. The most commonly invented writing system is called *ideographic* or *logographic*. In this system, one symbol stands for an entire word. In ancient Chinese, for example, the drawing of a tree represented the word for "tree." Ancient Egyptian hieroglyphs, similarly, are often drawings of what they stand for—you can draw an eye and mean "eye." And Sumerian cuneiform is, at its earliest level, crude drawings on clay tablets of the objects they represent. These earliest ideographic writing systems, unfortunately, ran into a simple problem: language is abstract, not always concrete. How do you draw "beauty"? The Chinese developed an ingenious system of combining characters, one that sounds like the abstract word to be represented, and one that indicates its general meaning. Or they combined two characters that represent the idea when combined. Sometimes this leads to clever combinations, such as the word for "good," which is "mother" combined with "child." Other times, it leads to what is apparent nonsense after millennia of language change: the word for "beauty," for example, is "sheep" combined with "man," because in ancient Chinese, the word for "sheep" sounded like the word for "beauty." The ancient Egyptians came up with a simple solution: they drew a musical instrument and allowed it to mean "beauty" in certain contexts. Or they added a special symbol, or even a sound or syllable of another word, to indicate if they meant a glyph to be read as an ideogram. Thus, they moved quickly toward two other kinds of writing: the syllabary and the alphabet.

In the syllabary, each symbol represents a single syllable of the word. For English this would require hundreds of symbols, but many languages have much simpler syllable structures. Japanese is still written with a syllabary to this day. A syllabary is apparently fairly easy to use and invent,

---

53. These languages, creoles, are often regarded as mixtures of two or more languages, but this is an oversimplification. While the vocabulary in a creole often comes from two different languages, creoles all have a strikingly similar grammar independent of the grammars of their origin languages, indicating that in some sense they're arising from some deep, underlying default grammar.

since it has been reinvented several times. Even Chinese could be considered not ideographic, but a very complex syllabary with ideographic elements. Ancient Greek was originally written with a syllabary, and when the nonliterate blacksmith Sequoyah wanted to create a writing system for his people, the Cherokee, he created a syllabary despite the fact that he had only ever seen (although never learned to read) alphabets.

The alphabet is the most flexible of all writing systems. An alphabet, instead of representing an idea, or an entire syllable, uses symbols to represent single sounds, known as phonemes. The alphabet has been invented only once, by the Proto-Canaanites, who gave it to the Phoenicians, who spread it around the world.[54] This early alphabet—actually an *abjad*, or alphabet without vowels—became the Hebrew alphabet and then, later, the Greek alphabet. The Greeks did the world the great service of adding vowels, a development the Romans and the Norse embraced. This same alphabet became the Latin alphabet this book is written in, the Greek alphabet, the Hebrew alphabet, the Cyrillic alphabet that Russian is written in, and the Northern European runes. In each of these, the letters changed shape slightly but maintained a family resemblance.

Magical Use of Writing in History

From the earliest records we have, we know that writing was used in magic. In fact, the first written characters we have of Chinese consist of markings on oracle bones. Bones or turtle shells were marked with characters and then heated; the cracks were interpreted according to which characters they passed through. We also know that Chinese characters, in a stylized form, were used by Daoist sorcerers as talismans and as gestures—they would "cut" a character into the air with a sword or fan, as a way of invoking its power. The stylized characters used by the Daoist sorcerers strongly resemble the style of the writing on the oracle bones,

---

54.   One could argue that the Korean writing system of Hangul is in fact an alphabet and therefore the alphabet has been invented twice. But since the Korean alphabet was invented relatively recently, and by people quite familiar with the concept of the alphabet itself, I'm hesitant to suggest that it was "invented" in the same sense as Sequoyah invented the Cherokee syllabary.

indicating either that there were two different forms of writing, one for magic and one for ordinary day-to-day work[55] or that the "magical" writing was just an earlier form of written characters before the invention of brush and paper led to their current characteristic shape.

The Hebrew qabalists used the written name of God as a magical talisman in its own right. The story of the Golem of Prague, for example, tells how the name of God in the golem's mouth brought it to life, while the word *ameth*, or "truth," on its forehead kept it alive. Furthermore, by erasing the first letter, the *ameth* was changed to *muth*, or "death," deactivating the golem. Merely writing a word invoked the force it represented.

In ancient Greece and Rome, this practice of writing a word to invoke its power led to the development of the *defixio* (*katadesmos* in Greek), which is a lead tablet or sometimes a poppet inscribed with a spell and thrown into a pit or well. Often these tablets were folded over and nailed shut—hence, the name *defixio*, meaning "something nailed." In archaeology, these tablets are mostly known as "curse tablets," because usually the thing written on them was not just any innocuous spell but a curse. These curses have very practical goals: confusing someone's speech in court, or making them lose a sporting event, or tormenting them until they love (or stop loving) the caster of the spell. These written spells are rarely for blessings or what we today might regard as positive goals. Perhaps the Greeks' ambivalent attitude toward writing (Plato calls it a poison that kills memory)[56] led them to develop a system in which writing is inherently suitable to negative magic. Moreover, while we might say incantations imagining that the god to whom we are speaking is nearby, most defixiones and katadesmoi were written to chthonic or underworld gods—what contemporary pagans sometimes call "dark" or "shadow" deities. Speaking aloud implies the presence of a speaker, at least until the relatively recent invention of recording materials and telephones, while writing implies a

---

55. This would be consistent with later Egyptian practice, too, in which the graphic hieroglyphs were used primarily for religious and magical texts, while other writing was done in a stylized, quickly written form of hieroglyphs.

56. Plato, *Phaedrus*. Benjamin Jowett, trans. New York: C. Scribner's Sons, 1871. Online at http://www.sacred-texts.com/cla/plato/phaedrus.htm (accessed 21 April 2008).

distance in space and time. To write down a spell and drop it in a well is to send it like a letter to the underworld. It simultaneously curses and keeps the curser at arm's reach from the powerful and sometimes unpredictable chthonic deities. More pleasant spells were probably spoken, not written, and therefore were ephemeral.

Defixiones are peculiar in terms of form, as well. In ancient Greece and Rome, verbal spells might be driven by emotion, such as Theocritus's description of the witch Simaetha's love spell, in which she passionately interjects in the middle of the spell, "Ah, cruel Love, why do you cling to me like a leech from the swamps and drain all the dark blood from my body?"[57] Written spells, however, make use of a language that to contemporary eyes might look more suitable on a legal brief. Part of the reason for this emotional coolness might be, again, the chthonic deities being invoked, against whom the best protection seems to have been cleverness and coolheadedness. But it might also be a bit of the monkey-paw motif,[58] in which one must be careful what one wishes for, in the certain knowledge that one will get it. Such careful language and precision implies that, for at least some users of defixiones, they did in fact get what they asked for. And other users *expected* to get exactly what they asked for.

An unusual element of the defixiones, arising particularly in later specimens, is the addition of *charactres* [*sic*], or sigils. These sigils have no conventional meaning, although they bear some resemblance to symbols used by early astrologers to represent fixed stars, and a large number of them resemble the magical alphabets described by Francis Barrett and others.[59] They are linear drawings with circles at the ends of lines, in various configurations. Sometimes they are also ideographic in nature—a drawing

---

57. Georg Luck, *Arcana Mundi: Magic and the Occult in the Greek and Roman Worlds*. Baltimore: Johns Hopkins University Press, 1985, 69.

58. Named after a short story, *The Monkey's Paw*, published in 1907, the motif refers to a wish fulfilled in an unpleasant and unexpected way.

59. Such as in Francis Barrett, *The Magus: A Complete System of Occult Philosophy*. York Beach, ME: Samuel Weiser, 2000. Mostly a cut-and-paste and regurgitation of Agrippa, Barrett did gather together several magical alphabets currently in use in the nineteenth century, as well as geomancy symbols and alchemical symbols that share some resemblance with the much older charactres.

of a person, for example, with pins or spears sticking in his limbs. The ideographic sigils were probably intended to have an iconic or sympathetic effect; by drawing what we desire, we can gain power over it.

The other class of characters on the defixiones are non-iconic or abstract. They lack conventional meaning, by which I mean it is impossible to determine what they might have meant to the person drawing them. While some characters repeat from tablet to tablet, these characters are fairly simple drawings in general and therefore repetition may not indicate any sort of set tradition. On the other hand, we have the handbooks of several magicians who record the characters they use for certain spells, and the care with which these characters are recorded and the seriousness with which they are recommended speak eloquently for their importance. It is possible that such characters were given by various tutelary spirits or gods in visions, in dreams, or through some method of scrying. It is also possible that such characters were attempts to approach a divine or transcendent language. The logic is that what cannot be understood by a human might be comprehensible by an angel or spirit. Other theories include the rather cynical idea that the characters provided an aura of mystique and arcane knowledge to the practitioner. They served an economic function, making the product of the defixio look more magical and powerful to potential customers. While that possibility might seem appealing to those who seek an economic explanation for human behavior, it doesn't explain the fact that some defixiones were probably prepared not by professional magicians but by individuals for themselves. Most likely, the characters were used because they represented something, either in the conventional or occult sense, that could not easily be conveyed in more ordinary words.

Sigils are and have been the pocket knife of magical practice. In medieval magic, for example, each spirit is often given a seal that is used to summon and control that spirit. Such seals are passed down from magician to magician, in letters or in books called grimoires. More recently, the early twentieth century magician A. O. Spare created his own sigils for idiosyncratic purposes. He composed his sigils for a single purpose, then destroyed them. This practice of creating single-use sigils for particular purposes has been revived in the chaos magic community and has spread in recent years to almost all branches of magic. The process is simple: combine the letters of a word or statement into a single shape. The advantage is that entire sentences can be composed into a graphic image that bears no resemblance to the original sentence of desire. Some theories[60] suggest that this practice bypasses the conscious mind that prevents magic from occurring. Other theories[61] suggest that the deep mind, from which magic comes, operates more efficiently through symbols than verbal constructions. Unfortunately, this theory ignores the fact that verbal constructions are in fact symbols, but the theory can be saved by recognizing that the information content of a sigil is greater than that of an equivalent sentence and therefore might be a more efficient transmitter of information to the deep mind.

The idea that a sigil contains more information than a sentence might require some explanation. A sigil contains so much information that a second person cannot decipher it. Even the maker may not know what a sigil means or meant in any conscious way; in fact, most users of sigils recommend forgetting the purpose of the sigil after use. It might seem paradoxical that the very thing that makes a sigil meaningless is its superabundance of information, but information and meaning are not the same thing. A tablet written in the Rongorongo script, a Rapa Nui script that no one can read, is meaningless, because no one alive can understand the information encoded on it. But it still contains information—we can even, theoretically, measure the quantity of information by analyzing the frequency of occurrence of certain symbols (although with the small sample size of the Rongorongo script, the results would be highly speculative). Similarly, until they were deciphered, Egyptian hieroglyphs were meaningless, although they still retained their original information. Too little information in a system is meaningless—as for example the word *the* by itself without context. Similarly, too much information in a system is what we commonly refer to as random—such as the string *uytoyhugbv*

---

60. Frater U.·. D.·., *Practical Sigil Magic: Creating Personal Symbols for Success.* St. Paul, MN: Llewellyn, 1990.

61. Jan Fries, *Visual Magick: A Manual of Freestyle Shamanism.* Oxford, UK: Mandrake, 1992.

created by smashing my hand down on my keyboard. The sigil contains so much information that it cannot be decoded back into meaningfulness by the conscious mind. Yet the information is still there, because the process of creating the sigil maintains the information throughout as it obscures the conventional meaning. Including such symbols in a text thus increases the information content, while the meaning is maintained by the text itself.

The use of magical letters or defixiones seems to have waned after the rise of Christianity. However, during the Middle Ages one could buy letters for protective, rather than cursing, purposes. Such letters often contained the invocation of magical figures—this time, saints, angels, and the Virgin Mary—and the authority of religious figures. Many such letters were decorated with the symbols of various saints or icons, or in Protestant traditions, the sign of the cross, or the chi-rho monogram of Christ's name (a sigil!). The American book *Pow-Wows; or, Long Lost Friend* is a grimoire or magical handbook of Hexcraft, an American folk magic tradition mixing Protestant (usually Lutheran) magical practices with Native American practices, as well as its own innovation. *Pow-Wows* ends with the statement: "Whoever carries this book with him, is safe from all his enemies, visible or invisible; and whoever has this book with him cannot die without the holy corpse of Jesus Christ, nor drowned in any water, nor burn up in any fire, nor can any unjust sentence be passed upon him. So help me."[62] The invocation is sealed with three crosses, although interestingly these are equal-armed or solar crosses rather than the more commonly seen Calvary cross. Most letters of protection and blessing were single pages, carried with one or hung up in the house, but adding such a blessing to a book guaranteed its popularity not just as a handbook but as a talisman in its own right.

---

62.   John George Hoffman, *Pow-Wows; or, Long Lost Friend* (1820). Online at http://www.sacred-texts.com/ame/pow/index.htm (accessed 21 April 2008).

Contemporary Use of Writing in Magic

In more recent times, the use of magical letters found a resurgence in the New Thought movement that prefigured the New Age. This movement taught the importance of positive thinking and visualization, and with the publication of the small pamphlet *It Works* in 1976, many people began using defixiones without realizing it.[63] Although *It Works* does not suggest that the process by which writing down desires to make them manifest is magical, it embraces some foundational magical principles: one is to write down one's desire in detail (establishing a statement of desire), think about it often as if it has already happened (reducing lust for results), and not talk about it until it occurs (encouraging the magical virtue of silence and preventing the doubts of others from intruding). A later book, *Write It Down, Make It Happen*, encourages a much more freeform approach—in fact, the thesis of the book is summed up in the title.[64] The traditions of characters, sigils, *voces magicae*, and the disposal of the defixio in a well or pit, are all absent from this practice.

In contemporary practice I have heard of magicians who have had success simply writing down and burning their statement of desire. "Thee Temple of Psychick Youth" (TOPY), now mostly defunct (although it's difficult for such an anarchic group to become completely defunct, and I occasionally still run into people who spell the definite article "thee"), had a practice of writing down one's desire in succinct terms, anointing it with saliva, blood, and semen (or vaginal fluid), and sending it to a central location. This process is textbook defixio, and makes me wonder if Genesis P-Orridge, the founder, hadn't studied classical magic. Unlike the *It Works* model, it includes the characters and sigils (potentially—it is not entirely clear whether the statement of desire was the only thing included), the sacrifice or ritual action, and the sending or transmission of the sigil itself. One could consider oneself a full-fledged member of TOPY after having performed twenty-three "sigils" or defixiones.

---

63. R. H. Jarrett, *It Works*. Camarillo, CA: DeVorss & Company, 1976.

64. Henriette Anne Klauser, *Write It Down, Make It Happen: Knowing What You Want—and Getting It!* New York: Fireside, 2000.

The practices outlined in *It Works* and similar pieces of New Thought gave rise to the practice of positive affirmations, short statements that were written and repeated over and over in order to give confidence to overcome difficulties, in the mundane interpretation, or to cause direct change in the universe, in the magical interpretation. Most magicians have at least experimented with such affirmations and found them lacking. On the other hand, their continued popularity indicates that they work for some people. Still, they lack most of the characteristics of classical defixiones, and this lack may be a reason for their limited successes for some people.

Innovation and Historical Inspiration

Defixiones seem unlikely to go out of style any time soon, and I think there's a lot of room for experimentation in the field of magical writing. The historical record is useful in exploring what our ancestors thought about magic, but it's important not to be too slavishly bound to historicity. For example, the use of lead as a medium of inscription in ancient Greek defixiones was partially because lead was readily available and easy to inscribe. Only in relatively late defixiones are the physical and magical characteristics of lead invoked sympathetically, by for example calling on the gods to turn the person named in the lead plate as heavy and cold as the lead itself. Early practitioners of defixio probably regarded the lead much as we might regard parchment or acid-free paper—a relatively permanent, somewhat special, but not entirely unusual writing surface. So for us, in the twenty-first century, to use lead as a writing surface surpasses our ancestors rather than imitates them. For us, parchment and rag paper are more appropriate choices, if we wish to maintain the relative symbolic significance of the materials. Of course, we might not want to maintain that significance at all; for whatever reason, we may consciously choose to disregard the ancient practice for the modern.

For example, in the ancient practice of defixio, the letters were inscribed into the lead with a stylus, a writing instrument consisting of a sharp point and a handle. This kind of writing instrument was not unusual; it was probably not as common as a ballpoint pen or a pencil is to us, but it was available to persons of limited means. It created letters by engraving, or removal of the writing medium (the lead). We almost exclusively write most of our material by embossing, or adding material to the writing medium (ink or graphite particles to paper, in most cases). While embossing as a means of writing wasn't unheard of in ancient Greece and Rome, engraving was just as common.

The point of this bibliographic digression is that when we sit down with pen, paper, and ink, we sit down with three objects, while the ancient Greek or Roman sat down with only stylus and lead, two objects. So symbolically, if we wish to make the act as maximally significant as possible (a good magical practice in general), we need to account for the ink. We don't know what correspondences ancient magicians used, if they even used any. Therefore, I'm not going to advocate a particular set of symbolic associations as superior to any other. But in my own practice I regard the special pen I use (a dip pen, a quill with a metal nib, given me by a friend) as the axis mundi, the center of the world and the entry point into all possible worlds. I regard the paper as the surface of consciousness itself, the substance upon which the universe is written, which I am now about to edit or add to. Finally, I regard the ink as the underlying fluid of my own unconscious, black but charged with the light of mind. So I am laying the substance of my own unconscious upon the surface of the universal consciousness, through the axis mundi which is the gateway to all possible worlds. Other symbolic systems may have a better aesthetic effect on other practitioners; I don't expect anyone to adopt my rather complex and esoteric cosmology unless they also find it compelling.

Originally, when I first began working with defixiones, I simply left them on the altar when finished and, when they manifested, burned them or disposed of them outdoors. Recently, however, I read an article that changed my approach to defixiones in a rather obvious way—at least, obvious in retrospect. The article was "Beneath the Pavement, the Beast," a discussion of the use of the situationist[65] technique of *derive*, or drift, in

---

65. The situationist movement, or Internationale Situationniste, was an artistic and anarchic political movement active in the middle of the twentieth century in France and elsewhere.

magic.[66] Derive (pronounced approximately "duh-REEV") was originally a way of integrating artistic sensibility with the environment, by deliberate derangement of the senses and drifting from locale to locale as if they were unfamiliar or alien. In other words, it was a means of changing an artist's consciousness to regard the familiar as unfamiliar, in hopes of refreshing one's perception and escaping the controlling economic and social pressures that the situationists believed underlay all culture. The practice of using the derive for magic is not entirely in line with situationist principles, such as they were, but it does provide a means of regarding the world not as an alien piece of art but as an analogue to the astral plane. What attracted me to the practice was that it mixes astral work (which I lean on heavily) and street magic (which I am also attracted to).

The practice, in a nutshell, consists of regarding some point as an entryway, sanctified and guarded by various gateway deities. (I use Janus Bifrons, having already developed a relationship with him.) One makes offering to those deities and passes through the gateway with the intention of remaining in the physical world but simultaneously interpreting the material world as a spiritual, or astral, message. So one is effectively traveling in two worlds.

There is a historical connection between this practice of magical derive and defixio. One of the most important elements of the defixio, as practiced in antiquity, was that it be deposited in an appropriate place—a well, a grave, or sometimes nailed to a particular wall. The magician inscribed the defixio in one location and then carried it to another location to be delivered. The magician traveled from place to place, just as the statement of desire traveled from potential to manifestation. While the classical practitioner probably regarded the depositing of the defixio in a well or grave as a means of delivering it to the chthonic gods, it is not hard to imagine delivering it not just to the chthonic gods, but to the chthonic depths of our own consciousness, where individual mind and universal Mind become the same thing. The defixio can be inscribed in

---

66.   Stephen Grasso, "Beneath the Pavement, the Beast." In Jason Louv (ed.), *Generation Hex*. New York: Disinformation, 2006.

one place and carried, physically and astrally, through a portal into the other world, and then deposited in a symbolically significant physical location and an astrally important magical location at the same time.

An Example of a Defixio with a Derive

I'll provide an account of such a working so you can see how it looks from the inside. Obviously, this account is of my process, not necessarily yours. It is a composite of various magical operations I've performed. An outside observer may regard some of these ritual actions as odd or even silly. Part of the point of ritual magic is to behave outside the ordinary to accomplish things one might otherwise not be able to. It works for me and brings me pleasure and success; it may work similarly for you.

I begin any such operation by carefully considering what I am going to say—what, in other words, the statement of desire will be. I achieve better success when I express the statement of desire in direct, positive terms. By *direct*, I mean with as few modifiers (adjectives and adverbs) and being-verbs as possible. Adjectives and adverbs are low in information content, and being-verbs are almost devoid of information. By the same rationale, one could also eliminate the articles *a* and *the*, but this produces ungrammatical sentences, which don't work for me. Many people prefer to eliminate negative words, such as *nothing*, *not*, *no*, and *nobody*, by recasting negatives as positives. The usual reason I've heard is that the subconscious mind cannot understand negatives and so deletes them; I've yet to see any evidence of this. I prefer to eliminate them from statements of desire simply because the positive statement that corresponds to a negative tends to be better written: more clear and direct. It also forces the conscious mind to admit the possibility, while the negative does not. For example, the statement "Let me not get a cold" is less direct than "Let me be healthy." It also doesn't strike at the heart of the true desire, which is for health rather than freedom from a single cold. "Make Mary not cheat on me" similarly suffers from poor style, while also guaranteeing that the magician does not manage to imagine a faithful girlfriend, but a cheating one. Of course, it also raises ethical questions, forcing Mary to do something she might not want to do. "May I find a faithful lover" might be more effective in that light—if Mary is it, and can be faithful, and will be of her own will, then there you go. If not, maybe you'll meet Ted at the bar next week and discover something new about yourself.

After deciding what my statement of desire will be, I go to my workspace where I have laid out my magical tools. For this operation, all I really need is my pen, ink, and some paper. I perform a banishing ritual, usually the Lesser Banishing Ritual of the Pentagram. Or if in a hurry I might just purify myself with sanctified water and sage smoke. Finally, I acknowledge and invite any gods and spirits that I might want to help me. Obviously, if you don't have a relationship with any gods or spirits, this step can be skipped.

Following the purification comes the shifting into another state of consciousness. There are lots of ways to do this, and depending on mood or time, I might try any of them. You want a state of consciousness that you can maintain long enough to write down the statement of desire. The fourfold breath, described in chapter 2, is an easy method of calming the mind and attaining a very light trance. The fourfold breath increases oxygen in your blood, which can help push you into an altered state of consciousness. Some people enjoy drumming; a rhythm of about four to five beats a second in a steady tattoo can entrain the mind into a trance. So can swaying, rocking, and shaking. Whatever method you use, once you attain that altered state of consciousness, pick up your pen, dip it into the ink (unless the two aren't separate, of course), and write your statement of desire.

I try to visualize the writing of the statement of desire as if I were inscribing my desire directly on the substance of reality itself with fire. Pay attention not to the meanings of the words but to the shapes and forms of the letters, as if they were abstractions. It may help to look at the space between the letters, the negative space as artists call it, and the shapes made by the adjacent letters. At this point, my hand will usually want to create sigils spontaneously—I may scribble three or four such sigils on the paper, not knowing where they come from or what they mean. I regard this automatic writing almost as a modem handshake—it lets me know that I'm in touch with something deep in my mind that's pushing messages in both directions.

Once finished, I fix the paper in some way, by rolling and tying with appropriately colored thread, for example. The ancient defixiones were nailed shut, hence the name, but I prefer the symbolism of tying. I've also experimented with sealing wax, but I have a white rug and a lack of patience. After fixing the defixio, I put it on the altar, offer thanks, banish, and clean up my tools. Then I grab my coat and the defixio.

My derive often begins at a nearby crossroads or at my front door. Both are example of an in-between space where one can access the astral plane. I say a prayer to Janus Bifrons, god of doorways and crossroads, under my breath, asking for permission to enter the derive. Then I imagine a doorway opening in front of me, and I hold in my mind the idea that this doorway leads to a world much like mine, but closer to the astral plane, and in which I'll find a place to "mail" my defixio. I step forward into the doorway.

Once I've symbolically entered the other world, there are several options. There is a park within walking distance and usually I will go there, but I could also turn toward the university or head toward town. Often I will watch for indicators of what direction to go to—the flights of birds, odd cars or significant-seeming bumper stickers, that sort of thing, or I'll use convenient puddles as scrying mirrors. Of course these are things that one could dismiss as coincidence, but I prefer to assume, in a derive, that coincidence is communication. Having chosen or been directed in a direction, I continue to walk. If I go to the park, there is a path that runs through it and a stream as well. The stream is a good place to deposit defixiones, as water is a common symbol for the deep mind. Also, there are hollow trees, animal dens, and various other holes and depressions, all of which could be traditional places to deposit a defixio. In the city, there are sewer grates, subways (although not in my city), and construction sites. The point is to find a place that clearly, symbolically identifies itself as the destination for your defixio. That identification may just be a sensation of rightness, or you may hold out, as I tend to, for a more unambiguous sign—an insect landing on the spot, or a dust devil, or some other indication. In the city, a snatch of overheard conversation can provide a clue. You may also be offered a challenge—go to a place that makes you uncomfortable or nervous. You have to decide if it's worth it. Throughout the entire trip, the key is to maintain a double consciousness, one of the physical reality and the other of the astral reality.

I usually accompany the depositing of the defixio with a small prayer, along the lines of "Deep mind, I deliver this desire to you, that you act on it and manifest it according to my will, with no harm to anyone." I make every effort not to think of the contents of the defixio at that moment but just to deposit it with faith in its eventual manifestation, whatever it is. Of course, saying aloud a short prayer on the city street may seem ostentatious to some, silly to others, and to yet others, entirely impossible. One of the values of this method, to me, is that it challenges my limits and forces me to confront my fears of social opprobrium. To that end, if the derive sends me into the city, as it well may, I force myself to say the prayer aloud or, at the very least, in a whisper. Shouting it, probably, would be overkill as well as historically inaccurate. We have several mentions in the classical corpora of incarnations being muttered, hissed, or whispered. Part of the reason for this tone of voice, however, may have been the illegality of such spells. We have the great fortune to live in a society that regards the practice of magic as eccentric, rather than criminal, and therefore while we might have to struggle against the disbelief and occasional disapproval of others, we do not have to struggle against armed guards taking us into custody (unless, of course, in the process of depositing your defixio, you break some mundane law). Most of these ritual actions are mental. To most observers, this ritual appears to be a simple walk with occasional stops to contemplate mud puddles or the flights of birds. On the other hand, there might also be call, on a defixio, to do something unusual and strange, even embarrassing. On one defixio, for instance, I felt compelled to kneel and compose an extemporaneous paean of praise to a small sapling growing near an abandoned parking lot. In another, I left an offering of a candy bar in the crosswalk of an intersection (timed with the lights). I've begun to rely upon the fact that people will ignore a lot of weird behavior, especially in a college town.

After depositing the defixio, I will usually retrace my steps back, unless some clear indication or sign signals me to do otherwise. In a de-rive, as the name implies, you are not entirely in control. You are drifting through a landscape that reflects the astral landscape to which you have taken your defixio. Therefore you might find, on the derive, signs of how to proceed with your desire. It's important, however, not to expect such things or think consciously of your desire. To accomplish this "don't think of the monkey" task, I usually mentally rehearse a mantra—anything will work, but if you can't think of anything else, try *Aum*, the traditional Sanskrit word that symbolizes the perfection of creation. You may also chant to yourself the name of a deity or spirit who seems appropriate—"Aphrodite" for love defixiones, or "Horus" for defixiones of defense and justice.

When I arrive at the crossroads, I make another prayer to Janus Bifrons, step again through a portal or doorway, this time intending to return home, and then take a few moments to ground and center. Grounding and centering consists of, in its simplest terms, becoming conscious of one's body and one's space within it, and the pull of gravity on that body. It's a way of making sure that you are present and aware and in an ordinary state of consciousness (whatever that is). Once in this state, I return home. I make an effort on the trip to consider trivialities or mundane things that do not involve my goal. I try to put the defixio out of my mind just as I symbolically placed it out of the world.

The elaborate ritual described above is only one way to realize the process of defixio. I have had equal success by just writing down the desire and putting it on the altar. However, the above elaborated ritual provides a framework for those who wish to experiment on their own, to simplify or to elaborate. Elaborations that some may prefer include particular ceremonial frameworks, such as the Golden Dawn method of creating talismans and the inclusion of objects of natural magic, such as particular herbs, stones, and so forth, into a packet. Other may prefer fewer elaborations—a friend of mine performs his defixiones by writing down his desire in as precise terms as possible. Often, he says, this requires writing for a while, to work through what he really wants. Finally, with the statement of desire clearly expressed, he goes about his business certain that it will manifest. He and I share a fundamental rule, Rule Zero, which says, "If anything—ritual elaboration, necessary materials, or whatever—prevents you from actually performing the magic, throw it away." In other words, if you like the ritually elaborate method I describe above, but find you don't have the time to do it or can always find an excuse to do something else, then throw away that method and find something that fits better in your schedule. As Goethe reportedly said, "What you can do, or dream you can do, begin it! / Boldness has genius, power and magic in it."[67]

Theory

In magic, the *practice* of magic is paramount. Theory is secondary. Magic is above all a practical thing, and the defixiones show that. They are for practical (if rather lamentable) goals: overcoming an enemy, winning a bet, getting a lover, getting rid of a lover. They existed alongside a more rarefied form of magic, theurgy, which was concerned with identifying and communing with the gods. Theurgy has its own attractions, especially to the magician interested in language, as we'll see in later chapters, but it is defixiones where language is used for its magical purpose, almost unadorned. Even the characters that appear on the tablets may have been considered a type of language-beyond-language, a language of the spirits or gods. So defixiones provide us with a clear example of language used for magical purposes, over centuries and, arguably, into the present.

While practice is paramount, it's hard to be a magician and not be concerned with theory. Being curious is a human trait, and humans love their theories. Defixiones work—stipulated. The question is, why do they work? Upon what mechanism do they depend to influence the world at large?

The ancient Greek or Roman using defixiones had a clear idea of the mechanism. The deities did it. Sometimes people have an idea of the Greeks and Romans being rather childlike in terms of religion, imagining anthropomorphic gods having sex with animals and the like. Although the anthropomorphic characteristics of the gods in Greek and Roman religions should not be underplayed, adherents to these religions also had a more sophisticated view of the gods, not unlike that held by many Hindus today. While the gods in Hellenistic Greece, for example, were multiple and anthropomorphic, many Neoplatonic philosophers regarded them as all aspects of the same higher deity. Stoics, similarly, all considered gods

---

67.   Goethe never actually said that, but he could have.

part of the mind of Zeus, who was most often characterized as a "fire" that underlay reality. This last theory is surprisingly like Spinoza's idea of God being the underlying substance of infinite qualities (or perhaps not so surprising, since Spinoza was familiar with Stoic thinking). The Romans often didn't even think of their gods anthropomorphically until their contact with the Greeks. The very earliest Roman religion was animistic, in that every natural phenomenon had a spirit, or *numen*. The *numines* of powerful and important natural phenomena became gods. To throw a piece of writing, a letter as it were, into a well or depression in the ground was to ask the numen of that place to operate in the world for you. In this sense, defixiones are shamanistic: they work through the spirits of natural phenomena.

A more contemporary view of magic is the belief that all magic is effected by a sort of subtle energy. In its most materialistic form, this paradigm suggests that there is an energy, undetected by science, that infuses all reality and we can move that energy with our minds. These tablets, then, are talismans—objects charged with this energy in a specific way and for a specific purpose—and to cast them away is to send the energy out to work in the world. Notice that all one need to do is replace "energy" with "spirits" in the above, and you return to the original, shamanistic conception of how defixiones work. The difference, of course, is that in the energy paradigm, the energy comes from oneself. I call this view of magic contemporary because it's influenced by eighteenth-century Western ideas of the nature of the world. For example, proponents of this paradigm sometimes say "everything is energy," while in the eighteenth century a natural philosopher might argue that "everything is magnetism." There are ancient paradigms that have similarities to the energy paradigm. For example, the idea of "mana," often borrowed for video games and role-playing games, is indigenous to the Polynesian peoples of the Pacific Ocean. They believe that everything in the universe has its store of mana (much like numen). This mana gives things a sense of awe, power, and efficacy. If a person has a lot of mana, he or she is powerful and naturally fortunate. One can become more fortunate by gathering mana, through particular rituals of worship or through magic. A good translation of *mana*, therefore, might be "personal power." "Energy" as a metaphor for this type of "personal power" strikes me as a fairly reasonable and useful paradigm for describing the effects of magic. One deposits the defixio in a well, therefore, because it has a certain type of mana, and some of that mana will rub off on you.

Another model or paradigm that explains how defixiones work is one that I particularly enjoy working with, partially because of its new-ness, and partially because it affords me insights I might not arrive at with other paradigms. The information paradigm, as readers of my last book will know, is the model of magic that explains the entire world as a system of interlocking symbols. Magic influences those symbols to cause physical change. One can think of the world as a froth of matter on top of a great sea of consciousness, and our little consciousnesses interact with that sea to communicate desires and cause change. Sending a de-fixio is a physical analogue of the magical act, which consists of sending a message to this underlying consciousness or deep mind.

Understanding how to perform magic is essential, but understanding why it works might be interesting. If we understand how magic works, we can refine our magical technologies to be more and more effective. Of course, it's possible—even probable—that there is no one way that magic works. Instead, magic, like the mind, works differently for each person. That one person gets success with one method and another with a different method testifies to this truth. Magic is as multiform as humans themselves. Still, there may be some principles, some guidelines, that we could uncover and explore to increase our own stores of mana or our own depth of communication with the deep mind. There is value in casting the defixiones our ancestors did a millennium ago, but there is also value in understanding how we might refine their techniques and speak our own postmodern magical language.

FIVE

From Babel to Enochian: The Search for the Primal Language

Scholars, ranging from magicians to philosophers and scientists, have struggled to find the primal language, a language spoken in heaven by angels or by the spirits or by the first *Homo sapiens*. Attempts to arrive at this primal language range from speaking in tongues to the carefully copied tables and charts of John Dee's "Angelic Language," often called *Enochian*. All of these kinds of primal language share the idea that somewhere in the distant, mythological past, human beings spoke a perfect language from which we have fallen.

The fascination with origins manifests differently in different cultures. The Judeo-Islamo-Christian tradition, which has dominated Western thought in part or in whole since the conversion of the Roman Empire, has a linear and progressive view of time. We have a beginning, we have a present, and we have a future, all relatively set; and while our present is imperfect, our future, we are promised, will grant us perfection. This view of time is not the only one available. Huston Smith describes time in what he calls the primal religions as circular and regressive. Aboriginal shamanic peoples often do not strive for some future redemption but instead hearken back to a period of perfection in the mythological

past. Life in the present is a matter of returning again and again to this
mythological "Dreaming," as Australian aborigines call it.[68] Our culture
places perfection in the future; primal cultures place it in the past. However, these two views are not as mutually exclusive as they might appear.
After all, at one point even the Hebrew tribes who founded the main
philosophical currents of Western civilization were tribespeople—in other words, aborigines. And we have evidence that they also had this idea of
a primal source privileged by its anteriority: Adam and Eve fell from an
original state of grace through an act of disobedience. Yet the Jews also
developed the idea of future perfection in the concept of the Messiah
who would free the Jewish people from slavery. On the other hand, even
this is a circularity, as Moses could be seen as the primal ancestor who
freed the Jews, originally, from oppression, and the Messiah would be a
hearkening back to this archetypal event.

The same sort of ambiguity is present in the origin myths of language presented by the Torah. Genesis gives us two origin myths for
language. In the first, Adam, the first man, is given the task of creating a
language that, apparently, consisted mostly of nouns:

> 2:19 And out of the ground the Lord God formed every beast
> of the field, and every fowl of the air; and brought them unto
> Adam to see what he would call them: and whatsoever Adam
> called every living creature, that was the name thereof.

> 2:20 And Adam gave names to all cattle, and to the fowl of
> the air, and to every beast of the field; but for Adam there was
> not found an help meet for him.[69]

Adam's primal language consists of names given primarily to animals.
This is not a complete language, nor is there evidence that language
did not exist before Adam. God speaks in a language in order to com-

---

68.   Huston Smith, *The World's Religions: Our Great Wisdom Traditions*. San Francisco:
      Harper, 1991, 373.

69.   All biblical quotes are from the King James Version, available online at the
      University of Michigan's searchable Bible, http://quod.lib.umich.edu/k/kjv/.

mand Adam not to eat of the Tree of Knowledge of Good and Evil. Adam therefore doesn't so much invent language as contribute to it. But language itself comes from God, given to Adam as an inherent gift. This passage embodies what we now know to be two truths about language: it is inherent in human makeup to develop and use some kind of language, and all languages are subject to change and innovation by the people who use them.

This particular myth is more about the purpose of the primal language than its origin. Adam is not merely naming the animals so that he has something to call them—otherwise, he would name the rocks, trees, and bushes as well. He's naming them in order to judge their suitability to be a "help meet" for him. He's seeking a partner, in other words, by assigning labels to the beasts around him. When he finishes, he discovers that he has not succeeded, and God intervenes to create a suitable partner for him: the first woman, whom Adam names *Ashah*, or woman, because, as he puts it, "she came out of man (*'ish*)." The words *'ashah* and *'ish* have a clear relationship in Hebrew that's lacking in English; they are spelled very similarly. He changes her name, however, when they fall from grace: "3:20 And Adam called his wife's name Eve; because she was the mother of all living." Eve, in Hebrew, is Khavvah, which comes from the Semitic root *kh-y-w* meaning "to live."[70] This root is source of the word *khai*, which one occasionally sees in jewelry depicted in Hebrew, meaning "life." Interestingly to us pagans, it's also the Semitic root for the Assyrian god Ea.

Language defines and probes Adam's relationship to the world around him. He identifies the suitability of his animal partners by giving them names, and when his relationship with his wife changes due to their fall from grace, he redefines her name to reflect that new, changed relationship. It's also interesting to note that she becomes a person with a proper name, rather than a derived name, at that point. She is no longer named literally "from-man" but is now "origin-of-life." She is no longer a destination, but a beginning; no longer an object, but a person. The Gnostics among us might make as much as they like out of that element of the

---

70. *The American Heritage Dictionary of the English Language.* Boston: Houghton Mifflin, 2000. Index of Semitic Roots.

myth. The other language origin myth in the Bible explains how we move from this primal state of language to one of extreme complexity. Hebrew speakers lived in close proximity with a large number of people speaking a large number of different languages, many of them only very distantly related to Hebrew. Rather than recognize what linguists now know, that language is incredibly mutable and even in just a few years can change dramatically, the Bible creates a myth—in a bit of a non sequitur—about how this complexity of language came about:

> 11:1 And the whole earth was of one language, and of one speech.

> 11:2 And it came to pass, as they journeyed from the east, that they found a plain in the land of Shinar; and they dwelt there.

> 11:3 And they said one to another, Go to, let us make brick, and burn them thoroughly. And they had brick for stone, and slime had they for mortar.

> 11:4 And they said, Go to, let us build us a city and a tower, whose top may reach unto heaven; and let us make us a name, lest we be scattered abroad upon the face of the whole earth.

> 11:5 And the Lord came down to see the city and the tower, which the children of men builded.

> 11:6 And the Lord said, Behold, the people is one, and they have all one language; and this they begin to do: and now nothing will be restrained from them, which they have imagined to do.

> 11:7 Go to, let us go down, and there confound their language, that they may not understand one another's speech.

> 11:8 So the Lord scattered them abroad from thence unto the face of all the earth: and they left off to build the city.

The key here is that we have a place and a time ascribed to the diaspora of languages: Babylon, shortly after the rise of cities. In a literal sense, we now know that language had already differentiated into many, many dialects and languages by the time of the building of the first cities. But metaphorically, this biblical story tells us that the author is suspicious of the development of cities, as an affront to God's power and secondarily as a hindrance to communication. This story also does not rule out the possibility of the primal language still existing somewhere on Earth.

Seeking the Primal Language

Various contenders for this primal language have been put forth, some of them bizarre from modern etymological and historical linguistic understanding. By popular acclaim, the winner of the title of primal language is Hebrew. After all, God speaks Hebrew in Genesis, and Adam answers in Hebrew, so Hebrew must be it. Hebrew's nearest neighbors were languages quite similar to Hebrew but clearly different, so it would be easy for a Hebrew speaker to imagine that others just spoke "bad Hebrew." Of course, it would be equally easy for an Aramaic speaker to think the opposite, but Hebrew had already garnered a reputation as an important cultural language. The opinion that Hebrew must have been the first language survived until fairly late, but it should be kept in mind that linguistics as a scientific field is only a century or so old.

The lack of a formal linguistic science did not prevent some people from conducting experiments to discover what the primal language was. Herodotus recounts a rather dubious experiment by one Psammetichus:

Psammetichus, a king of Egypt, wished to determine which nation was the oldest. Rather than relying on research or archaeology, he took two newborn children and shut them up in a hut in a sheep field. No one was to speak to them, until the children themselves spoke.

1. Psammetichus did this, and gave these instructions, because he wanted to hear what speech would first come from the children, when they were past the age of indistinct babbling. And he had his wish; for one day, when the shepherd had done as he was told for two years, both children ran to him stretching out their hands and calling "Bekos!" as he opened the door and entered.

2. . . . Psammetichus then heard them himself, and asked to what language the word "Bekos" belonged; he found it to be a Phrygian word, signifying bread.

3. Reasoning from this, the Egyptians acknowledged that the Phrygians were older than they. This is the story which I heard from the priests of Hephaestus' temple at Memphis; the Greeks say among many foolish things that Psammetichus had the children reared by women whose tongues he had cut out.[71]

Contemporary linguists and historians regard the entire story as a bit of a "foolish thing" in its own right. More recent incidences of children left isolated from exposure to language (fortunately quite rare) show that they develop no language ability at all, and if the "critical period" of puberty passes before exposure to language, there's a small amount of evidence that a person's linguistic ability will be forever stunted. To be fair, the only evidence we have are a couple instances of very badly abused or abandoned children, who may have suffered other physical or emotional problems due to their abuse.

Psammetichus places importance on discovering this primal language, because he reasons that a language is the same as a people, and if one can identify the primal language, it must have been spoken by the primal people. Languages change, however, and shift from group to group. Language, therefore, is not the same as a people, but it is tied to a culture. Herodotus is unconcerned with these ideas, but the original story that Herodotus records fulfilled the purpose of providing an assurance of primacy to a particular group. It illustrates the importance placed on "the original" and "the first" in cultures without a linear model of time. Herodotus, it seems, embraces such linearity; he regards the anecdote much as we might—an interesting story that provides a bit of evidence, perhaps, for some historical truth. The original story, however, shows the lengths to which people may be willing to go (or more likely, imagine themselves going) in order to prove their an-

---

71. Herodotus, Book II, chapter 2. Perseus Digital Library Project, Tufts University, A. D. Godley, ed. Online at http://www.perseus.tufts.edu/GreekScience/hdtbk2 .html (accessed 22 April 2008).

teriority. It also illustrates an assumption a contemporary scientist would not make: that anteriority is both past and present. The fact that children in the present of the story are expected to recall the ancient and historical past indicates that time for the tellers of the myth of Psammetichus was not linear.

The idea that all languages derived from one single language is not controversial scientifically—most linguists are willing to accept that idea, • since there's no evidence that humans developed language more than once. But the idea that this original language is superior (more accurately reflects reality, say, or gives people the power "to do anything that they set their hands to do") is not a scientific idea but a poetic metaphor. The notion of the superiority of the Ur-language (original language) is part and parcel of the notion of the superiority of the distant past, of our origins. We believe that we have fallen from some superior historical state: this idea manifests spiritually as the "fall from grace" and it manifests mundanely as "the good ol' days." In language, people often have the notion that we spoke "better" in years past, and that slang and colloquial language have degraded English. Part of this notion comes from the existence of writing, which both records our earlier ways of speaking and gives them a power and presence that, in a completely oral culture, we would lack. In other words, we can see language changing from Shakespeare's day to ours, and because we value Shakespeare, we reason that he must have spoken "better" than we do. Linguistically, this entire notion is nonsense: the principle of parity, one of the fundamental axioms of language, states that all languages are adequate to express any human idea. The slang of "Ebonics" is no more a degradation of English than French is a degradation of Latin. Still, in popular thinking we hearken back to our original, and imaginary, good English. British accents sound "posh" to American ears, and American accents sound "like idiots with head colds" to British ears, partially because of the value we place on origins.[72]

---

72.   So a British friend once described American accents to me. A French person I met at a party described our accents as "two cats f***ing in a paper sack." Beautiful.

The Invention or Discovery of Enochian

While dismissed in scientific circles, the idea that we could arrive at some language that more accurately or efficiently communicates with spirits or our own deep minds is a common one in magic. The most famous of attempts to do is often called Enochian, although the creator, John Dee, called it "the Angelic Language." John Dee, who was court astrologer to Queen Elizabeth I in the sixteenth century, specifically characterized his attempt to contact angelic beings and learn their language as an attempt to recover an anterior Ur-language that was spoken by Adam before the fall.

What Dee ended up with, thanks to the help of his friend Edward Kelley, is a collection of short poetic utterances and many, many names, all derived from complex tablets. While Kelley was well known to be a charlatan in other things (he was famous for attempting to pass off fake gold as an alchemical success, for example), and while there are places in his records of his work with Dee where he tries, quite obviously, to lie about what the spirits are saying, it's not so easy to dismiss the entire proceeding as a fraud. Dee would ask Kelley to sit at a table and look into a shew stone or scrying device. Kelley would, presumably, enter some sort of trance while Dee prayed for angels to appear. Eventually, Kelley would announce the presence of an angel, and Dee would converse through the interpretation of Kelley. This procedure led to a series of complex tablets, filled with letters, whose general internal consistency must have meant Kelley, if a charlatan, had a profound memory. From these tablets, by some means or code now obscure to us (despite the fact that we have Dee's notes), the angels would point to certain letters, which Kelley reported and Dee transcribed. These letters spelled out eighteen angelic keys or calls, word by word, backwards. Once composed, the angels would provide translation, which Dee would try to match up with the calls line by line.

The main attraction of Dee's system is that it provides an almost infinite number of angels that, as Donald Tyson points out,[73] are associ-

---

73.   Donald Tyson, *Enochian Magic for Beginners: The Original System of Angel Magic*. Woodbury, MN: Llewellyn, 2005.

ated with regions of the earth. Dee, being active in politics in Queen Elizabeth I's court, would of course find such a thing attractive, particularly because Renaissance magic was primarily conceived as begging the aid of certain spirits, whether demonic or angelic. Dee's system provided a very flexible system of magic, with many angelic (and therefore good) names to call on, to accomplish any number of tasks in various regions of the earth. Dee composed, in other words, the ultimate grimoire of "white" magic.

The evocation of such spirits has been dealt with in multiple books, and while there is controversy I'm no more qualified than the next fellow to elucidate it. What interests me are less the names and more the keys or calls. Linguistically these provide a puzzle, in the form of a series of questions: (1) Are they a language, and if so, from where? (2) What is their purpose? (3) What is their origin? (4) To what purpose can we put them now?

The first of these questions, is Enochian a language, is easily answered: no. Not, at least, by any standard definition of language. While there are elements that look language-like, such as grammatical endings, a cursory examination shows them to be completely random. Unless this language has nothing but irregular verbs,[74] which could mean it is indeed the language of nonhuman entities and largely unlearnable by people, the verb endings are random. The fact that verb endings also seem to differ in words with the exact same case, tense, gender, number, person, and mood would indicate that these endings mean nothing. Of course, if it's not a human language, and is indeed the language of angels, then it very well may mark verbs for something no human language does, or even for some purpose no human could comprehend. If that's the case, and I doubt that it is, then human analysis couldn't possibly avail much.

While not a language, Enochian also isn't random. Words mean the same things consistently, and vocabulary is rarely mixed up. If Kelley or Dee fabricated Enochian, they did so very, very carefully—and if they

---

74. While a human language with all irregular verbs is exceedingly unlikely—the human tendency to generalize one ending to another word would quickly kill it, just as the plural *shoen* of *shoe* died out in favor of the more common *-s* ending in English—there are some languages with exceedingly complex verb systems.

did so, why not be just as careful about grammar? What Enochian appears to be is not a language but a sort of complex substitution code called a relexification. In a relexification, words from one language are replaced with different, or made up, words. One famous example of a relexification code is that used by Navajo code talkers during World War II. Navajo speakers were hired by the military to replace common and important words with Navajo code phrases. Such a code is incredibly difficult to break; one needs to collect a large number of messages and link them to various contexts to break the code, and by then the relexification could be changed. While it has been suggested that Dee developed Enochian for just this purpose, there is exactly zero evidence that he ever used the language to spy or pass messages, and there simply isn't enough of the language to do either. Plus, the language lacks some important words a spy might need—no words for *soldier* or *war*, for example.

So that raises the second question: what's the purpose of this language? The angels, if they just wanted to transmit a grimoire, could have transmitted the tablets and the means of drawing names from them, and left the keys out of it or provided them in English. Yet the angels seem to focus, largely, on the question of the language. They want Dee to learn it. To what end? Donald Tyson suggests that the keys may have been a means of bringing about the end of the world, or immanentizing the eschaton (speeding up the end of the age), as some might put it. What he overlooks is the fact that while the keys are filled with apocalyptic language, they are no more filled with such images than sermons of the time, and even sermons stretching back to the beginning of written English. There's a long tradition, in other words, of apocalyptic writing in English; Dee and Kelley's Enochian keys hardly stand out in the genre. While an interesting idea to "conjure with," there's simply not much reason to think so other than the eschatological imagery of the keys themselves, which are common in the religious literature of the time.

Dee frequently asked about a book he had in his possession, filled with similar tablets, that he suggested might come from Adam's own hand. The angels eventually reluctantly agree that, in fact, that book descends from Adam, as does, they say, the Enochian language. In this is the key of the language: the angels mean it to be a primal code for interpreting the magical world. Just as Adam defined his relationship to the animals with a series of labels, so Dee is—I suggest—to define his relationship to the world with a similar series. The keys are the beginning of that redefinition. Yet the language is incomplete, and the means by which the angels transmit it guarantees that it could not be finished before Dee's eventual death. If, indeed, Dee was in contact with some sort of supernatural entities, they must have had something else in mind. Tyson convincingly argues that Dee was not the one who was supposed to complete the work of Enochian.[75] He doesn't suggest who might be.

That, of course, raises the question: is the origin of Enochian supernatural or human? While most scholars would argue that Kelley deceived Dee and created Enochian himself, I come down on the side of at least some supernatural influence. Kelley frequently didn't understand what was going on. He would often ask the angels questions about alchemy, which they were loath to answer. Kelley knew little Latin and no Greek. On one occasion he carried on a long conversation in Greek, which he didn't understand. In another, he created a complex Latin acrostic, something difficult to do with a language you don't know well. Furthermore, the information often channeled by the angels was heretical to a degree not seen for hundreds of years; it would have gotten both men killed if it had been discovered, and so there's no benefit for Kelley to fake such heresy. On the other hand, early drafts of some diagrams had been found on his person by Dee. Kelley explains them away with feeble excuses. The angels also spoke in bad Latin, when they did speak in Latin. They also contradict themselves, and in several places give blatantly wrong predictions. Often, they play up to Dee's paranoia. Dee, however, was not completely credulous. He called the angels on their contradictions, and demanded independent confirmation of many claims. The most unusual circumstance is when the angels demand that Dee and Kelley swap wives. I've written elsewhere that I did not think they had done so; I have now changed my mind. After examining the source material, I think there is some veiled reference to the swap. This may have been Kelley's attempt

---

75. Tyson, *Enochian Magic for Beginners: The Original System of Angel Magic.*

to get kinky; it also may have been a ploy by the angels. Even if Enochian did come from one of their minds, what a mind to create something so complex and yet consistent. Even the inconsistencies in grammar do not negate the careful memorization a hoax would imply. Such a hoax would be more work than getting an honest trade! And considering that neither Dee nor Kelley ever made money, as far as we can tell, out of Enochian, it would have been an elaborate hoax for little or no material gain. Dee even locked up most of his notes, to prevent being tried for heresy. That's hardly the way to engineer a hoax.

The Use of Enochian

The final question, to what purpose can we put Enochian now, is a tricky one. Almost no one (with a few exceptions) practices Enochian the way John Dee did. Creating the wax tablets upon which he placed his equipment can take a few months alone. Those who do practice Enochian magic probably do so in the Golden Dawn tradition, a magical tradition with its origins in the nineteenth century, quite a bit after Dee died. That leaves us with a lot of tables, a few keys, and a bucket of questions. One can summon the angels and spirits—but what can one do with the language? The Golden Dawn has an elaborate system of associating the keys to various Enochian angels.[76] There's no evidence those keys were meant to be used that way. The Satanic church of Anton LaVey uses them as a liturgy—amusing, considering how often they mention God. LaVey tries to replace mentions of God with mentions of Satan, but he misses quite a few and often produces gibberish with the ones he hits. Such ridiculous uses of the language don't really concern me. What I find interesting is people using the language to create new compositions.

Aleister Crowley used Enochian to create an evocation based on that in the *Goetia*. But even Crowley needed to invent a few words. Any attempt to use the language will involve inventing new words, and even making grammatical decisions. The grammar of Enochian is largely that of Elizabethan English, but there's no reason to suppose that there's anything

---

76.   Israel Regardie, *The Golden Dawn*. St. Paul, MN: Llewellyn, 1986.

sacrosanct about that. We could just as easily use the grammar of American English if we're so inclined. If we do, we can create our own Enochian incantations. Doing so without inventing vocabulary can be a headache. But I offer, in the spirit of experimentation, the following short invocation of the Higher Genius, written in Enochian, without the invention of new words (although I've used Crowley's neologisms when necessary):

> Ol vinu drilpi hami, obelisong od arp de ors. Ol gru noan pire, ar ol biah a-gi a salman de iaiadix. Ofekufa-ol od prdzar hoxmarch, gohed.

> I invoke the great being, deliverer and conquerer of darkness. Let my deeds become holy, so that I stand with you in the house of honor. Exalt me, and diminish fear, to the end of the ages.

Anyone brave enough to experiment with my composition, or better yet, create his or her own, should let me know.

Perhaps now that we have what Dee never could have imagined, a quick means of sharing knowledge, we could begin composing in Enochian and gathering new vocabulary together to create a neo-Enochian more suited to the practice of magic. Of course, any attempt to do so will lead to divergence of vocabulary; therefore, dogma must be scattered and diversity embraced. Some such attempts to create magical languages already exist, but no one has yet tried to organize one around Enochian. If we are to compose in Enochian, I'd suggest some basic rules, which I've followed above.

First of all, it is best to treat verbs as indeclinable, and select the proper verb according to aesthetic preference rather than attempting to impose conjugations on the verbs. Second, I would advise using words as parts of speech largely interchangeably. If, for example, there is a word like *arp*, which means "to conquer," use it also as the nouns *conquerer* or *conquest*. There are many natural languages that do this. Chinese is one example. On the other hand, if there is a word for the noun form of the word, I'd use that instead, as long as I could find it. I'd advise using basic English grammar: adjectives before nouns, subject before verb, object following verb, and so on. I'd even go so far as to suggest the use of *de*, "to," to mark the indirect object. It's also probably permissible to use *de* as an all-purpose preposition for those that are lacking—some languages get by with only one or two prepositions. In coining new words, I'd recommend relying first on compounding—creating, for example, the word for "computer" by adding the words *angelard*, "thought" and *aviny*, "millstone." A mill for thought would be a computer, presumably, so the word for computer could be *angelardaviny*.[77] I advise you to record your coinages so you can use them later.

In creating completely new words, we can use Dee's method if we are brave. This involves going into a trance and staring into a crystal while invoking the angel. Dee used prayers and psalms to do so, but we can also compose our own evocations. If you are not particularly skilled with evocation, perhaps this would not be such a useful method. A more useful method might be one used by the Golden Dawn: scrying in the spirit vision either into the squares of the tablets or into the Aethers said to surround the earth. If you wish to attempt this method as a means to increase your personal Enochian vocabulary, then I recommend seeking out the Golden Dawn sources, particularly Regardie's *The Golden Dawn*. If you and I begin creating and discovering new Enochian words, what we will likely arrive at is not a coherent Enochian (although that's possible!), but a series of ideolects, or personal languages. Everyone already speaks an ideolect: in mine, *cool* is a word of approval and *gonna* is a future tense marker, for example. The Enochian ideolects are likely to diverge further from each other but still hover around the core of Enochian, just as all ideolects of speakers of English hover around the imaginary construct of "standard English."

Other Attempts at the Primal Language

Dee was not the only thinker who tried to discover a primal language. The philosopher and polymath Gottfried Leibniz, for example, not only invented binary code and anticipated, in the seventeenth century, the existence of the computer, but he also tried to create a language of "real

---

77.   It does not escape me that *millstone* is usually used in metaphor to describe something weighty and cumbersome that bears us down, almost to destruction. Some days, I feel that way about computers.

character" that could express any idea with perfect truthfulness and logic. His method, unlike Dee's, was analytic and mathematical, and his results were not nearly so impressive. On the other hand, his discoveries and theories did lead to revolutions in formal logic and computing, so perhaps we ought not dismiss the scientific approach so readily.

The Western hermetic effort to achieve a primal language has largely been systematic, perhaps even scientific, in that we have conducted experiments and sought information from the world outside ourselves. The attempts of early scientists such as John Dee are not what we would call science, as he did not follow the then-nascent scientific method. In fact, while the scientific method was invented shortly after Dee, it wasn't applied to language until fairly recently. The science of linguistics really did not start as a science until the nineteenth century, and the reconstruction of Proto-Indo-European is only about a century old, with much of it still under debate. Indo-European is the language of a group of people who invaded or settled in Europe roughly ten thousand years before the present. They did not have writing, but they had tamed horses and had the wheel and a system of laws and contracts. They were not a unified culture (or, probably, language) but spread out all over Europe.

In time, their language evolved into branches such as Romance (i.e., Latin, then Spanish, French, Italian), Slavic (i.e., Russian, Slovak, Polish), Germanic (i.e., German, English, Icelandic), and Gaelic (i.e., Irish and Scots Gaelic). Outside of Europe their language became Sanskrit and Hindi, among others. The Indo-Europeans were the second most successful language group, based on area of diffusion (the first being the Polynesian language groups, which spread to cover most of the Pacific). We know all this because we can take these languages and work backward. Sound change is regular, although meaning change isn't, so we can work back to what an original form of a word is, although not necessarily what it might have meant. For example, we can derive the word *ekwo*—[78] by looking at the words in various Indo-European languages that refer to horses and working their sound changes backward as far as we can. When

---

78. By convention, reconstructed words are marked with an asterisk to indicate that we have only indirect evidence of their having existed.

we take, for example, the Greek *ippos* and the Latin *equus*, there may not seem to be much connection, but what in Latin became {qu} became an emphatic {pp} in Greek. Knowing this, we can see that these are really the same word: **ekwo–*, "horse." Yet *horse* is English, which is Germanic, but there's no way that *horse* came from **ekwo–*. No one is entirely certain where the word *horse* came from, but it probably came from the Latin root *curs–*, meaning "to run." All of which illustrates the careful and tentative nature of such reconstruction.

Proto-Indo-European wasn't the first language spoken on Earth. Attempts to reconstruct even further back, to the actual original language—and few linguists would argue that we didn't have, at some point, just one language among a small band of us—have been made, but linguists mostly ignore them. Since, most linguists reason, we can only tentatively reconstruct a mere ten thousand years back, even with the help of many ancient written languages to compare and work from, there is no way we can stretch back our reconstructions all the way to the beginning of humanity about 200,000 years ago. Even attempts to work one step back and find a protolanguage for Indo-European have proven fruitless. However, one particularly interesting attempt uses a loose form of the comparative method that led to the reconstruction of Indo-European and applies it to a large number of languages from across the world. The very tentative results of this method have yielded what may be a few words of a very early human language; among these words are *tik* for "one" and *ak'wa* for "water."[79] The linguistic scientific community is almost united in regarding this as a good attempt that nevertheless has almost no scientific validity.

For our purposes, what this scientific attempt proves is the importance in our minds of the idea of anteriority. Yet anteriority need not necessarily refer to time. Dee's anterior language was the language of Adam and therefore situated in time, but it was also the language of the angels, and therefore anterior in the Great Chain of Being—closer to God. Any attempt to reconstruct the first language in terms of temporal

---

79.   Merritt Ruhlen, *The Origin of Language: Tracing the Evolution of the Mother Tongue*. New York: Wiley, 1994.

anteriority (i.e., the first language actually spoken 200,000 years ago) is doomed to failure. We simply do not and cannot have the data, unless we develop some radically different archaeological technology. Scientifically, such an effort is impossible. Magically, such an effort is dubious at best, if you demand historical accuracy. Enochian, for example, is interesting and useful for many people—but there is no evidence that it was spoken originally, in Eden, as the first language. In fact, it couldn't be, since it seems to lack the systematic grammar a language must have.

Personal Attempts to Achieve a Primal Language

One thing we can do, however, is construct an anterior language of our own, looking for the terms that resonate mostly strongly within our own minds. Mundanely, such a task is on par with tilting at windmills; creating a personal language is, at best, regarded as an eccentric hobby. Magically, however, it allows us an opportunity to reconstruct our own minds, or at least, explore them more fully. Like Adam in Eden, when we name the objects of our environment we give them a relationship to other ideas and discover how they interact with our perceptions and the personal reality that arises therefrom. For example, if I wake up some morning laughing at a dream that amused me and feel good for the rest of the day, I might discount that complex emotional event because there is no word (as far as I know) for it in any language. But if I can give it a name, either completely made-up (let's call it the emotion of *filliastor*, say) or composed of Latin and Greek roots, as many English words are (call it *somnifellicity*), then I can address it if it occurs again, deal with it as a real emotion, and analyze it according to my needs. Moreover, I can create words that embody complex ideas that would take many words to define and manipulate those ideas more effectively. Just as we might use algebra to say "x = 4 + y" and then use x as a signifier for the operation 4 + y, we can also use a simple word to represent a complex idea and therefore think about it more efficiently. It is hard to think about something that has no name.

In magic, we can discover labels for complex desires that allow us to manipulate them, like algebraic expressions, in magical operations with more efficiency. The British magician and artist A. O. Spare developed such a system, which he called the "alphabet of desire." It's not clear exactly of what his alphabet consisted. In homage to Spare's work the chaos magician Peter Carroll developed his own alphabet of desire consisting of twenty-two symbols representing twenty-two separate and distinct emotions, mostly arranged in opposites like love/hate.[80] There's some evidence that Spare's system, however, included grammatical elements—for example, he clearly used a looping line after a sigil to represent plurality. The alphabet of desire may have been a constructed language in its own right. It probably did not have a vocal component—Spare probably couldn't speak it, only write it—but there's no reason we can't construct one that does. There's also no reason to balk at the idea of constructing a whole language; for magical purposes, a few vocabulary words at a time may be sufficient. Frater U.·. D.·., in his book on sigil magic, suggests creating sigils for particular desires and recording them for later reuse. This way, the language grows organically, as you need it, as natural languages do.

Let me provide an example of how this can be useful. Let's imagine that you wish to do a candle magic ritual in order to attract a lover. You have prepared two candles to symbolize you and your lover, and you have anointed the first candle with oil of rose to represent yourself. The second candle, however, you wish to inscribe with the qualities and characteristics you desire in a lover. You could simply write them out in English on the candle with a pin while chanting them during the anointing. The problem with that is that we often have ambivalence about the things we're looking for. If one of your qualities or characteristics is "listens really well" then you might find yourself imagining partners who didn't listen very well, or what it might mean to listen well, or doubting that you deserve to be listened to, and so on. One way around that is to translate it into another language like Enochian or Latin, so it becomes a series of sounds. Still, the idea of "listening really well" might lose something in translation. You have a clear image of what that would look like in your head, but expressing it in existing languages is difficult.

---

80.   Peter J. Carroll, *Liber Null & Psychonaut*. York Beach, ME: Samuel Weiser, 1991.

So instead, you sit down before the ritual with a pen and some paper and you relax as completely as possible. Imagine what someone who "listens really well" would look like in as much detail as you can. Focus on how you feel being listened to, and so on. You should, at least for a moment, be able to put everything outside of your thoughts except the idea of this quality, at which point you can create a symbol by doodling or a magic word by muttering randomly. Having done so, you have a signifier that represents this rather complex state of mind. Now, when you are performing your candle ritual, you don't need to imagine "listens really well" and banish all your doubts—which might be difficult if you've also got other qualities, such as "attractive to me" and "has a nice car," all of which have some of their own ambivalence. All you need to do is use the sigil you've made or the word you've spoken (or both) to mention these qualities, without even necessarily consciously remembering exactly what the words mean in English. You may forget your original English formulation and just remember that this symbol has something to do with listening or, better yet, just represents one of several qualities you want your lover to have. Forgetting such things is an indication that you are moving away from the usual codes with which you interpret your world to a new code that gives you the leverage to change it. It also saves room on the candle.

The search for the original, Ur-language is a search for the ultimate and original code. Probably such a code is impossible; there seems no reason to imagine that humans would have developed six thousand separate and distinct languages if one were any more primal or perfect than another. What we can do, however, is create a code that reflects our own mind, whether hieroglyphic or jargon or a full language. We can achieve a primacy of our own minds that way and delve deeper and deeper into what it is to be ourselves.

One interesting way to do this, particularly if you are of a systematic bent, is to compile a list of nouns (one could also use verbs or some other class of words, but nouns are a bit easier to start with), all belonging to the same semantic domain. So, for example, one could use "weather" as the semantic domain and list, just off the top of one's head, "thunder, lightning, wind, rain, snow, sleet, hail, cloud, sunshine." Such a list must always be partial, of course, and in later consideration you may decide to unite some terms or delete others—*thunder* and *lightning*, for example, are very closely related terms, and in some languages are expressed by the same word. Once one has a list, even a partial list, a ritualized contemplation of each of its terms can yield wonderful symbolic material. Consider, for example, how each symbol relates to the others—thunder and rain are clearly related, while sunshine and cloud are clearly opposed. Similarly, consider what emotions each represents: thunder might represent anger, rain, sorrow; and wind, joy. The process of creating a table or chart of correspondences among these terms and between these terms and other ideas is a meditative exercise in interrogating one's own magical codes. What gods do you assign to each term? What plant? Mineral? Day or time? Do they link in a cycle, a web, a line, or some complex feature? For those interested in pursuing such an exercise—which can turn into a magical system in its own right—I recommend Bill Whitcomb's *Magician's Reflection*,[81] which lays out many symbols and suggests culturally common meanings.

For Spare, his alphabet of desire involved emotions, as does Peter Carroll's. Yours may involve metals, stones, weather phenomena, and so on. The important thing to consider is what you will use as your base symbols. The Qabalah, for example, contains information on the relationship between stones and herbs, but its base symbols are the ten numbers and twenty-two letters of the Hebrew alphabet. The codes governing those things also govern how their secondary symbols relate. Using a different set of base symbols will lead to a different system of codes governing relationships between terms. Breaking out of the preconceived codes of the magical system you usually use can be a powerful way of moving beyond your current understanding; in other words, creating a new magical system from your own mind can be a catalyst for initiation.

---

81. Bill Whitcomb, *The Magician's Reflection: A Complete Guide to Creating Personal Magical Symbols and Systems.* St. Paul, MN: Llewellyn, 1999.

SIX

Speaking in Tongues: Glossolalia and Barbarous Words of Invocation

A s I mentioned in the last chapter, one way to think of the "first language" is in terms of time—the language closest to the beginning of *Homo sapiens* as possible. Another way to think of the first language is in terms of closeness not to some temporal point in history but to some primordial "ideal." This view of language is Platonic; it assumes that somewhere outside of all of our mere instantiation of language lies the Ur-language. In Plato's philosophy, this ideal or "form" language is manifested by all our individual languages but unreachable itself except through reason and logic. This view of language is exactly the one held by many, if not most, linguists. Following Noam Chomsky,[82] most linguists believe that underneath all of the various human languages there is a "universal grammar." This grammar isn't the sort of grammar we learn in school—like "form plurals by adding -s." It's more a set of on-off

---

82. Chomsky may be more famous to most of my readers a political theorist writing on anarchism and libertarianism. By profession, however, he is a linguist and his theories have defined the current state of the science. Although controversial, his theories are referenced even by those who do not adhere to them.

switches in our minds, and when we learn our native language we flip those switches into various positions. For example, one of those switches is "Does my native language mark plurals on nouns?" In English, we flip that switch to "yes." Speakers of Mandarin Chinese flip that switch to "no."[83] But all languages have the switch and flip it to one position or another. There are no languages, for example, that mark past tense of verbs on their nouns—although there's no reason why not to do so. These rules of language, presumably coming from the universal grammar, are called *linguistic universals.* The existence of linguistic universals is evidence that all languages share a similar underlying grammar, even if the manifestations of that grammar vary dramatically in reality.

I say that this view of language is particularly Platonic because Plato argued that for everything that exists in the world, there is an ideal form existing in an ideal world. So for example (and this is for some reason the example everyone uses), we have a chair. Now, in our world, we have all sorts of chairs—we have folding chairs, chaise lounges, recliners, and beanbag chairs. But we regard them all as "chairs." We recognize that they partake of "chairness." But where, Plato asks, does that chairness lie? He suggests that it has its origin in the world of forms, where there is a form of a chair of which all other chairs are just dim reflections. There are also, much more importantly, ideal forms of beauty, truth, goodness, and so on—and that's how we can recognize that some act is good without necessarily being able to define goodness to cover all possible good activities. According to Plato, we are born with an inherent understanding of these forms, a memory from before birth, and our confrontations with the less ideal versions of the forms in the physical world sparks our memory. We can also arrive at an understanding of the forms through pure reason—for example, mathematics is the closest we can come to forms. Specifically, for Plato and other Greek philosophers, geometry is an example of the ideal in reality. We can define the rules for

---

83. Actually, there are two switches: one for regular nouns and one for people. Languages that don't mark plurals on most nouns sometimes mark them on nouns referring to people. Mandarin, for example, has a plural suffix -*men* that can only attach to nouns referring to people.

the ideal triangle, for example, that work well enough in reality to predict the shape of an actualized triangle—say, one sketched in the sand. But we can also recognize that our ideal rules, when applied to real triangles, are not perfect representations. Or, from a Platonic perspective, the triangle we sketch in the sand, no matter how carefully we sketch it, will never match our ideal triangle for which the angles add up to 180 degrees.[84]

Language, from the Platonic perspective, is a representation in reality of a perfect ideal that never sees full expression. It's interesting that Plato's theories are ignored by most scientists as irrelevant or false, but accepted in linguistics. Or more accurately, linguists have re-arrived at Plato's theories without realizing it. From a magical standpoint, this parallel with Plato is interesting because much of magic owes its development to the Neoplatonists. The Neoplatonists believed that the physical world is a result of a progressive series of manifestations all coming from a single source, usually identified as The Good or The One. This ideal form led to Mind, which gave manifestation to Soul, which led to Nature.[85] The Neoplatonists advocated a form of magic called theurgy, or "godwork," that involves working back up this list of manifestation through analogues or symbols to the ultimate godhead. Thus, Neoplatonism heavily influenced the development of the Qabalah, which underlies most of Western ceremonial magic.

If we wish to use the Neoplatonic understanding of reality to arrive at The One—or The Good—through language, we need to discover the original language. As discussed in the last chapter, one way to do that is through revelation or reconstruction. Reconstruction is, at the present time, a dead end. We cannot reconstruct that far back—the furthest we can currently go is about ten thousand years and humans are probably about 200,000 years old! Revelation leads us to Enochian or languages like it, and while they might be useful as magical languages, they are probably

---

84. Because of variations in the surface, the thickness of the line, and other imperfections, most real-world triangles do not, actually, add up to 180 degrees. Or, to put it another way, most real-world triangles are not technically triangles at all.

85. David Godwin, *Light in Extension: Greek Magic from Homer to Modern Times.* St. Paul, MN: Llewellyn, 1992.

not actually the original language as spoken by the very first humans. So if we wish to arrive at the first, ideal form of language, we are left with redefining "first" or "original" to mean not first in time but closest to the ideal form. Attempts to arrive at that language have been more successful than the historical approach, if personal reports can be believed.

Barbarous Words

It's not hard to find examples of words that, supposedly, have a closer link to underlying reality than our everyday languages. Many of them—like abracadabra—have become famous as magic words, but others have simply troubled scholars. Some such words are clearly just transliterated Hebrew, sometimes corrupted through copier error. But many other words are not Hebrew at all, nor any other language. For example, in one classical spell the magician addresses the magic lamp with the words "Ieou, Ia, Io, Ia, Ioue."[86] While *Ia* could be a transliteration of *Yah*, a Hebrew name of God, and Ioue could be a transliteration of *yhwh*, it is difficult to tell for sure, and such speculation is merely speculation. More likely, these "barbarous words" are meaningless in a strict sense. The word *barbarous* in the phrase *barbarous words* really just means "foreign," as in, not Latin or Greek. Such barbarous words were considered powerful simply because they came from other languages—they had an inherent strangeness that made them salient and "weird." In some spells, the magician even claims to be speaking languages like Persian, when really he or she is reciting nonsense (from our perspective) syllables.

One of the most famous examples of a spell containing barbarous words of power is the "address to the god drawn upon the letter," more commonly called the Bornless Ritual. This ritual aims to invoke a god "without beginning" or "without head" (akephalos) to exorcize a patient of some spirit.[87] It is used in Golden Dawn-style magic as a general pur-

---

86.   F. Ll. Griffith and Herbert Thompson, *The Demotic Magical Papyrus of London and Leiden.* New York: Dover, 1974 [1904]. Online at http://www.sacred-texts .com/egy/dmp/dmp19.htm (accessed 22 April 2008).

87.   Godwin, 82.

pose invocation, and Crowley modified it in his *Liber Samekh* to serve to invoke the Holy Guardian Angel. In his modification, he defined the many passages of barbarous words by giving them "meaning" based on letter and sound symbolism. For example, he defines *Ar* as "O breathing, flowing Sun," because the Hebrew letter *alef* is related to air and the letter *resh* is related to the sun. In other places, he relies on direct translation—for example, the Greek word *iskhure* occurs at one point, which means "mighty" or "strong." Crowley simply glosses it with its meaning: "Mighty art Thou!"[88] There is no doubt that, historically, these words had no such meaning (with the exception, of course, of *iskhure*). *Ar* may have been dimly conceived as an Egyptian or Persian deity, or as the name of some spirit somewhere, but probably wasn't given a precise designation or gloss. When Crowley does so, he lends form to the formlessness of the words of power—and often, his form is particularly related to his own brand of magic. There is certainly nothing wrong with this, and many people have found *Liber Samekh* useful. But it's wise to keep in mind that granting qabalistic meaning to the names is not the original practice but an innovation.

It's sometimes common for scholars studying barbarous words of power to assume that they are simply blinds to confuse a magician's clients. Textually, however, there's some evidence that those who used these barbarous words meant them to be meaningful. Often, the barbarous words are described as "true names." Such claims of a long string of vowels or meaningless syllables being a "true name" imply that barbarous words were not just foreign-sounding phrases, but were also attempts to achieve a type of anteriority—an original language of true names.

The term *barbarous* to describe these words is a hint of their original purpose. They were meant to be unknown, to be mysterious words of power. This mysteriousness may have served two purposes: first, it provided the magician with an aura of mystery in the eyes of his or her clients. Second, and more importantly, it confounded the magician's own conscious mind with words it cannot understand. If you have ever listened to

---

88. "Liber Samekh: Theurgia Goetia Summa Congressus Cum Daemone." In *Magick: Liber Aba : Book 4*. Boston: Weiser, 1998. Online at http://www.hermetic.com/ crowley/libers/lib800.html (accessed 22 April 2008).

a long conversation in a language you cannot understand, you may have noticed yourself focusing on those elements you could understand—facial features, tone of voice, and so on. Similarly, by shifting meaning away from semantic content, the use of barbarous words of invocation allows us to look for other kinds of meaning. Words, with all their semantic content, cry louder than other, more subtle vehicles of meaning. "Nonsense" helps shout down the clamor of words.

Glossolalia

One way to achieve this "nonsense" is the time-honored method of glossolalia, sometimes called "speaking in tongues" in a Christian perspective. Some (including me) theorize that some of the strings of vowels and the like in Greek spells were actually attempts at recording originally glossolalic utterances. Some of the oldest evidence we have for glossolalia used in a religious or magical context is the babbling of the Pythia, the priestess of Delphi, in her oracles. These babblings were translated into meaningful Greek couplets by the priests. The translation from nonsense to sense illustrates the need for an intermediary between the language of the god and the language of the priests. Christian practice also occasionally includes "translations" of the glossolalia, providing messages and oracles for those present.

Linguistic analysis of glossolalia shows that it contains neither semantic nor syntactic information. Language, to be language, must exhibit syntax (the way words fit together to make sentences), semantics (the particular meaning of individual words), and pragmatics (the way that words are used in context and the way that context changes their meaning). If something lacks one of these three elements, we say it is not language, but that doesn't mean it lacks information. The cries of most animals, for example, have semantic content, such as "Food over here" or "Danger!" but lack syntax or grammar. A dog can say "Danger!" by a certain bark, but it can't say "Danger yesterday!" Yet such animal cries have meaning—semantic meaning. Glossolalia is not language, but it does contain meaning—pragmatic meaning. Pragmatics in linguistics is the study of how language interacts with context. For example, the phrase "Could you pass the salt?" literally (semantically) asks about your ability to move a salt shaker. But because of context, we know pragmatically that, if you ask me this, you are really politely asking me to pass the salt.

The translations of glossolalia, at least according to one study, are widely inconsistent with one another.[89] It's easy to explain away the translation of glossolalia in a religious setting as deliberate fraud. Evidence for this interpretation includes its lack of meaning, but in my experience glossolalia does contain meaning. While the syllables may not be language, there is often voice intonation, gesture, and pragmatic context. To describe discovering meaning in glossolalia as "translating" is a bit inaccurate; more likely, one is constructing meaning based on pragmatic content and personal intuition and insight. The discovery of meaning need not be fraud, and creating such meaning could feel very much like translating from one language to another. In fact, "translating" a piece of glossolalia—i.e., constructing a meaning in your mind based on the sounds you hear—is what we do when we translate another language or even our native language into meaning. We use verbal cues to construct a meaning in our mind. In actual language we have more channels of clues—the syntactic, semantic, and pragmatic—while in glossolalia we have only one channel and so must construct much more of the meaning ourselves. But in both cases, meaning is constructed in the mind based on verbal cues, not transferred in the language itself. Meaning exists only in the mind.

It's interesting to note that skeptics are not the only people who like to point out the supposed lack of meaning in glossolalia. A select number of Christian churches will go so far as to suggest that speaking in tongues is Satan's work, and in what must be one of the most risible statements on the subject ever written, a supposed "cross-disciplinary" religious website concludes: "In fact, it has been found that the *speaking in tongues' practiced in Christian churches* and by individual Christians *is identical to the chanting language of those who practice voodoo on the darkest continents of*

---

89.   "Speaking in Tongues." Religious Tolerance.org, http://www.religioustolerance .org/tongues1.htm (accessed 22 April 2008).

this world"[90] (emphasis original). Since Voodoo or Vodun is a syncretic religion created in North America out of African beliefs and Christianity, I have to wonder what our author would think is a "light" continent. Derision aside, it's clear that glossolalia has a powerful effect on people. The fact that critics often bring up its use in other religions—of which there are many—in my opinion endorses it as a practice discovered and rediscovered by earnest seekers of all types.

Most people who use glossolalia in a Christian or other context do so for personal prayer, often in private or small groups. It may seem strange to describe what they do as "prayer," since prayer implies the communication of some thought to a deity, and glossolalia contains no semantic or syntactic information. Instead, glossolalia communicates pure pragmatic content—which contains information about attitude, emotional state, and context. It is a way to pray without intellectualism and conscious thought. In fact, many Christians claim that they could not pray effectively at all in the traditional manner until they began praying in tongues or with glossolalia. What value does prayer without semantic content (or "meaning" in the traditional sense of information that can be decoded accurately) have for the worshiper? The actual effect of pragmatic communication without semantic content is not hard to discover, because there are many such utterances that people make every day to accomplish specific goals.

These nonsemantic communications are sometimes called *phatic* communication, or "presymbolic" communication. They consist of polite noises, such as "Good morning" and "How are you?" as well as such banalities as "Watch your step" after someone trips. What they mean is not their semantic content, which might as well be null, but their pragmatic or emotional expression. For example, "Good morning" really means "I see you and recognize the time of day and am disposed to you in a friendly manner." "How are you?" unless asked with the peculiar inflection that connotes that it should be taken literally, usually means "I see

---

90.   "Glossolalia in Contemporary Linguistic Study." Metareligion, http://www.meta
       -religion.com/Linguistics/Glossolalia/contemporary_linguistic_study.htm
       (accessed 22 April 2008).

you and am friendly toward you." "Watch your step," said after someone trips or stubs his or her toe, can clearly not be a warning against future such actions, but instead has the pragmatic content of "I sympathize with your pain and embarrassment and would prevent it if I could." S. I. Hayakawa, a philosopher of language, writes in regards to ritual utterances that contain no or little semantic content for their audiences (the Latin mass, for example, or Sanskrit mantras): "What is the good that is done us in ritual utterances? *It is the reaffirmation of social cohesion*"[91] (emphasis original). The case of praying privately in tongues would seem to argue against Hayakawa's suggestion that the purpose of ritual language is the creation of community, except that by praying in tongues the worshiper creates a community between himself or herself and the divine. Part of the advantage of glossolalia in creating this community, as Hayakawa points out, is that presymbolic language contains emotional, though not intellectual, content. It is a way of communicating one's emotions without having to analyze or explain them.

Christians are not the only ones who create a community between themselves and deity through glossolalia. Tungus shamans will occasionally mutter in glossolalia, claiming that it is another language spoken by their *udha*, or guiding spirit. Sometimes they identify the language: it's Chinese, they'll say, or Mongolian. In this case, they're claiming a community not just with their udha, but with their udha's country of origin.[92]

Techniques of Glossolalia

What happens when we, you and I, speak in tongues? The only way to know is to try it. The methods are various, and although many different

---

91. S. I. Hayakawa, *Language in Thought and Action.* New York: Harcourt Brace, 1990 (fifth edition), 61.

92. Apparently it is not unheard of for udha spirits to come from another country. I am doubtful, as a linguist, that the languages spoken in this glossolalia are actually an identifiable language, although I'd need more evidence to make a firm claim; from a magical perspective, of course, it doesn't much matter if this factual claim is accurate or not, if the process is efficacious. See Sarangerel, *Chosen by the Spirits: Following Your Shamanic Calling.* Rochester, VT: Destiny Books, 2001.

cultures use glossolalia, we can most easily find instruction in the method from those in our culture who use it most often: Pentecostal Christians. Before I delve into the advice offered by Pentecostal Christians on how to speak in tongues, I want to address the various delicate issues raised by the borrowing of a Christian (in our culture) technique to elucidate a practice many Christians might disapprove of (i.e., magic).

Borrowing any cultural practice, especially one connected to religious beliefs, is a sticky proposition. Some Native Americans, for example, are angry because of white people "borrowing" their traditions without full understanding or proper initiation. Similarly, I can imagine some Christians being offended by the use of glossolalia outside of a Christian religious context. Pentecostal Christians regard speaking in tongues as confirmation of God's grace and as a gift from the Holy Spirit, one of the three aspects of God. For someone unbaptized (like me) to speak in tongues might be considered at best ridiculous and at worst Satanic deception. Yet glossolalia occurs worldwide in diverse contexts. It is an ubiquitous spiritual technology. Therefore, we have every moral right to employ it if we choose to, as long as we do not do so in the context of Christians speaking in tongues. The moral issue arises when we seek instruction in the technique from those who do not regard it as a technique but as a sacred practice.

To learn the technique without encroaching on the spiritual territory itself may placate some, but it may enrage others. Some may ask why bother placating Christians? There is often an attitude in the occult community, I've noticed, of distrust or dislike of Christianity and Christians. I strongly disagree with such an attitude, perhaps because I was not raised Christian and do not therefore have a personal investment in the religion, but also for logical reasons. To give respect even if one cannot be certain that respect will come in return is to establish oneself as a truly respectful person. A person who only respects people like himself or herself is not really respectful at all, but narcissistic. Certainly there are some Christians who disapprove of the practice of magic, of paganism, or of any number of other things that we might be or do, but there are also a large number of Christians who do not disapprove. I even know several

Christians who practice magic! To immediately label someone and exclude him or her from one's social circle is to diminish the self. Therefore I will make every effort to describe the Christian technique of glossolalia without disrespecting the spiritual gift of speaking in tongues.

The Christian technique of achieving glossolalia is interesting in its mixture of automatism (somewhat reminiscent of surrealist poetic techniques of the early twentieth century) and deliberate instigation. Accusations of "faking it" are irrelevant—the question is "faking what?" Faking the fluent production of syllables? To produce syllables fluently is to produce syllables fluently. Some people apparently "jump-start" (in the words of one Christian I spoke to) by forming random syllables deliberately. Others feel a physical sensation come over them; one Christian described the term "come over" as literal, explaining that he felt he was enveloped in a blanket just before he began to speak. Alternately, he said, he sometimes feels an electrical sensation in his face, lips, throat, or upper jaw. The physicality of the experience is interesting; it either engenders or grows out of a twitch or what in yoga is sometimes called a *kriya*, a spontaneous ecstatic movement. The production of glossolalia among Pentecostal Christians is sometimes accompanied with involuntary bodily motions, as well, such as raising up, throwing about one's arms, or falling down (being "slain in the spirit"). It's important to point out that some Christians also pray in tongues quietly and without such ecstatic movements; the idea of people rolling about and shouting in tongues is something of a stereotype.

Larry Christenson, in his book about glossolalia, describes a method for gaining the gift of speaking in tongues in a Christian context. It is important to keep in mind that for a certain type of Christian, speaking in tongues is a gift and not just a technology, and therefore God must grant it by grace. The first step, therefore, is to pray for the gift—to express an earnest desire and willingness to speak in tongues. Christenson devotes considerable space to this method and ultimately suggests that, in your prayers, you fall silent with the firm intention to speak no known language. At that point, having strongly formulated that desire, the worshiper opens his or her mouth and speaks out loudly and confidently. Christenson points out that the beginner may start by uttering syllables that occur to him or her and subsequently allow the stream of sounds to carry him or her away. He points out that the final goal is a fluent stream of syllables "in which the words are prompted not by the mind but by the spirit."[93] He also addresses the issue of "faking it," or pretending to speak in tongues. He suggests that worries about faking it are at least in part a temptation away from doing the practice, and one can lay them to rest in the assurance that God desires the worshiper to manifest the gift of speaking in tongues and therefore is willing to give it. This reassurance seems designed to address the issue of the practice being "too easy" or simple. He points out that we often imagine speaking in tongues to be something that comes over the worshiper without his or her will, but often the worshiper instigates the gift.

The method of speaking in tongues shares similarities with the automatism practiced by the artistic movement known as surrealism. While the word *surreal* has come to mean "dreamlike" or "bizarre," the artistic movement of surrealism was dedicated to achieving an organic art through automatism. The term refers more to the method than the content (although content can also be an issue). The surrealist sits down with artistic materials and allows something to come forth without conscious direction. So, for example, an artist may splatter a canvas with random paint and then modify the splatters to create an image. Or an artist may hold a canvas over a fire so that the soot stains it, and then following the lines of soot create an image. Writers developed "free writing" or "automatic writing," or more accurately modified and borrowed from the technique as developed by the spiritualist movement current at the same time, the early twentieth century. This method consisted of writing at speed without self-consciousness. The technique is still used by some writing teachers because it helps students break through their self-doubt and preconceptions about writing. The surrealist, however, used the technique to create organic writing—and often surreal writings are bizarre and dreamlike, although other times they are poignant, bitter, or funny.

93.   Larry Christenson, *Answering Your Questions About Speaking in Tongues*. Minneapolis: Bethany House, 2005 [1968], 126.

A surrealist school of performance, in which the poet composes "mouth music" on stage, is also relevant to our discussion of methods of achieving glossolalia. This school of poetry, if such it can be called, consisted of the poet babbling or making animal noises. Clearly such performance never particularly caught on, partially because it was largely divorced from community and did not have the tradition or cultural context behind it that glossolalia does in the environments in which it is used. The method of such extemporaneous surreal composition consists of mental preparation beforehand. The poet clears his or her mind, internally touches his or her emotions and physical needs, and "speaks" them forth without language. Notice that this method, simply opening your mouth without any intention to speak a known language and speaking forth, is the exact secular parallel to what Christenson describes as his method of speaking in tongues. He claims that the words come not from the mind but the spirit, and the free-voice poet claims that his or her syllables come not from the mind, but the emotions or body. It's interesting, as an aside, that both create a dichotomy, but where the Christian dichotomy is mind/spirit, the surrealist dichotomy is mind/body. In constructing a cosmology of his or her own, the magician might choose to create a three-way distinction between spirit, mind, and body, making glossolalia a valid tool to link either spirit or body with the mind.

From the surrealist technique and the Christian technique, we can extrapolate a simple series of instructions for the magical use of glossolalia. Of course, these instructions differ slightly from those of the Christian speaker in tongues, because what I am suggesting for the use of magic is not speaking in tongues per se, but glossolalia, which has some of the same benefits but may be used for a wider range of purposes. We can break down the procedure into three steps:

1. **Preparation.** One of the advantages of glossolalia is that not only does it not require a deep trance state, but it also helps to induce a deep trance state. So preparation can be simple—a prayer or statement of desire, some calming breaths, and some introspection.

2. **Silence.** Take a few moments of saying nothing at all, during which you firmly decide that you will not speak a known language but will speak the primal language of your body or spirit. If you can make this silence total, by which I mean quell the inner dialogue of your mind, you may find it easier to allow glossolalia to arise. But even if you can't, I've noticed that glossolalia helps to shut off that inner monologue effectively on its own.

3. **Speech.** At some point some syllables should arise out of the silence: open your mouth and let them come out, even if it just feels made up. I've noticed a certain "priming the pump" experience, in which a few syllables can lead to more and pretty soon a long stream of syllables is coming out of my mouth. Speak as if you were speaking real words, which is to say with real intonation and animation. One of the interesting things about glossolalia from a linguistic perspective is that it seems the syllable stream is broken into intonation units, which are units of information in a linguistic sense. This fact implies that the meaningless syllables nevertheless contain information that the mind strives to package as it packages our day-to-day informational utterances.

At this point, the effects can vary. I'd like to finish this chapter by talking about some of the uses of glossolalia in magic. In Christianity the speaking in tongues is decidedly focused on maintaining a closer relationship to God. Christenson mentions that it can also be used to pray in situations in which you cannot find the words or do not know what to pray for. In shamanic contexts, glossolalia is often used as a way of creating a relationship with the spirits by "speaking their own language" as it were. So clearly one of the chief uses of glossolalia is the cementing of relationships with the Other through distancing yourself from human meaning. The speaker of glossolalia becomes Other himself or herself, by embracing the meaninglessness of his or her utterances. From a magical perspective, we would regard this use as primarily invocational.

Invocation

Invocation is the calling into one's sense of self an outside entity, usually an angel or deity. It makes up an important part of several religions, including charismatic Christianity, Santeria, and others. It also makes up an important part of a branch of magic known as theurgy, from the Greek *theourgeía*, "divine work." The usual procedure in Western ceremonial magic is to identify with the god through a series of successive incantations, or invocations. These incantations loosen the sense of self or ego and allow the other consciousness to take over or, more often, "overshadow." By means of this overshadowing, shamans will—for example—walk through fire or endure extreme cold, perform healings, and so on. Charismatic Christians, overshadowed by the Holy Spirit, prophesy, experience ecstasy, and also perform healings. Taking on some of the characteristics of a spiritual beings allows the magician to accomplish miracles associated with that being, as well as experience changes to his or her consciousness itself.

Glossolalia has particular utility here, since it can help silence the stream of internal dialogue. In fact, I find this silencing effect useful in most magical contexts. We constantly maintain our identities by means of this internal dialogue, telling us the things we like and don't like, are and are not. By silencing that dialogue we can allow other parts of our identity to arise, or even invite exterior identities to inhabit our minds. This shouldn't be done lightly, but when done it is effective. Many religions that employ invocation make heavy use of glossolalia. Often this glossolalia occurs when the worshiper is already in a state of being ridden, as it's called in Voodoo, but I suspect it is also sometimes used to induce such a state. At some point, one gets the sense that one is not in charge of the speech stream, and from there the perception of an external consciousness is almost inevitable.

Evocation

Evocation is the calling of a spirit or spiritual entity into an external space. In Western magic, this is often a triangle or a magic mirror or crystal, but of course other options exist. The verbal element of the ritual of evocation is an incantation in which the magician lists his or her credentials, recalls mythological stories to establish his or her authority, and forms a mental link with the spirit. Many of these invocations include long strings of barbarous words, and Crowley actually went so far as to replace traditional evocations with one he composed in Enochian. Other magicians use the Bornless Ritual, already mentioned for its barbarous words of invocation, as a means of establishing authority. Few magicians seem to use glossolalia, although it has several advantages over more traditional formulas. First, evocations are often heavily Judeo-Christian, something that many non-Christian magicians cannot relate to. Second, they rely on a firm mythological background in Christian scripture and apocrypha. I sincerely doubt that anyone who has not made a serious study of the Bible will be able to derive much symbolic value from most of them. Third, they are long, dull, and sometimes offensive affairs, in which the spirit is exhorted again and again to come, and if the spirit does not make itself known, the entire evocation is to be repeated verbatim. Unlike other types of repetition for rhetorical or poetic effect, Donald Michael Kraig points out that such repetition of evocation is a tacit admission of the possibility of failure.[94] Yet it may very well be that it takes the spirit longer to arrive, or the magician or seer longer to perceive the spirit, than the evocation can be drawn out.

The advantages of glossolalia over more traditional forms of evocation are equally manifold. First, a glossolalic utterance creates trance in the speaker, mitigating to some extent the need for a seer. In traditional evocation, it's often useful to have a seer to communicate with the spirit and a magician to perform the ceremony.[95] The magician reads or recites the evocation and concentrates on the appropriate symbols, while the seer attains trance. However, with glossolalia the need for conscious activity by the magician is obviated, and the magician may attain his or her own

---

94.   Donald Michael Kraig, *Modern Magick: Eleven Lessons in the High Magickal Arts.* St. Paul, MN: Llewellyn, 1988.

95.   Donald Michael Kraig suggests this two-person team evocation, and it's also the working method that John Dee developed. Its pedigree stretches back to ancient Greece and Persia.

trance and act as his or her own seer. Second, glossolalia has no structure demanding that it come to an eventual end, like a usual evocation. On the contrary, glossolalia can be uttered for a long time, with greater ease than semantic speech, because it operates on a level behind the conscious mind. Finally, glossolalia is culturally neutral. A Christian magician can make use of it just as a Pagan magician can, and neither need feel compromised in his or her beliefs.

My own experiences with the use of glossolalia rather than a usual evocation is that it offers a freedom not often seen in evocational techniques. The preparation needn't involve the usual memorization and organization. A chair, a crystal, a simple banishing ritual to set up a circle, and a seal drawn on a piece of paper are all that are necessary to begin the ceremony. The ceremony itself is also shorter. I notice a much quicker response from the spirits and a much stronger mental image of each spirit. I've also noticed, however, that it is a bit more difficult to return to normal language to question the spirit after the evocation. The advantages outweigh this disadvantage for me, however, and I now do most of my evocations with glossolalia. Of course, while it's possible to do an entire evocation in glossolalia, I find it somewhat easier to begin with normal speech, usually a prayer to Janus Pater, and then a short address to the spirits and angels, if any, that rule over the spirit I intend to call. This approach also makes it marginally easier to return to normal language after the glossolalia. And obviously one may drop in and out of glossolalia as the situation demands, using it to deepen trance and using intelligible incantation to focus the mind. "Surfing" the difference between the two types of speech can be very effective.

Enchantment

Enchantment is using magic to have a direct effect on the world. For example, creating and activating a sigil for some goal is a type of enchantment. As I've already discussed, one of the hardest parts of enchantment is maintaining a state of "need not be/does not matter" or detachment after the ritual is finished. For magic to work effectively, the conscious mind must stay out of it to some extent, at least after the act of enchantment itself.

The silencing of the internal monologue is one way that glossolalia can be useful in enchantment. The "forgetting" of a spell's purpose and goal is one of the most difficult parts of magic, and few people have offered techniques for how to go about this. One method is to do a banishing ritual every time the thought arises, but very persistent thoughts—i.e., things we want very much—tend to occur so often that it would be impractical to stop and do the Lesser Banishing Ritual of the Pentagram every time one remembers the goal. Others distract themselves with another attractive thought, but this only works if there is a thought more attractive than the fantasy of fulfillment of one's desire. Glossolalia can be used, silently or aloud, to stop the self-talk that leads to lust for results.

For example, if I create and activate a sigil for extra money, I may find myself during the day experiencing self-talk such as "It'll be great when I get that money" or "I wonder if that spell will work." Neither of these thoughts is useful, so I may condition myself to run them over, mentally, with a burst of glossolalia. If one is new to glossolalia as a technique, it may be necessary to do this aloud, but eventually one can subvocalize the glossolalia and not draw stares from people on the Chicago El.[96] You'll find it quite hard to carry on two different monologues at the same time, and the glossolalic utterance, being unique and unusual, will probably claim more attention, at the moment, than the lust for results. You can keep the glossolalia running until you find something more interesting to fix your self-talk on, and by then the original lust for results should be firmly banished, at least for a while.

Another use for glossolalia in enchantment is attaining trance or gnosis. Gnosis is a state of mind in which the conscious monologue stops. Many magicians find this state a useful one for the implanting of suggestions, whether in the form of sigils or rituals, as well as for divina-

---

96. Actually, now that I think of it, one could probably perform the entire Greater Invoking Ritual of the Pentagram, and one still wouldn't draw stares on the El.

tion. One often returns from gnosis with insight into a problem or, occasionally, prophecy about the future. Most techniques for achieving gnosis involve either lulling the mind into a state of relative quiet or shocking it into a momentary silence. The inhibitory methods involve hypnosis, meditation, and slow repetitive movement. Excitatory methods involve orgasm, intense pain, or rapid dancing to exhaustion. Some people also describe a third method, chemognosis, which uses drugs to achieve a state of mental quiet. Glossolalia can be both excitatory and inhibitory, depending upon the speed, intensity, tone of voice, and so forth. Much like physical movement (which, of course, it is—just movement of the mouth, tongue, and diaphragm), glossolalia can be done gently so as to lull the mind into quietude, or intensely in order to shock the mind into quiet. Moreover, just like physical movement, glossolalia is flexible in that one can start slow and work up to an ecstatic climax, or vice versa, in order to achieve various effects. Unlike orgasm, a popular yet sharply limited technique, and chemognosis, an often discussed method, glossolalia can be repeated in a short time, so that one can build up intensity, internalize the desire through sigilization or some other method, and then achieve a second peak of gnosis shortly thereafter to drive it further into the mind.

I've found that following one gnosis with another, or mixing different types of gnosis, can have an intensifying effect. For example, achieving an excitatory gnosis in the midst of an inhibitory gnosis increases the intensity of the former. Following a gnosis of any kind with another gnosis in short order can serve to clear the mind of the original intent, and preceding the internalization of the sigil with a low-grade gnosis can prepare the stage for the internalization. Some people have characterized the sigilization technique as "fire and forget," but I would modify this to "fire and fire to forget." Glossolalia is an effective and flexible tool for lighting gentle warming fires, or great roaring blasts, as the occasion demands. Of course, glossolalia may also be mixed with other types of gnosis—for example, one can lead up to an excitatory gnosis through orgasm or pain with glossolalia, or accompany self-hypnosis with quiet glossolalia.[97]

Meaning

Glossolalia as a magical technique calls into question what we mean by "meaning" and demands at least a brief explanation of how meaning interacts with information. While to my knowledge no one has discovered a mathematical relationship for meaning,[98] we can make some rough and handy general statements about meaning that are useful for a magician to be aware of. After all, magic isn't science—if it were, we'd call it "science."

We know that for small messages, those containing very little information, meaning increases as information increases. For example, the word *the* contains little information (it just indicates that the noun following it is definite) and little meaning. The word *banana* contains much more information and much more meaning (it denotes a particular kind of fruit). At this point, we could simply decide that meaning and information are exactly the same thing, but at higher levels of information, meaning begins to lag behind information, and at some point, meaning actually decreases as information increases. For example, in an ambiguous statement, two possible meanings exist at the same time, and it's impossible to determine which was really "meant." Does the word *unbuttonable* mean "can't be buttoned" or "can be unbuttoned"? Furthermore, when we increase information dramatically, meaning all but disappears—take for example the incredible amount of information available on the World Wide Web. Much of it is meaningless simply because there is so much

---

97. If one is using sex magic, and begins to speak in glossolalia, it helps to have an understanding partner.

98. Part of the problem is the obstacle of operationalizing meaning. I'd like to offer this operational definition as a possibility: "Meaning is the ratio of the message correctly decoded by the receiver." Of course, this definition is still useless from a scientific perspective, because a sort of uncertainty principle intrudes: any attempt to find whether the message was correctly decoded involves two further acts of communication (one with the sender and one with the receiver), both subject to the inevitable corruption of noise, and therefore each requiring yet two more acts of communication, and so on.

of it. In fact, "noise" is simply too much information to make meaning from—imagine a crowded restaurant with many people talking at once. This is an information-rich environment, but it becomes increasingly difficult to construct meaning from the randomness.

Meaning, therefore, is subtractive after a certain point—meaning is what we extract from a body of information and decide to highlight. It may be that one person has a higher threshold of meaningfulness than another, and this is why a magician can look at a random array of tarot cards, for example, and find meaning, or why a Pentecostal Christian can hear the meaningless information of someone speaking in tongues and reduce it to at least one meaning. With the *unbuttonable* example, when we select a meaning, we collapse the word into meaning and discard the other possibility. No one has actually done this with *unbuttonable*, but the word *inflammable* used to mean "likely to catch fire." The *in-* prefix, however, contains two possible meanings: an intensifying meaning and a negative meaning, so many people assumed that *inflammable* meant "not likely to catch fire." It's important to make that distinction clear! One might argue that it "really meant" the prior meaning, but in fact it meant what people wanted it to mean. By sending the message, I may have meant "Watch out!" but you may have discarded a different part of the message (one of its possible meanings) and decided it meant "Don't worry." We solved this language problem by coining a new word, *flammable*, which no one could misinterpret.

I've already argued that glossolalia is not devoid of information, but that it contains pragmatic and emotional information rather than semantic information. It is also not devoid of meaning in the subtractive sense—on the contrary, it contains so many meanings that it is possible to extract several different, conflicting messages from it. Many scientists would argue that this fact proves that glossolalia "means nothing," but in fact quite the opposite is true. It means so much it's possible to uncover multiple, perfectly correct meanings from the information stream. It sounds like gibberish to us because every meaning-rich stream of information sounds like noise. (No wonder: it *is* noise. Noise is just unwanted or undecodable information.)

If the universe could talk back to us, it would sound like glossolalia or static. Any such message would contain more meaning than we could easily decode, and we'd require or lean on some supernatural help in deciding what part to discard. Yet even with the grace of God or our own higher genius guiding our subtraction, we must be aware that someone else might subtract some other meaning. In fact, I suspect that if the universe could communicate back to us (and I think it can, and does), then its communications would contain, at least in a nascent state, all possible meanings. What would that look like? Something easily dismissed as gibberish, coincidence, or static. One way to learn to decode such static is to participate in it and allow oneself to become a mouthpiece for nonsense, from time to time.

SEVEN

The Qabalah:
The Grammar of Number

When a lot of people think of the Qabalah, they think of the glyph known as the Etz Chaim, or Tree of Life. This diagram of ten emanations of deity linked by twenty-two conduits, channels, or paths is particularly important in Hermetic Qabalah, but the Qabalah is much more than this glyph and the relationships of its parts. This glyph is only a surface representation of the underlying structure that the Qabalah seeks to elucidate: the Hebrew language. To understand why a system describing the Hebrew language might be central to Western ceremonial magic requires understanding the view of the Hebrew alphabet and language held by Jewish mystics. An understanding of the mystical role of the Hebrew alphabet in creating, sustaining, and manipulating the universe is essential if we are to understand the magical use of our own language, at least from a qabalistic perspective. Very little has been written on the qabalistic features of English, but after a short discussion of the Hebrew and Greek Qabalahs, I'll show that English has its own mystical relationships.

The written Hebrew language and the base-ten numeral system are intricately linked. Hebrew-speaking peoples (and probably speakers of related languages like Chaldean and Aramaic) represented numbers with letters in a base-ten system in which the place value of each digit was encoded in the number. So where we might write the number 12 with the numeral 1 and the numeral 2, placed in a specific order, and 21 with those numerals in reversed order, the traditional Hebrew way of representing those numbers is with the letters yud-bet in the first case and kaf-alef in the second. The way it works is simple: yud in every situation equals 10, and bet always equals 2, so yud-bet is 10 + 2, while kaf (20) plus alef (1) equals 21. Note the table in appendix 2 of this book for the shapes of the Hebrew letters and their values. I've also included handwritten or "linear" forms of the letters for those who don't have calligraphy pens handy. Note that any given number can be represented in manifold ways. For example, because order doesn't matter, one could represent twelve by writing YB or BY, but one could also indicate it by writing WW, or ChD, or even AAAAAAAAAAAA!—as long as the values of the letters used add up to twelve. Now, because Hebrew lacks regularly written vowels,[99] it's distinctly possible that one of these ways of writing the number could make a word—in fact, WW, pronounced "waw," is the word for "nail," and ChD (khad) is the verb "to be sharp."

You may have noticed a relationship in meaning between waw[100] and khad: a nail, of course, is sharp. Such relationships between meaning

---

99.   I've occasionally heard the claim that "Hebrew has no vowels," which is absurd—every language has at least one vowel, and most have many. I've also heard "Hebrew never wrote its vowels," which also isn't true. In fact, scripta plene, a system of representing at least some vowels, was well known and often employed during biblical times. Scripta plene, however, only recorded long vowels in some syllables, but Hebrew has a very complicated vowel system. A later series of innovations eventually led to the current system of representing vowels with points and lines around letters. I've rarely seen it used in modern Hebrew outside of dictionaries and children's books. Since the pattern of vowels is grammatically significant, it's predictable from context in most situations.

100.   Different dialects of Hebrew have slightly different pronunciations, just as different dialects of English do. One will occasionally see the letter waw spelled and pronounced *vav*. This variation is simply a dialectical difference.

leads to the practice of gematria, which attempts to derive mystical insight from comparing words with similar values. For example, the phrase *abba we'amma*, meaning "father and mother," and the word *ben*, meaning "son," both add up to 52—the son comes from the union of the father and mother. Similarly, the word *milah*, which means "circumcision," and the word *kohen*, which means "priest," both have the value of 75. The covenant of circumcision marks the holiness of the priest. Plenty of such relationships can be found by the earnest student with a handy copy of Godwin's *Cabalistic Encyclopedia*.[101]

Before you become too impressed, however, understand that many words show no obvious relationship. For example, why should the words for "ice," "stomach," and "Gomorrah" all add up to 315? What relationship do they have to each other? One can approach that question in two ways: the first answers "There may be a relationship too subtle to see without contemplation" and the second answers "None, because it's all random and you only tend to notice the relationships that stick out by coincidence and chance." The two explanations are really variations on each other: we observe closely, and even in random noise, we find a pattern. Once we find the pattern, the pattern is there. To say that there is no real pattern once we have observed a pattern, even in randomness, is to deny the possibility of gathering data through our senses. Surely we might be deceived about what the pattern signifies, but to observe a pattern is to prove the existence of a pattern. So what does ice have to do with one's stomach? Probably not a lot. But maybe what it's telling us is that the sin of Gomorrah was the freezing of community (represented by the stomach, since to eat together is to become a community). What seems random is random, but it is also something out of which we have yet to perceive a pattern. Once we perceive the pattern, we create it—we set the world in order and make a cosmos out of chaos. Which is, ultimately, the whole point of gematria.

---

101. David Godwin, *Godwin's Cabalistic Encyclopedia: A Complete Guide to Cabalistic Magick*. St. Paul, MN: Llewellyn, 1989.

Uses of Gematria

Gematria does not stop at the mere identification of words with the same value. The word *gematria* is a borrowing from the Greek for "geometry," *geometrein*, or "measurement of the earth." Geometry, as the Greeks conceived it, was the investigation of the relationships between ideal forms of pure reason. To link these ideals with the symbols of words makes possible a more rarefied investigation of an entire symbol system. We can perceive not just the geometric relationships between objects in ideal space, but the symbols that we use to describe and construct our day-to-day lives. Many qabalists have used mathematical relationships and series to explore the relationships of various ideas.

For example, the Fibonacci sequence, named after Leonardo Fibonacci of Pisa, a thirteenth-century Italian mathematician who among his other accomplishments promoted the use of Arabic numerals, is a sequence of numbers that describes a natural spiral. Starting with 1, add 1, then continue to add the two previous numbers to yield the next number: this results in the sequence 1, 1, 2, 3, 5, 8, 13, 21, 34 . . . If one draws squares with sides equal to each of these sequential numbers, and then connects the diagonals of those squares, a spiral is created (see figure 2). This spiral is the one seen in the shells of sea creatures, the arrangement

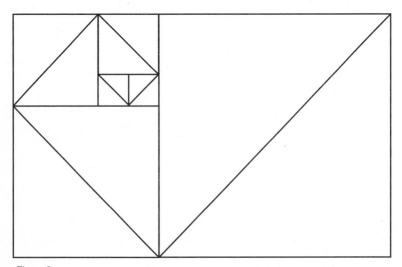

Figure 2

of seeds in the heads of sunflowers, and the growing of leaves. In other words, everywhere in nature where one observes spirals, one usually observes a Fibonacci spiral. While this phenomenon has a fairly mundane explanation (the Fibonacci spiral is a very efficient shape for packing a large quantity of substance into an ever-expanding small area), its frequent occurrence in nature gives it a certain mystical resonance. Furthermore, we are conditioned, perhaps by seeing the spiral everywhere, to feel that proportions based on the Fibonacci sequence exhibit a pleasant harmony. For example, one can construct an interlocking sequence of golden rectangles in a Fibonacci spiral. A golden rectangle is the graphic representation of a proportion we often find in classical art. This proportion, the golden ratio, is 1.618 . . . , an irrational number. The ratio of successive numbers in the Fibonacci sequence approaches the golden ratio. Examining some of the numbers in the Fibonacci sequence, we might notice a pattern in their gematria. For example, 13 is the value of *aheva*, meaning "love," and 21 is the value of *Eheieh*, a name of God meaning "I am." Thirty-four, the sum of these two, is *gala*, meaning "to reveal." So the love of ultimate Existence is revealed in the spirals of nature.

Gematria has more uses, however, than the generation of platitudes through numerical significance. Some people argue that gematria actually encodes complex mathematical knowledge directly into the Torah. For example, the verse 1 Kings 7:23 describes a circular sea: "And he made a molten sea, ten cubits from the one brim to the other: it was round all about, and his height was five cubits: and a line of thirty cubits did compass it round about." Clearly, 30/10 does not equal pi, but all circles bear the same ratio of circumference to diameter: 3.14159 . . . This irrational (i.e., not able to be expressed as a fraction) number is called pi, and it does not equal three. Many people use this verse as an example of the Bible's lack of scientific sophistication, but the Gaon of Vilna, an eighteenth-century skilled Jewish qabalist and philologist,[102] realized that

---

102.   Immanuel Etkes, *The Gaon of Vilna: The Man and His Image*. Jeffrey M. Green, trans. Berkeley, CA: University of California Press, 2002.

there is a peculiarity in this chapter: the word for "compass" in the original Hebrew is misspelled. This misspelling of some words in the Bible isn't unusual—frequently "he" is written for "she" or some other simple error. However, the misspelling of "compass" is peculiar because it contains an extra letter, whereas most misspellings contain the same number of letters.[103] Instead of writing *quw*, the scribe writes *quwah*. The numerical value of quwah is 111, while the numerical value of quw, the correct word, is 106. One hundred eleven divided by 106 equals 1.047169. If one multiplies this number by three, it yields the value 3.14151. This number is closer than most rational estimations of pi used at the time. Is this value for pi, hidden in the midst of 1 Kings, really intentional, or just a strange coincidence? A skeptic, such as myself, might well ask why not hide the value of *e*, or of Planck's constant, somewhere in the Torah as well? And a believer, such as myself, might well answer, perhaps they are there and have just not been found.

Gematria, Isopsephia, and the English Qabalah

The Torah is most frequently used as a source for gematria and speculation thereof, but it need not be the Torah from which we glean our insights. I once translated a comic book into Hebrew to demonstrate gematria, and discovered some fairly interesting insights. Similarly, Aleister Crowley frequently used gematria to analyze his own holy book, *The Book of the Law*. The problem with this approach is that the *Book of the Law* was written not in Hebrew, but English. In fact, it specifically states "Thou shalt obtain the order & value of the English Alphabet; thou shalt find new symbols to attribute them unto" (II:55). Crowley's attempts to do this is rather abortive. Most of those who follow Crowley also follow

---

103. One of the ways scribes checked their work was to count the number of characters and compare that number to the number of characters known to be in the book. This makes spellings like "he" for "she" easy to slip by, since they have the same number of letters in Hebrew. But an additional letter would throw off the count, so is less likely to be accidental. Or so the argument goes.

his method of transliterating (or sometimes translating) significant terms into Hebrew to determine their values.

It stands to reason, even without the divine revelation of the *Book of the Law*, that there would be a gematria related to English. Hebrew is not alone in having a system of numerical significance; Greek has its own method, called *isopsephia*. In isopsephia, each letter is given a numerical value, as in Hebrew. Words with the same value, again, have similar meanings. For example, *thelema* (will) and *agape* (selfless love) both equal 93. Crowley uses this fact when he named his system of magic "thelema." Similarly, *aetos* (eagle) and *pneuma* (spirit) both equal 576. So one can conclude that an eagle is an appropriate symbol of the spirit. Unfortunately, since the Greek alphabet is longer than the Hebrew alphabet, and letters at the end of the alphabet (such as omega) are common, words in Greek span a much larger range of values than in Hebrew. This makes Greek isopsephia less useful than Hebrew gematria because fewer words share values. The nonexistence of a complete isopsephic dictionary[104] also probably contributes to the lack of popularity. Still, almost no one outside of Jewish mystics and occultists know much Hebrew gematria, but almost everyone knows one piece of isopsephia. In the last book of the New Testament, the verse Revelation 3:18 reads: "Here is wisdom. Let him that hath understanding count the number of the beast: for it is the number of a man; and his number is Six hundred threescore and six." The number 666, the number of the beast, is said to be the number of a man—this clearly means that a certain important man has a name which, when added up, will equal 666, and that man is the Great Beast. The reason for this claim may be that in Greek (the language this book is written in), the phrase *to mega therion* ("the great beast") equals 666. Figuring out who might have been meant by this obtuse occult allusion has occupied philosophers and commentators for generations. Crowley even found several ways of spelling his own name in Hebrew that add up to the number,

---

104. David Godwin's *Light in Extension* contains a small isopsephic dictionary in the back. I would be willing to compose a more complete one, if I felt there were any demand for it.

to justify claiming the title of Great Beast.[105] Probably, the person meant was Nero, the emperor at the time of the composition of Revelation, as the Greek *Neron Kaesar*, or "Nero Caesar," adds up to 666.

Hebrew and Greek share a commonality: both were at one time used to write numbers. The numerical values of their letters, therefore, was set by tradition before the adoption of the practices of gematria and isopsephia. English, however, developed after a widespread adoption of alternate ways of representing numbers, most notably and successfully the so-called Arabic numerals of 1, 2, 3, 4, 5, 6, 7, 8, 9, and 0. To determine the value of the English alphabet, therefore, is to impose a value on it in a way that isn't quite what one does when one decides, for example, that yud = 10 or kaf = 20. Many methods have been designed for doing so. Some simply borrow the phonetic values of the Hebrew alphabet and transfer the numbers, thus:

---

105.   None of these spellings would be accepted by a Hebrew speaker as a valid
       transliteration of his name, however. Interestingly, by adopting his rather loose
       rules, I can make my own name add up to 666 as well. It's an entertaining game.

A	1	P	80
B	2	Q	100
C	20 if hard, 60 if soft	R	200
D	4	S	60
E	5	T	9
F	80	U	6
G	3	V	6
H	5	W	6
I	10	X	90
J	10	Y	10
K	20	Z	7
L	30	Sh	300
M	40	Th	400
N	50	Ch	(when hard) 8
O	70		

As far as I know, while this system is sometimes used to create a value for a word in, for example, talismanic magic, it's rarely used in actual gematria. Nema uses it in conjunction with Hebrew gematria,[106] but I've seen few other people do so. Of course, one could create a system of English gematria by simply following the same pattern used in Greek and Hebrew, and numbering each letter sequentially up to ten, then numbering by tens until a hundred, and then hundreds until the end. But in both Hebrew and Greek, the alphabet was numbered this way before the advent of the mystical practice, so to do it with English is working retroactively, imposing a system on top of the existing alphabet. There's nothing wrong with that, and perhaps it could yield some interesting results, but I haven't found it useful.

The English alphabet does have one native numbering system, however. It's often been overlooked in its simplicity. Remember back to those dreadful high school English classes in which you were required to create an outline: you used multiple numbering systems for different levels of information. One of them was the alphabet, which proceeded from A all the way, sequentially, to Z. Therefore, it might be reasonable to assign the letters of the English alphabet the numbers 1–26, from A to Z.[107] Doing so yields some interesting, not to say exciting, results. For example, *God* equals 26, the same value of the Hebrew four-letter name of God, YHVH. Other words display mathematical relationships, such as *square*, which equals 81, itself the square of two perfect squares.

Many words with the same value display a semantic relationship. For example, *base* and *ball* both equal 27, or less trivially and more mythologically, *snake* and *apple* both equal 50. Other relationships, such as 48's *blood, sex, son,* and *live,* seem suggestive of mysterious symbolic links. Such links are worthy of meditation, even if gematria is random. For example:

---

106. Nema, *Maat Magick: A Guide to Self-Initiation.* York Beach, ME: Weiser, 1995.

107. The six people who remember how to make a formal outline will probably point out that after Z, in this system, you start over with AA, which would make double-A equal to 27, double-B equal to 28, and so on. I'm going to cough and pretend this fact doesn't exist.

- 52 = earth, salt, mass
- 45 = milk, cheese
- 46 = cry, shame, body
- 42 = war, gun
- 38 = fire, boil, change, death
- 34 = cold, heat
- 89 = complete, unity, summer, winter, memory, religion

On the other hand, one can just as easily find associations that seem not to make much sense, such as 42 = boy, female; 100 = hospital, writing, ornament; 17 = ice, acid; 71 = soup, snow; and so on. Yet although such entries from one standpoint are nonsense, from another they may be too profound to immediately perceive.

The criticism of the Qabalah is, and always has been, that one can find in it anything one wishes. Crowley answers this argument thus: "When the sceptic sneers, 'With all these methods one ought to be able to make everything out of nothing,' the Qabalist smiles back the sublime retort, 'With these methods One did make everything out of nothing.'"[108] While this riposte may seem a glib dismissal of the point, I think that Crowley meant that the question was an adequate and reasonable one within a certain context—namely, the empirical context. In fact, the essay preceding this comment is dedicated to ridiculing and criticizing the rather lax methods of some qabalists. In another context, the context of faith, whether or not the values of gematria "mean" anything, is as unimportant a question as whether or not Shakespeare wrote the plays attributed to him. In the mundane case, we have these plays, all demonstrably written by the same person, and all paragons of Elizabethan literature. In the magical case, I have a number of infinite associations, and I sit at my desk with a pen and trace out as many of those associations as I like, and at some moment I have a brief "aha!" that strikes me with a sense of order and structure to the universe. When I feel chills hearing the

---

108. Aleister Crowley, *777 & Other Qabalistic Writings*. York Beach, ME: Weiser, 1986, 25.

Saint Crispin's Day speech in *Henry V*, it doesn't matter who wrote the play (or that Henry V never gave that speech outside of fiction). When I stand in awe at the substance of the universe, the underlying consciousness that swims with numbers and words, it doesn't matter if the associations I have been tracing are "chance" or placed there by secret masters or any other explanation. All such speculations fade into meaninglessness in the face of the moment of transcendent awe.

As a person trained in the scientific method, I opine firmly that, in the empirical universe of measurement and observation, the associations of words with numbers in Hebrew, English, or Greek is random. No person planned it out (except, perhaps, in particular cases in late Hebrew writings), because no person could possibly have so much control of language. However, as a person trained in the occult, I opine firmly that the association of words with numbers in Hebrew, English, or Greek is *not* random, in the sense that it does have meaning that engages my consciousness. While no person might have placed these correspondences in the letters and numbers of holy texts, perhaps some entity greater than a person did. That, I cannot know empirically. But I can have faith.

Faith, however, in the sense that I mean it, is not credulity. Much of the history of the literal Qabalah (which includes methods of gematria, among others, which I'll explain shortly) is riddled with questionable claims. For example, Christian qabalists attempted to convert Jewish qabalists by finding (or creating) qabalistic evidence for the identity of Jesus as Messiah. Such evidence is often questionable. For example, the letters of the first word of the Torah, *breshith*, can be expanded into a sentence, a practice known as "notariqon." Usually, notariqon is used to create a shorthand word for a larger phrase, but it can also work in reverse, to expand an unusual word into a sentence. Christian qabalists in an attempt to convert Jews took the first word of the Torah and expanded it, by creating a sentence whose abbreviation spelled "breshith." One such attempt, by a qabalist calling himself Prosper, was *bekori rashuni asher shamo yeshuah thaubodo*—"Ye shall worship My first born, My first, Whose name is Jesus."[109] Mathers claims that Prosper actually converted a Jew with this method, which puzzles me, since one could argue that, just as easily, one could create an infinite number of sentences, including such bits of nonsense as: *baholand ra'a immekha shalikh yamma'i thumim*, or "In Holland your mother saw the messenger of an innocent sailor." So in order to use the literal Qabalah—through gematria and the other methods I will discuss in a moment—we need a method that will help prevent such self-serving or downright silly results.

Methods of Gematria

In gematria, there are five basic operations. We can compare, add, subtract, multiply, and divide. In comparing, we find what other words equal the value of the number under question. If, for example, we are analyzing the word *deity* in the English Qabalah we might discover that it equals YHVH, a common way of writing the four-letter name of God called the tetragrammaton. Or, in the Hebrew Qabalah, we might note that Boaz, the pillar of Severity, and Jachin, the pillar of Mercy, both add up to 79, along with the word *'ideh*, meaning "union" or "conjunction." From this we can conclude, through comparison, that the duality of the Qabalah is really unity expressing itself through duality.

Adding gives us another range of numbers—we can compare two different numbers by adding them together to yield a third number. If we take 79, with its ideas of union, and "test" it by adding 93, the number of the Greek words *thelema* (will) and *agape* (love), we get 172, which equals the verb *baqa'*, "to cut, divide," among other things. So it is love, acting through will, that creates the separation between opposites, because without such division, there can never be the pleasure of union. If you work with gematria, you will eventually develop a range of "test" numbers that are personally significant to you.

Subtracting can be used like adding, to test a number with another number or compare two numbers. So if one takes 79, and subtracts 13

---

109. S. L. MacGregor Mathers, *The Kabbalah Unveiled*. York Beach, ME: Weiser, 1992.

(symbolic of love and unity, because the words *aheva* and *ekhad*, meaning "love" and "one" add up to it), the result is 66. We learn from Crowley's *Sepher Sephiroth*[110] that this number is the Mystic Number of the Great Work as well of the qlippoth or qabalistic hells. So it's a dangerous number—to understand unity is to achieve the Great Work. But it's also, potentially, to fall into solipsism. We also find that the word *gilgul*, "wheel," is also equivalent to 66, so that we can understand 66 as a number of the magic circle. The Sefer Yetzirah specifically mentions gilgul in numerous places as the swirling of creation itself, so understanding this unity, separating it into opposites, and reuniting them again is a cycle of creation. We can examine the number further, continuously subtracting 13 from each preceding result, until we cannot subtract 13 any more; this gives us a series as follows:

- 53:   ma'heva—"lover"
- 40:   gazal—"to cut off" and khaval—"to bind"
- 27:   zakh—"purity"
- 14:   dawid—"beloved"
- 1:   The number of unity

Clearly, this reveals a pattern of union and separation. Ultimately, we end in the perfect unity of one. We also learn that all our opposites are united by love, yet this isn't the wishy-washy love of chicken soup and crackers. It's the love that purifies. It's the love that drove King David (his name comes from *dawid*, above), and it's the love that simultaneously makes distinctions in order to collapse them. This subtraction method often yields a string of results that elicits complex insights.[111]

Multiplying and dividing also have their uses. Each number is a product of factors. Some numbers have only themselves and one as a factor;

---

110.   Published in Crowley, *777 & Other Qabalistic Writings*. York Beach, ME: Weiser, 1986.

111.   Henrietta Bernstein, *Cabalah Primer*. Marina del Rey, CA: De Vorss, 1984. One of the few books to explore the English Qabalah; it contains other methods of testing through subtraction, including one based on the Fibonacci sequence.

we call these numbers prime. All other numbers are products of one or more prime numbers. One can investigate a number by looking up its factors. For example, one can analyze the famous 666 as 6 x 111, or the sephirah of the sun (numbered 6) times 111, which is the numeration of the word *alef*, the name of the first letter of the Hebrew alphabet. So 666 is a solar number. Or one can take 65, the number of *Adonai*, a name of God, and analyze it as 5 x 13, or the five elements manifested through unity and love.

Obviously, any of these methods also works with the English Qabalah, or should if the English Qabalah has any validity. Let's explore some important concepts in the literal Qabalah, and see what we arrive at.

Notariqon

I've already discussed notariqon. Notariqon comes from a Latin word, *notarius*, meaning a shorthand-writer. Latin shorthand was not like our shorthand—instead of inventing new symbols for sounds, Latin simply used a large selection of abbreviations and relied on the scribe's memory. In Hebrew, notariqon can work two ways: one can take a word and extend it out by making a word out of each of its letters, or one can take a sentence and condense it into a word. I've already given a couple examples of the first method. The second method leads to a class of magical words, such as the famous *Agla*, as a name of God, condensed from the Hebrew sentence *atah givur l'olam, adonai*, meaning "Thou art great forever, my Lord."

Simply digging through a dictionary looking for various words isn't an appropriate method for extending a word into a meaningful sentence. One needs some other criterion—for example, the sentence expanded from a single word should have a numerical value that bears an interesting relationship, perhaps in general or perhaps when compared to the original value. For example, one can expand the initial word of the Torah into the sentence *breshith raah elohim sheyiqbelo ishrael torah*, meaning "In the beginning God saw that Israel would accept the Law." The value of this sentence is 2626, or 26 x 101. Twenty-six is the value of the four-lettered name of God, and 101 is the value of the noun *mlukah*, meaning "kingdom" or "royalty." So the first word of the Torah can be expanded

into a sentence that establishes God's plan—the Torah—and shows how
it manifests in reality (mlukah) through his divine name. This also works
in other languages; alchemists referred to their sulfur by its Latin name,
vitriol. They also expanded out *vitriol* into a sentence: *Visita Interiora
Terrae Rectificando Invenies Occultum Lapidem*, meaning "Visit the interior of the earth, and you will find in rectification the Secret Stone." This
sentence is an instruction for the Great Work, a handbook of alchemy
in one word.

The method of condensation, in which a sentence is reduced to a
word, is most often used to create a shorthand reference for an entire
prayer. It's interesting to note that one of the names of the scriptures of
Judaism, *Tanakh*, is in fact a notariqon condensation of Torah, the first
five books setting out the Law; Nviyim, the books of the prophets; and
Ksuvim, the "Holy Writings" including the psalms and proverbs.[112] It's
possible that *amen*, as well, is a condensed notariqon of the sentence
adonai melekh na'amon, meaning "My Lord is a faithful king." Probably,
the word *amen* precedes its notariqon, but the use of this method of abbreviation is a common one even in secular modern Hebrew.

Part of the advantage of Hebrew's predictable and often unwritten
vowel structure is that one can plug together a string of consonants and
easily guess at a plausible pronunciation (assuming, of course, that one is
familiar with Hebrew vowel patterns or rhymes). This method is useful
for the creation of words of power and spirit names. For example, with
a little brushing up on one's Hebrew, a Hebrew dictionary, and some
time, one can write out a sentence of desire in Hebrew and reduce it to a
single word. For example, imagine that you want a new car: *yesh li mobil
tov* ("I have a good car"). Taking each initial letter in Hebrew gives you
Yud Lamed Mem Tet, or the word *yelmet*, which one could use to name a

---

112.   Israel Regardie, *Foundations of Practical Magic*. Wellingborough, UK: The
       Aquarian Press, 1979, 117. This, and my examples of *vitriol* and *amen*, come
       from this book, and while they are repeated in work after work as examples of
       these methods, they're rarely cited.

servitor or artificial elemental, or as a word on a talisman for a new car.[113] One could also use it as a mantra or word of power, repeating it until gnosis, to implant the idea in the deep mind.

This method is mighty handy if you happen to know some Hebrew. Most of us, however, get by with a little Hebrew and a lot of English. Yet this method can also be used in English. For example, in the secular domain the word *scuba* is a notariqon of "self-contained underwater breathing apparatus." Yet such notariqons in English are a bit tricky partially because we have, unlike Hebrew, a full alphabet rather than an abjad. In other words, we have vowel letters, so if we take the letters of a sentence, such as "I make more money" or "I want a new car" we end up with something unpronounceable, like "immm." Or, worse, something pronounceable and absurd (chanting "iwanc" will likely not lead to gnosis, but to laughter). Of course, being fluent in English, we can play with the statements of desire to create names that can be pronounced, such as changing the infelicitous "I want a new car" to "I have a good auto," leading to *ihaga*. Or, if we simply cannot interpolate a word beginning with a vowel, we can just add neutral vowels to aid pronunciation. So "I make fifty thousand dollars a year" becomes "IMFTDAY," or *imaftaday*.

Temurah

Temurah means "permutation"; the English equivalent is probably *anagram*. This is the method of rearranging the letters of a word to spell out a new word. Obviously this method isn't as open to interpretation and abuse as notariqon, since only a few words are possible. Some such relationships are interesting—for example, *ani*, "I" in Hebrew, is composed of the letters alef, nun, yud, which when recombined into the order alef, yud, nun, spell *ein*, "nothing." So the personal identity is, in some sense, nothing. Obviously words derived through temurah should have the same numerical values,

---

113. If you just grabbed a pen to calculate the numerical value of the word *yelmet*, congratulations, you're a qabalist. It's 89, which equals *guf*, meaning "body."

In a way, a car is like a surrogate body—it allows us to do things our bodies don't. We could also use gematria to determine what the spirit Yelmet would be like: he'd be silent, because *demamah*, "silence," also equals 89. Unfortunately, Crowley disapproves of this type of silence; perhaps a new car, after all, is not such a good idea.

unless you count the final forms of letters in your gematria, so that in some cases a nonfinal letter might become final—such as in the above ani/ein example, when the nun becomes final and is counted as 700 rather than 50. However, most people, I've noticed, do not count final values. Another interesting example is the temurah of the words *hilel* (morning star), *yilelah* (wailing, lamentation), *laylah* (night), all composed with the same letters, heh, yud, lamed, lamed. So we can conclude that, by temurah, there is some link between night, the herald of its ending, and lamentation. The advantage of Hebrew is that it consists of three-letter roots with various prefixes and suffixes, so any given three letters are likely to create a word, and if rearranged, other words as well.

English is not so lucky. However, with some modifications, temurah can be useful in English as well. Obvious examples, such as *heart* and *earth*, provide plenty of material for meditation. There are also imperfect anagrams, in which each word of the anagram is composed of the letters of the word, but letters can be repeated. This method allows self-deception, but can be an entertaining game in a meditative state as well as enlightening, although I'd always be careful to validate any insights gained through it by some other means. For example, take the name Clint Eastwood, the famous American actor, whose name aptly creates the anagram "Old West Action." That seems fairly significant, but Abraham Lincoln can produce "Calm Banal Rhino," which is hard to imagine could be relevant to the former president. Nor can one imagine that Dick Cheney is really a "Needy Chick." A much more useful application of anagrams is the creation of words that encapsulate an entire sentence of desire. For example, "I want a new car" can be "incant raw awe," a phrase that could be worked into an incantation to achieve the original goal. Or nonsensical words of power can be created, such as "anatwi canwer." Frater U.·. D.·. suggests the repetition of such anagrammatic words of power until trance to exhaustion.[114]

---

114.   Frater U.·. D.·., *Practical Sigil Magic: Creating Personal Symbols for Success*. St. Paul, MN: Llewellyn, 1990.

Tziruf

Qabalists also employ substitution ciphers, called tziruf, to gain insight about certain words, or more commonly, to create words of power. These usually have a name based on the ways they modify the Hebrew alphabet. For example, one such method, Athbash, is called that because it takes the alphabet, breaks it in half, and matches it up, so that alef is associated with thav, beth with shin, and so on, spelling Ath-bash. To permute a word, one takes its letters and replaces them with the ones they match to. With Athbash a name like Adonai, ADNY, becomes ThQTM, which is then given the same vowels to become *thaqotam*. Often, because of the way Hebrew roots are constructed, a word will become a different word through tziruf, while in English this method would lead to a mishmash of consonants—that new word, and its numerical value and so on, become linked to the original idea. More often, one uses tziruf to derive the names of angels and spirits. For example, if one wants to find an angel of love, one would take the Hebrew word for love, *aheva*, and permute it through Athbash (or one of several other systems) to yield the word *Thatzeshatz*. Adding the suffix *-el* turns it into an angel, "Thatzeshatzel." One could then invoke, evoke, or summon this angel as one wills, to accomplish whatever desire one wishes. It's been said that each blade of grass has its angel; this is the method by which one discovers their names.

In English, tziruf runs into the problem of our vowels, but it's easy enough to fix. If we follow the Hebrew method and simply delete our vowels, we can create a table equivalent to Athbash by bending our alphabet in half in the same way:

B	C	D	F	G	H	J	K	L	M	N
P	Q	R	S	T	V	W	X	Y	Z	

This system, Bapcaq, is not entirely satisfactory, since the English alphabet without its vowels creates an odd number. This means N doesn't change. A word like *love* becomes LV with the vowels deleted, then YH, with the vowels reintroduced becoming *yohe*. One can still use the suffix *-el* to denote an angel, creating the angel of love in English: "Yohel."

A more aesthetically satisfying method is a three-part table in which each letter is replaced by the one below it, and the bottom row is imagined to "wrap" up to the top row, so:

B	C	D	F	G	H	J
K	L	M	N	P	Q	R
S	T	V	W	X	Y	Z

With this system, which I'll call "Bakas," *love* becomes the word of power *tode*, and the angel "Todel." *Hate*, on the other hand, becomes *qace*, and its angel becomes "Qacel." The advantage of this system is that, since vowels are kept the same, there's a chance of arriving at an actual English word, in at least some cases, especially if one makes the concession that a {u} can be inserted after {q}, even if there isn't one in the original word. For example, *one* becomes *owe*, because we owe our existence to the concept of unity. However, other words are still likely to become unpronounceable, because of English's complex syllable structures—for example, *sleep* becomes the train wreck "bteex"!

Testing Experiences

It's wise not to take these qabalistic games *too* seriously. They're entertaining and occasionally enlightening, and they can provide us with the names of spirits to work and experiment with, but ultimately they're games with letters. The skeptic scoffs at such things as superstitious numerology, pointing out that, for each startling correspondence, there are dozens of meaningless ones, and several silly ones. Temurah, notariqon, and tziruf are even more subject to such criticism than gematria. They lack any sorts of regulatory brake to slow their potential slide into absurdity. The skeptic is largely right, and no less authority than Aleister Crowley agreed. The Qabalah is, or rather can be, a collection of irrational, silly word games proving nothing. One might as well seek out ultimate truth in a crossword puzzle. Yet Crowley, and many other intelligent and skeptical people, continued and continue to use the Qabalah with full faith that it works. Why?

The idea that gematria or notariqon or tziruf reveals some secret code hidden in a word or text is a superstitious one, owing more to rigid materialism than to a magical mindset. In a cause-and-effect world, there must be a cause for a link between words, an apt anagram or a suitable enumeration. But the magician does not live in such a rigid cause-and-effect world. At least, he or she admits to the possibility of causes nonmaterial and effects unpredictable. Instead of trying to tease out the code God placed in the Bible, the magician (and any other reputable qabalist of any stripe or spelling) uses the manipulation of letters and numbers to accomplish three things: to test his or her perceptions, to break free from the tracks of well-worn thought habits, and to achieve a state of consciousness in which the interrelationship of all ideas becomes evident.

Crowley himself, for all his skepticism about the methods of the literal Qabalah, highly endorses gematria to test one's experiences. He suggests analyzing the name of any spiritual being numerically, to make sure that it is connected to suitable symbolic associations. For example, he describes an astral vision of an entity named "Ottilia," which he spells "OTYLYAH." (Crowley's *Magick Without Tears* here has a typographical error of a tzaddai in place of the 'ayin.) The value of this name is 135, which is a product of 3 x 45, both of which numbers are particularly Saturn-like. Since images of Saturn surround the entity Ottilia in the original vision, these numbers are appropriate, and so one can be certain that Ottilia is truly a Saturnine entity and not a figment of Crowley's imagination.[115] One can also learn something about an entity by its choice of words, or by asking the entity for a number that best expresses its nature. On one such occasion, I asked a spirit for a number and a name. The name was an unusual one, not clearly fitting Hebrew phonotactics, so I asked the spirit to spell it. The spirit spelled it oddly, and I asked if another, simpler spelling might be more suitable, to which the spirit disagreed. When I returned to normal consciousness and added up the odd spelling of the name, it equaled the number exactly. Of course, one could argue that I unconsciously chose a name with a sum that would be appropriate. At

---

115. Crowley, *Magick Without Tears*. Scottsdale, AZ: New Falcon, 1991, 146.

the time, however, I knew almost no Hebrew aside from the alphabet, and that imperfectly! I would not formally study Hebrew for another two years. Interestingly, no other spirit has offered such simple proof—the more sophisticated I become in the practice of Hebrew gematria, the more complex the proofs become, as if to skate on the edge of my capabilities, both to assure me of their validity and to stretch my limits.

Using gematria to test your experiences does not require that you have memorized long lists of numbers and their significances, nor does it require you to be fluent in Hebrew or Greek. The entities you meet will always choose a method, if they wish to communicate with you, that you yourself can understand. A principle of communication, called the Cooperative Principle, states that any two people who attempt to communicate will operate under the assumption that the other is cooperating, or trying to be understood. It is this assumption that allows us to understand metaphors; we hear someone say, "It's a war zone out there!" and, if we are not actually engaged in a war in the northern Illinois area, we might think, "Oh, traffic must be pretty bad." We assume that a person isn't speaking nonsense or telling a deliberate lie, because we assume people cooperate in communication. Similarly, we can assume that a spirit isn't going to choose some complex and difficult gematria for us to perform unless that is within our capabilities. To put it simply, when you speak to someone you choose a language you believe that they can understand. When an angel or spirit speaks to us, it chooses a language it knows we can understand.

In using gematria to test experiences, I find it useful to ask a spirit to spell a name, if possible. Sometimes, the spirit will refuse to do so for some reason—perhaps figuring out the spelling is part of the puzzle. Other times I may ask the spirit to spell a name in Hebrew, and they'll tell me that the name isn't Hebrew. If the spirit offers a name that doesn't seem to match the experience I've had of the spirit, then I know that one of several possibilities may be true:

- I've deceived myself and created the spirit out of my imagination. If that's the case, the next question to ask myself is, is there any way I can still get some benefit from this? Self-deception is a danger, but it's also a bit puritanical to be paranoid about deceiving ourselves. Sometimes these "fake" spirits can become servitors or reveal something about my personality that is of value to me, even if they are just part of myself.

- The spirit is lying. Spirits can lie, but they cannot use symbols that do not belong to them. Just as we, made (partially) of matter, must obey physical laws, so spirits, made of symbols, must obey the logic of metaphor. A spirit's name must, in some way, reflect its nature—although in this case, it might not be obvious. If the spirit is lying, I can choose to banish it, or explore its real nature (a bit more dangerous, but sometimes valuable).

- I just can't understand the spirit. Communication does go wrong. In fact, communication *never* goes right! There is always some degree of error in any attempt to communicate. Maybe the spirit said its name was spelled one way, but I heard something else. Or perhaps communication went wrong in some other way. The best way to deal with this is the same as with mundane communication: ask for clarification.

Using gematria to test experiments can keep one from hying off on a fantasy or being deceived by nonbeneficial entities. Still, it's best not to become paranoid about the whole thing.

Breaking free from the tracks of well-worn thought habits is the second way in which one may use gematria. Many of the contradictory or confusing correspondences can encourage us to think more deeply about the relationship between ideas than we might otherwise. For example, 13 equals *aheva*, "love," but it also equals *'iv*, "hated." So how can love and hate be related? We might, in meditation, consider how these two concepts relate. First, they're both strong emotions. They both represent attraction, although one is positive and one is negative. We might also recall that Plotinus, the Neoplatonic philosopher, argued that the universe was governed by two equal forces, *eros* and *aneros*, or "love" and "unlove." We might also notice that the 13th path on the Tree of Life connects Tiphareth and Kether, or personal identity and the divine. That might remind us of the story of the Hindu murderer who demanded that a Saddhu or saint give him a mantra that would make him all-powerful. The Saddhu offered him the mantra "Mara," the name of the Lord of Death and Deception. Well-pleased, the murderer recited his mantra over and over, until a feeling of love and good will filled him. He returned to the Saddhu, angry about the results but unable to do anything about the love for God bubbling up in him. The Saddhu asked him to recite the mantra, at which point, the murderer began to repeat "mara-mara-marama rama-rama-rama-rama." The name of hate became the name Rama, one of the avatars of the god Vishnu, of whom Krishna is an avatar. And the Saddhu explained that hating God isn't as good as loving him, but both are better than indifference.

We might also use gematria as a way to understand people, or even learn to appreciate difficult people. If you enumerate a person's name, you may discover qualities about that individual you might otherwise have thrown away. For example, if you take a person many Americans don't really appreciate as much as people do in, for example, Germany, and translate his name into Hebrew, you might get DVD HSLHVP. Which adds up to a nice round 200, adding up to words like *archetypal* and *spring*. So perhaps what the Germans see in David Hasselhoff is an archetypal appeal and a freshness that we Americans miss. Of course, any name not originally written in English could be written in a number of ways, since there's never a one-for-one correspondence between sounds in English and Hebrew. The point is not to get the "right" name but to open ourselves up to new ways of thinking about a familiar topic.

The final reason for using gematria, to link all ideas together to promote a consciousness of the interrelationship of all things, is the result of breaking our most pervasive mental habits. We begin to see that habits are just that—habits. We think in the patterns we are used to, but all of those patterns are flexible, especially the one that gives rise to the illusion that objects are separate in place and time. For example, I think that I'm typing on this keyboard, but in reality the keyboard is part of me, as is the computer, the metals in the earth, the dinosaurs that provided the oil for its plastic, and you—and everyone you interact with, the trees the paper came from to make this book, and therefore the sun, moon, stars, earth, galaxy, and universe. All of it links together, and I cannot meaningfully say that I am different from any of it in any but the conventional sense. Gematria helps us learn to accept that truth by breaking apart our delusions. One traditional way to do this is to find a way that any number can be said to represent perfect unity.

Mere unity is, however, sometimes just too easy. For example, any number divisible by thirteen is a pretty straight track to unity, since 13 is the number that adds up to *ekhad*, or "unity." One can just sit down, say, "Huh, all numbers are divisible by one," and be finished with the whole bloody business. It's more challenging and useful to take two different ideas and, rather than trying to link them to "unity," just try to link them to themselves. A Hebrew dictionary is a handy toy for this: simply flip it open at random, as I'm about to do, and pick two words, such as: *nistar*, NSThR, "to be hidden," and *nishshesh*, NShSh, "to feel, grope, or track." Now, I've happened to pick two words that seem pretty similar conceptually, but let's run through them anyway.[116] Nistar equals 665 and nishshesh equals 650. Wow, these are some high numbers! With numbers this high, it's a good bet that Crowley's *Sepher Sephiroth*, a dictionary of gematria, is silent on the matter. But let's see: 665 also equals the idiom *beyt ha-rakham*, which means "the womb." The idea of being hidden and the idea of the womb—aha! But our goal is to link the ideas, not just explicate one of them—we want to make everything become everything else. So let's look at 650 . . . oh, curses, it only adds up to *nither*, or "nitre," another name for the mineral saltpeter or potassium nitrate. KNO_3 isn't particularly interesting in connection with tracking or groping (although if one is groping one's way in a hot, dry cave, one might come away with a handful of it . . . but no, that's a stretch). Too bad; things were going so well. But we're not done yet.

The difference of 665 and 650 is 15. The first thing one might notice, looking in Crowley's *Sepher Sephiroth*, is that 15 is the value of *khavah*, "to hide." So when we grope toward the hidden, we just serve to hide it more deeply, perhaps. It's also the value of a name of God, *Yah*,

---

116. By the way, I use Ben Yehuda's *Pocket English-Hebrew Hebrew-English Dictionary*, but any dictionary will work. If you are a purist, you may prefer to use a biblical concordance, a special dictionary of biblical Hebrew. I personally see no reason not to explore the rich field of modern Hebrew (or, for that matter, English!).

meaning "He is," so we could link the two ideas as expressing the fact that God is simultaneously hidden and sought. But we don't need to stop there, even yet. Both 665 and 650 are divisible by five, yielding 133 (7 x 19) in the former and 130 (5 x 13 x 2) in the latter. Nineteen equals the noun *khawwah*, which can mean, among other things, "to manifest" and "Eve" (as in, the woman in the garden). *Avad*, meaning "lost" or "ruined," is one word with the value of 7—so 133 represents, by one interpretation, Eve's loss. Five, the number of humanity, indicates this represents an archetypal human condition. Similarly, 130 represents 65 x 2, or 5 x 26, both indicative of humanity's relationship with the divine (in the case of 65, it's Adonai, ADNY = 65, while in the case of 26, it's YHVH). Either way, we can link these two words together in that old archetypal myth of the loss of innocence in Eden, when we tried to cover up our nakedness before the demiurge. But hidden in that disaster was the womb of our eventual humanity.

Or something like that. It's vital not to take such things too seriously. Gematria and literal Qabalah is a game; however, it is a sacred game, and there are moments at which the hairs rise up and one catches one's breath. Elsewhere I have spoken of the universe as a vast sea of information or an infinite web of constantly self-referencing symbols. But gematria teaches us another way of seeing the universe, not as a vast and infinite sea, but as a single monad, in which every word becomes linked to every other word, every number becomes linked to every other number. It also teaches us to look more closely at the words we use, and realize their connection to each other in other than purely grammatical or semantic senses. Some accuse gematria of being the random application of numbers to letters, no more meaningful than stabbing randomly at the words in a dictionary. But I wonder, if one were to do so and discover, again and again, that those words revealed rich material for contemplation, would such random pointing really be random? Randomness is meaninglessness, but when we discover meaning in the midst of the random, we create order and destroy entropy. That's a powerful magical act to accomplish with a pencil and some paper, whether in Hebrew, Greek, or English.

EIGHT

Mantras:
Formulas of Power

Many religions and magical traditions make use of repeatedly chant-
ed "magic words." The generic name for such things is a mantra.
In Hindu and Buddhist esoteric tradition, the word *mantra* designates a
specific type of magic word, something halfway between a prayer and a
spell. The etymology of *mantra* reveals one of the purposes of these words
in esoteric Hinduism and Buddhism. *Mantra* comes from the Sanskrit
root *man-*, meaning "mind," and the suffix *-tra*, meaning "tool" or "instrument." In English, we might calque the word as "minder." The mantra
is a tool that is used by, or used in order to change, the mind.

Eknath Easwaran compares the mind to an elephant, whose trunk
is always moving, getting into trouble. He points out that it is common
practice to give elephants a stick to hold, to occupy the trunk and prevent the animal from getting into mischief. The mantra, he says, is like
that stick, which "can steady the mind at any time and in any place."[117]

---

117. Eknath Easwaran, *Meditation: A Simple Eight-Point Program for Translating
Spiritual Ideals into Daily Life.* Tomales, CA: Nilgiri Press, 1991, 58.

For him, the mantra serves a utilitarian purpose: it is simply a word one repeats to prevent one from getting distracted. So, if hounded by obsessive thoughts or anxieties, for example, one can simply say one's mantra silently or aloud until those thoughts go away. This rational, almost materialistic view of the mantra is not, however, the most common view in Hinduism. Mantras are accorded powers well above those of simple concentration aids: they release shackles, transform bad karma, create beneficial luck, and so on.

The most famous mantra from the Sanskrit traditions is the syllable *Aum*, or sometimes *OM*. Aum is sometimes called the three-syllable mantra, because in Sanskrit phonotactics each vowel is regarded a syllable, as is a nasal falling at the end of a word. The *Upanishads*, a collection of teachers' sayings to their students, explains: "For as the earth comes from the waters, plants from earth, and man from plants, so man is speech, and speech is OM."[118] Humanity is speech, because it separates us from animals, but we also come out of speech just as plants come out of the earth. What it is to be human and to have a relationship to God is defined in the codes of speech, of which, the *Upanishads* tell us, Aum is the seed:

> AUM stands for the supreme Reality.
> It is a symbol for what was, what is,
> And what shall be. AUM represents also
> What lies beyond past, present, and future.[119]

The seed syllable Aum is the symbol of time and what lies outside of time. The reason why might seem obscure until one understands that the proper intonation of Aum is actually a physical, not just a verbal, gesture.

Even if you have little interest in Hinduism, you might experiment with Aum. Begin by sitting up straight. Merely straightening the spine through conscious effort isn't, by the way, the easiest or best way to do this, since sitting "straight" actually involves having a curved spine. Instead, imagine being pulled up by the top of your head, and let your spine and

---

118.   Eknath Easwaran, trans. *The Upanishads*. Tomales, CA: Nilgiri Press, 1987, 176.
119.   Ibid., 60.

body arrange themselves naturally under your skull. Touch your tongue to the roof of your mouth, relax your jaw, and draw in a deep comfortable breath (about 60 to 80 percent of your full lung capacity) with your diaphragm. Take a couple such deep breaths, and then with one of them begin to vibrate, very low in tone, the sound "ah" in *father*. Feel it as deep into your pelvis as you can; drop the tone until it physically vibrates the area under your diaphragm and in your pelvis. Now shift slowly to the sound "u" in *put* and feel the sound slide up to your belly and lungs. Finish by making the "mm" sound and feel the vibrations wrap around your skull. You may feel a sense of opening up, a greater awareness of the world around you, or an emotion of peace. I often use the recitation of Aum to start my day, not only to pay homage to the underlying consciousness of reality but also because it takes a while for my coffee to brew, and Aum wakes me up like a shot of espresso.

Understanding Aum—or any mantra, really—as a physical gesture underlines how language and the body are linked, and how language forms the bridge between matter and mind. Much Hindu writing on mantras explores the idea of "vibration" of various sounds, which I think has been somewhat misunderstood. This focus on vibration isn't a foreshadowing of modern scientific understanding of frequencies, but a recognition of the effects various sounds have on the body. Each vowel, for example, has a pitch all its own; that's one way we differentiate between them. If you're speaking at a fairly level pitch (all complexity of intonational contours and the like aside), you'll speak the vowel /i/ in *feet* at a higher pitch than the /a/ in *father*. As a general rule, the smaller the space you leave in your mouth, or the more closed your mouth is, the higher the tone will be. Poets sometimes use this to hide very subtle melodies in poems, and mystics frequently create mantras with these tones in mind.

Yet mantras are not merely sound—they also mean. For example, Aum is sometimes used as an affirmative or expression of agreement in the dialogues of the *Upanishads* (much as we might use *amen*), and many mantras can be translated. The famous *Aum Mani Padme Hum* contains two words that can be translated: "jewel" and "lotus." People often interpret this mantra as "O hail to thee, Jewel in the Lotus." The mantra teeters between pure sound and meaning. It also signifies a particular relationship with the entity it is dedicated to, the Bodhisattva Avalokiteshvara, the Bodhisattva or Enlightened Being of Compassion. Saying this mantra is supposed to encourage his attention and release us from suffering. The Jewel in the Lotus can refer to Buddha, but it can also refer to the precious nature of reality. The lotus, which has its roots in mud and its blossoms in the water, is a symbol of the world of duality, while the jewel in Hindu and Buddhist symbolism represents the precious and magical nature of the mind. With those symbols in mind, the mantra can represent the miracle of mind in the world of duality. Aum, like the lotus, has its roots in the mud of our pelvis and the blossom in the skull, while Hum vibrates the throat, face, and brain, the center of our mind in many cultures.[120] So the whole mantra represents rising from below in the physical gesture of the Aum and the symbol of the lotus, to bloom in consciousness with the physical gesture of the Hum and the symbol of the jewel. In this process, we are to see the workings of cosmic Compassion. It is a beautiful poem in two words and two sound gestures, a song and a dance of sound.

Many mantras, such as Hum and Aum, have sounds with no semantic or dictionary meaning. These *bija*, or "seed syllables," are sounds that encourage particular physical sensations—sound gestures, in other words—that match the meaning and purpose of the mantra itself. But not every mantra gains all of its power through these sounds alone; in the tradition of Tantra, many mantras must be activated by an enlightened teacher before they are useful. This activation is required both in Buddhist and Hindu Tantra.

Tantra is a tradition of yoga or union with God that works slightly outside the main traditions of yoga. There are both Buddhist and Hindu tantric practices. Often, Tantra involves systematic violation of proscriptions; for this reason it is often thought of as the yoga of sex in the

---

120.   It's interesting to note that other cultures, such as that of the Egyptians, placed the mind in the heart or liver. It's easy to assume that they were simply naive, but in reality, while the brain seems a logical and correct placement to us, imagine how well your mind would work without a heart or a liver. In reality, our body is dependent, in whole, upon our mind, and our mind can dwell in any part of it at will.

West.[121] In reality, it is a complex body of practices requiring discipline and elaborate training, only some of them dealing with sexual behavior. Many tantrikas are even celibate. I suspect that no one outside of the cultural traditions in which Tantra grew up can fully come to appreciate it—although one can certainly try.

The mantra in tantric practice is a result of initiation. The guru grants the chela, or student, a mantra that he or she has activated. These mantras are traditional, but often have a discernible structure and meaning. For example, they may alliterate, or repeat initial sounds. The bija, or seed syllable, might be chosen just because it alliterates with the name of a deity. Or the name of a deity may be permutated in much the same way as a qabalist permutes the names of God. For example, the rain god Heruka's mantra is a permutation of his name: "He he ru ru ka."[122] Palindromes are not unheard of, and some mantras resemble incantations: poetic utterances often referring to historical or mythological events. After this initiation, the student must activate the mantra for himself or herself. This involves repeating it a certain set number of times, usually in the thousands. After this process of activation, the mantra can be used not just to attain certain states of consciousness, but to affect reality.

From a linguistic perspective, the mental effect of repeating a word or sound over and over offers a clue to the mantra's function. As any child knows, if you take a word and repeat it again and again it will seem to lose its meaning. This phenomenon has actually been studied by linguists and psychologists, who have named it *semantic satiation*. No one can agree exactly what causes semantic satiation. Some claim that it results from the divorce of context, but I find this explanation a bit thin: after all, if I say "truck driver" out of the blue, even if you find it an odd statement because of its lack of context, you still know what the word means. Why constant repetition should divorce it from context is difficult to ascertain.

---

121. One of these practices that some tantrikas in the Hindu tradition use is the ritual eating of beef, forbidden by Hinduism. Had Americans been less neurotic about sex, Tantra might have entered America as the "yoga of steak."

122. Robert A. Yelle, *Explaining Mantras: Ritual, Rhetoric, and the Dream of a Natural Language in Hindu Tantra*. New York: Routledge, 2003, 14.

Moreover, the phenomenon also occurs in writing. I suspect the effect is a result of *Verfremdungseffekt,* or "the alienation effect," the effect of making something ordinary seem strange. Why repetition should accomplish this effect, however, I am uncertain.

If you wish to explore the satiation effect for yourself, you can do so easily by choosing a word and repeating it out loud over and over in the same tone of voice. I recommend a word of two or more syllables, but any word will do—even your own name, although some might find the result of that particular experiment disturbing. Try not to daydream—just focus on saying the word as quickly as possible. You will find, at some point, that the word simply becomes a physical motion of your mouth, lips, and tongue. It will start to sound strange and foreign. Interestingly, you can get a similar effect if you open your word processor, print the word in the center of a page, then print it out and stare at it for a prolonged time.

Oddly, the repetition of words has another effect, exactly the opposite of semantic satiation, called semantic generation. If one repeats a nonsense word over and over, it will eventually begin to feel significant. For example, imagine that you are learning Spanish, and you first hear the word *cuchillo,* or "knife." As you are introduced to the word, it is a nonsense sound. You might learn, by rote, that it means "knife," but you are merely translating from one code to another. At some point in your study of Spanish, however, as you are exposed to Spanish speakers and hear them talking, you will find that *cuchillo* no longer sounds like nonsense. It now sounds like a word, and instead of thinking "*cuchillo*—that's the sound that, in Spanish, means the same as the English sound 'knife,'" you automatically think of a knife when you hear *cuchillo.* You may have known the definition of the word, but repetition has given it significance. Similarly, if you repeat a nonsense syllable long enough, it will stop sounding strange and you will have a subjective sense of it having a meaning, even if it truly has none. You may even begin to attribute one to it.

In fact, all the words that you know have their meanings only due to repetition. Meaning in a language is citational—when I say *chair,* I am citing every other time you have heard that word. Because you have always heard it applied to a certain physical object, you know what piece of furniture I mean. Children learn few words through formal definition; most words are learned by hearing them repeated in context and making the semantic links. Sometimes the mistakes children make are revealing of this process. For example, children rarely hear the word *hallowed* outside of the context of the Lord's Prayer. So many children think that God's name is Harold.

Repetition, therefore, both creates and destroys meaning. The side effects of semantic satiation and the citation effect are relevant to our discussion of mantras and formulas of power. When you experience semantic satiation, you may also find that your mind slows down and empties, briefly, of other thoughts. This state of consciousness is important in magic—it's one description of gnosis. From a semiotic perspective, you have completely denuded the word of signification, and having done so, you've momentarily unwoven the semiotic web—like pulling a thread from a sweater, you've unraveled meaning. Now, as meaning returns, as it inevitably must, it begins to coalesce around the repeated word. That word once again takes on meaning, and the semiotic web is rewoven around it. As I discussed in the first chapter, we can imagine this as a theory of how magic works, and therefore in reciting a mantra we are unmaking the complex world and reordering it around the idea expressed in that mantra.

Ancient Sanskrit grammarians had a sophisticated view of the symbolic nature of mantras. For example, the grammarian Bhartrhari in the seventh century argued that mantras, which might seem nonsensical, actually were symbols. He divided the mantra into sound and meaning, and suggested that both pointed toward *sphota*, a word that defies translation but that means something like "that from which meaning bursts or shines forth."[123] As one repeats a word over and over, both sound and meaning give way to sphota, and the experience of sphota leads to *Sabdabrahman*, or the truth of the divine.

Most of us lack gurus to teach us how to activate mantras. In chapter 2, I discussed the symbolism of sound. Those sound-symbols can be used

---

123. Harold G. Coward and David J. Goa, *Mantra: Hearing the Divine in India and America*. New York: Columbia University Press, 2004, 38–39.

to create original mantras. For example, you can create a set of mantras for the four elements:

fire   si
water   lu
air   na
earth   ke

After activating them for yourself—since you probably lack a guru—you can use them to commune with those elements. If you prefer to use more traditional mantras for the elements, however, the Golden Dawn[124] lists the following:

fire   ram
water   vam
air   pam
earth   lam
spirit   ham

The {a} here represents the "uh" found in the last vowel of *sofa*. So they sound more like "ruhm," "vuhm," "puhm," and so on.

Activating a Mantra

The key to activating a mantra is repetition and devotion. It helps to regard the sound itself as a sort of intelligence with which you are trying to communicate. If you find that a difficult idea to accept, merely accept it provisionally. Like most theories in magic, it needn't be a hard and fast truth to be useful. Regarding the sound as an intelligence, you need to repeat the syllable until it automatically, without cognition, leads to the idea you're trying to link it to. For example, if you're working with the elemental mantras, repeat the syllable "lam" until you automatically think of all the attributes of earth when you utter it. At that point, you continue to repeat the word until you experience semantic satiation. It's almost impossible to experience semantic satiation with a nonsense syl-

---

124.   Israel Regardie, *The Golden Dawn*. St. Paul, MN: Llewellyn, 1986.

lable, obviously, so you have to give it meaning before you can lose it. Once you experience semantic satiation, you've unwoven reality enough to reweave it around this new symbol.

This whole process could require thousands of repetitions. It's often useful to count repetitions through some simple, repetitive, manual procedure, not because you necessarily need to know how many repetitions you've made, but because it gives your hands something to do and seems to help achieve both citational meaning and semantic satiation. One traditional and pleasant way to count mantras is with a mala. A mala is a string of wooden, bone, stone, or even plastic beads. On a full-sized mala there are usually 108 beads, but other malas have twenty-seven (so that four repetitions make a full 108). The number 108 is significant in both Hinduism and Buddhism.[125] Other religious practices that repeat mantras or prayers also use malas of varying sizes. For example, the Catholic rosary has fifty beads and is used to count prayers and focus meditation on a sequence of mysteries. One can easily make one's own mala with a personally significant number. I use a Buddhist sandalwood mala, because I like the smell and feel of it. You use a mala by moving each bead over the index finger with the thumb as you recite the mantra you are counting. At the end, when you reach the large bead, you flip the mala around and count in the other direction, so that you never actually cross the center bead.

You may find counting your mantras useless. In that case, you may want to incorporate some physical motion anyway. I find rocking while chanting mantras to be very soothing, if not particularly traditional in Hindu practice. However, the practice of davening during Jewish prayer[126] does have a long-standing tradition: while reciting your mantra or prayer, rock slowly back and forth from the hips. Do this gently; there's no need to be a headbanger during prayer. You may also like to use hand motions, as some Sufis do while they recite the mantra called the dhikr: "There is no god [or reality] but God." Physical motion helps occupy the body

---

125. And baseball. It's the number of stitches on a regulation ball.

126. *Daven* actually refers to the prayer itself, but it has become connected in the popular imagination to the rocking motion that some Jews use during prayer.

and emphasize to the mind that you mean to use your words to bridge matter and mind.

Magical Formulas

Making, activating, and using one's own mantras is a century-long tradition in Western magic. Aleister Crowley, for example, discovered the Word of the Aeon, Abrahadabra (notice the spelling—his version contains "had" in the middle, which is the name of one his principles of reality). He claimed that the word formulated the Great Work itself. His explanation for how this formulation works is at best a smidgen abstruse. Most likely, such works are at least partially personal. Nema, for example, has discovered other words of *her* Aeon, the Aeon of Ma'at. One of these words is Ipsos, which she advises using as a mantra.[127] But where do these magicians get the idea for these formulas? Simply enough, they get them from the Greek magical tradition, which provides us with the so-called *voces magicae*, or magic words. I classify voces magicae into two categories: the first and least interesting are simply badly transliterated Hebrew or Coptic. In this category, a word or name is borrowed and written, as well as can be, in Greek letters. So the Hebrew *Adonai* ("my Lord") occasionally appears as "adonaos" or "adonael." Similarly, the Hebrew *tzava'aoth* ("armies, hosts") often appears as "sabao" or "sabaoth." The second category, more interesting to me, includes long strings of vowels or, sometimes, consonants. The line between the two types of *voces* isn't always clear; Coptic often involves strings of vowels, and it's possible that the most famous string of vowels—IAO—is actually a transliteration of the Hebrew YHVH. This second category, however, can be taken in much the same way we might regard the Hindu bija. They are seed sounds that represent ideas unrepresentable in regular language.

Just as a mathematic formula can express a complex idea more efficiently than an explanation of the same idea in English, so these magical formulas express the ineffable. We can try to translate them to some degree, and Crowley and other magicians of the twentieth century found

---

127.   Nema, *Maat Magick: A Guide to Self-Initiation*. York Beach, ME: Weiser, 1995.

that a worthy endeavor. However, any meaning we arrive at is likely to be—at best—personal. For example, the name IAO has been famously explicated by the Golden Dawn as follows:

The I stands for Isis, the goddess who was married to Osiris. The A stands for Apophis, the destroyer of souls, whom the Golden Dawn conflated with Set, the slayer of Osiris. And of course the O stands for Osiris, a god of grain, rebirth, and the sun. Therefore, IAO is a formula for the redemption of humanity through the death of a vegetative deity. This analysis is interesting in its own right, but it's even more interesting when combined with the analysis of another famous magical formula: INRI, the letters written on the cross upon which Jesus was crucified. The usual explanation of these letters is that they stand for "Jesus of Nazareth the King of the Jews." But the Golden Dawn translated them into Hebrew (which is rather unlikely historically, but acceptable magically) and used traditional correspondences to equate the I to Virgo, the N to Scorpio, and the R to the sun. From this equation, it is a small step to equate Virgo with Isis (who was at least somewhat virginal), Scorpio with Apophis (both symbols of destruction, although Scorpio includes ideas of sexuality and therefore re-creation), and the sun to Osiris. Interestingly, although never developed at all by the Golden Dawn that I've seen, the original myth of Isis has her becoming pregnant from a scorpion carrying the semen of Osiris. How this changes the formula might be grist for speculation.

Such formulas always say more about the decoder. The just-post-Victorian Golden Dawners were interested in the thesis, now largely abandoned, that all myths were a retelling of a primal vegetative god who dies and is reborn. While such motifs are common in world mythologies, most people have given up seeking evidence for such a theory. Still, the GD's attempt to analyze these two very diverse formulas in terms of this motif reveals a lot about their concern with death, resurrection, and redemption.

Crowley's famous translation of the Stele of Jeu[128] reveals much about the process of such translation. Taking each of the letters of the words of power from this ancient Greek spell (usually called the Ritual of the

---

128.   Lon Milo DuQuette, *The Magick of Aleister Crowley: A Handbook of the Rituals of Thelema.* Boston: Weiser, 2003, 129–153.

Bornless One but in Crowley's version called Liber Samekh) as a symbol, he creates rather peculiar phrases for each of the words. For example, he translates AEOOU as "Our Lady of the Western Gate of Heaven!" The sentence may seem incomprehensible, but it's really quite clear once you understand that each letter has a significance for Crowley. His translation of AR, for example, as "O breathing, flowing Sun!" makes perfect sense once you understand that A signifies air for Crowley, and R signifies the sun. Obviously, if you chose different correspondences, you would arrive at different "meanings." Crowley was a bit obsessed with systematization, I suspect, and wanted there to be a logical meaning to these logically meaningless strings.

Rather than translating formulas from thousands of years ago, we can create or discover our own formulas. There are two ways to create a formula: a spiritual entity can provide it (the preferred method of most modernist magicians) or one can create it from scratch and one's own ingenuity (preferred by many postmodernists). Of course, once one discovers a formula, there's the question of how to use it. Our exploration of mantras can give us some ideas to play with in using formulas.

Finding a formula from a spiritual entity requires communication with that entity. That's not as hard as it sounds. There are several ways of achieving communication with a nonphysical entity, many of which I cover in my first book, *Postmodern Magic: The Art of Magic in the Information Age*. All of these methods hinge on the active use of the imagination. By imagining, in a state of deep relaxation, an environment for the spiritual entity you wish to talk to, one that's perfectly symbolically congruent, you can make it more likely that you'll achieve contact. For example, if you wish to speak to a spirit of Mars, let's say Phobos the God of Fear, you'd imagine an environment (and maybe even create it in a physical, ritual space) of acrid scents, iron, the color red, the sound of clanging steel, perhaps the Mars theme from Holst's *The Planets*, and so on. Into this environment you would build an image of Phobos, and then communicate with him. Some of the information you receive might be just your own ego. For this reason it's a good idea to lean on a simple rule: if the spirit hasn't told you something true that you didn't know beforehand, or if the spirit has told you something not consistent with common sense or the symbolic nature of that spirit, then record what it said but do not act on it. If, on the other hand, the spirit tells you something useful—or at least, symbolically consistent—then you might consider using it.

For example, I made contact with a spirit during the hypnogogic state between sleep and wakefulness. This spirit was performing a ritual that seemed to involve honoring the sun in some way. When I woke up, I wrote down the word the spirit was chanting: *hayasana*. I tried several methods of analyzing the word, including translating it into several languages.[129] Nothing yielded much meaning until I transliterated it into Hebrew. Hebrew doesn't write its vowels, and there are two ways to write the sound /s/. So I tried both possible spellings of the word: *heh yud samekh nun* and *heh yud sin nun*. Neither of these spellings created an intelligible word, but the second spelling yielded the number 5 + 10 + 300 + 50, or 365, an important number in connection with the sun. Knowing this was the likely spelling, I analyzed each of the four Hebrew letters in the obvious fashion, as symbols of the seasons, taking sin, which is equated to fire, for the summer. This makes nun, the letter associated with Scorpio and death, symbolic of the autumn. Heh, therefore, becomes the winter, which is rather hard to explain symbolically, but yud is associated with spring, which makes a certain amount of sense, since yud is the "seed" of the other letters. I have theories about heh, some of which connect to Crowley's writings on the tarot, but I have not yet plumbed the depth of this formula. Clearly, however, it's a generative formula equating manifestation of a desire (since the spiritual figure seemed to be creating a talisman) with the inevitable revolution of the seasons and the sun.

What a lot of people don't seem to realize is that spirit communication isn't always thunderbolts and earthquakes. For example, on one

---

129. I have an interest in other languages, so spirits often couch messages in the terms of languages I have imperfectly studied but have the resources to look up. If you have no such interest, the spirits will, in my experience, couch their messages in other terms. They tailor their messages to our own symbolic preferences—which might be evidence for them existing within our own minds, except they sometimes know words and phrases in a language that I don't.

occasion I performed a lackluster invocation and was doodling on some scratch paper afterward, thinking, "It'd be nice if I had gotten some sort of communication from that spirit," when I realized I had doodled a Hebrew phrase. That's not unusual—being fascinated with language I doodle in lots of different languages. But I added up the phrase through gematria (see chapter 8), and discovered that it added up to the same value as the name of the spirit I was trying to invoke. Doodling in Hebrew is my own little peculiarity, but keep an eye on the things that just spring to mind after a ritual. Such things could be meaningless, but what differentiates the magician and the nonmagician is that we attach meaning to them.

Making It Up

Another way to receive formulas is to invent them yourself. No doubt our magical ancestors would frown at me for suggesting it, but why must every magical formula from a spiritual entity automatically be superior to one you develop yourself? You can take formulas from famous occult quotes, such as "as above, so below." You can analyze this not as a meaningful statement in its own right, but as a formula. For example, the first part has a two-letter word followed by a five-letter word, and so does the second part—therefore, it emphasizes the unity of two opposites. There's some historical precedence for this: the formula *vitriol*, which means "sulfur," was discussed in the last chapter. And the word *azoth*, often used in magic and alchemy to describe the mysterious "essence" of things, is constructed from the first letter and last letter of the Latin, Greek, and Hebrew alphabets. Since the first letter of all those alphabets is the same, that yields *a a a z o th*, or *azoth*. This formula also illustrates that out of one thing comes three different eventual results, an important idea in alchemy.

Or you may create a formula to express some complex idea that you want to understand more clearly. Let's imagine that you wish to pierce the illusion of a self separate from the world—a common enough goal in spiritual systems as varied as Zen and Vedanta Hinduism. To do so, you might decide that you need to break down the barriers between Self and Other. One way to do this is to intersperse the letters of "self" into those of "other." This gives you the formula *ostehlefr*. In analyzing this formula, you may notice that it would be hard to pronounce, but it occurs to you that in breaking down the barrier between Self and Other, you also break down the barrier between beginning and end, so why not symbolize that by starting the formula with its last letter, thus: *rostehlef*. I'll discuss how to use this formula, and other formulas, in a bit.

Another way to create formulas is to rely on the correspondences of the Hebrew alphabet. The Hebrew alphabet of twenty-two letters has been equated to the twenty-two major arcana tarot trumps. Therefore, you can create a "word" that represents an entire tarot layout to express any idea you like. This method shades into magical word territory, but imagine that you want a formula that you can use to understand the nature of true love. You might choose tarot cards expressing this idea, such as the Empress (III) and the Lovers (VI), and look up their Hebrew letters in appendix 2 of this book. Doing so, you discover that they create the word DZ, which you may freely envowel as you like (although I suggest /a/ in most cases). This yields the formula *daz*. Now you can do some Hebrew gematria on that and discover that daz equals 11, one of the numbers expressive of the Great Work of uniting the upper and the lower (5 + 6), as well as one of the numbers expressing the qlippoth, the "shells" of creation that go too far (10 + 1) beyond perfection. So 11 is a dual number, of dual use, and you can see that love can either lead us to the Great Work or to the qlippoth, depending how we wield it. It can be a door (the literal meaning of dalet) or a sword (the literal meaning of zayin.) Of course, if you don't happen to speak or read Hebrew, you can use the associations of the English alphabet. A possible table of correspondences can be found in appendix 3.

But how does one use such formulas? Obviously, one way is as I have above: to explore an idea in new ways, understand it from new perspectives, and break out of old habits. One may also, however, use such formulas as mantras, repeating them over and over to solidify their results in your consciousness. Another way is to use them as words of power in ritual. For example, you may create a formula for manifestation and repeat it in a ritual of evocation to encourage the spirit to appear. This last way is most common in ceremonial magic.

We can also use the formula as a magic word in another sense. We can anchor specific formulas with specific magical goals. For example, if we wish to create a word for the magical goal of overcoming obstacles, we might begin with the card the Chariot (for its idea of forward motion), follow it with the Devil (to symbolize physical, rather than mental, obstacles), and end with the World (symbolizing perfect success), which yields the Hebrew word ChOTh. We can place any number of vowels in this word, of course. If we're heart-set on figuring out a fairly accurate Hebrew word, we'd end up with *kha'ath*, but we could just shrug and say "Ayin is often associated with the letter O, historically, even though it didn't have that sound in Hebrew, so I'll just call the word 'khoth.'" Or we could use the English correspondences, and say the Chariot is J, the Devil is S, and the World is Z. Then we need to decide on vowels. We could decide that overcoming obstacles best belongs in the suit of wands, and create the word *Jisiz*. Whichever method we use, we have a magical word that we can charge for its purpose.

The easiest way to do this is to enter a mild trance and visualize, in as much detail as possible, the desired outcome while chanting the word a certain number of times, say 108. To use the word when faced with an obstacle, recite the word over and over like a mantra while you deal with the obstacle. Even in the mundane sense, such an approach can help you focus your mind on your goals. But it also, magically, prevents you from creating a semiotic code of failure. It holds, in your mind, the code of success over obstacles, and this pattern held in the mind has sway upon the world.

The one thing all of these approaches have in common is that the formula is a word that rearranges other words. It interacts with the semiotic codes that make our world and adjusts them. So, for example, when I find myself caught in the semantic code of duality, in which the world is either matter or spirit, people are either friends or foes, and information is either true or false, I can employ Crowley's Word of the Aeon, which unites (so he says) the upper and lower, and say "Abrahadabra." If I've invested that word with meaning and power, it can break me out of such a worldview and into a new one, a new Aeon in Crowley's nomenclature. A magical formula, like glossolalia, looks nonsensical, because

words have meaning only within the codes, and a magical formula comes
from outside the code to break it up and destroy it. Interestingly, the
word Abracadabra, from which Crowley presumably derived his formula,
originally appeared in amulets in the form

abracadabra
abracadabr
abracadab
abracada
abracad
abraca
abrac
abra
abr
ab
a

This inverted pyramid was common with words of power designed to
destroy fevers. Metaphorically, the codes through which we view our lives
are fevers. Formulas and mantras can help us break the fever and have a
moment of possibility.

NINE

Magical Narrative:
Metaphor, Myth, Ritual, and Theurgy

So far I have described a theory that emphasizes the importance of language and symbolism in Western magic. This theory has no necessary scientific validity, but a magical theory serves to evoke the possibility of new ideas and new approaches. This theory implies a cosmology, or an imagined shape of the universe. In this cosmology, there is potentially an underlying reality that cannot be expressed—the Ineffable. Above that floats a sea of undifferentiated Information, out of which come Symbols, organized according to Codes of interpretation. Not all symbols are created equal. Some symbols, called metaphors, have such power over our thoughts that we sometimes don't even recognize them as metaphors. We assume them to be truth.

Linguists are always looking for patterns and structures. The dominant theories of linguistics concern how, for example, words fit into phrases and phrases fit into sentences, all in an effort to break down the infinite variety of language into a simple "underlying grammar." Most of those seeking such structures focus on the level of syntax, or phrase and sentence. But there are also linguists who study how language works out in larger chunks—multiple sentences, paragraphs, entire stories or essays.

Usually, such study is relegated to the field of rhetoric, but some linguists still insist that we can study larger language structures using the principles of linguistics. This field is called pragmatics, and has borne some interesting fruit, most of it outside the scope of this book. One avenue of investigation that is relevant to the study of magic is how we organize information in our minds, and the research of George Lakoff suggests that we do so through metaphor.

To refresh your memory, a metaphor is a figure of speech in which one thing is equated to another thing. So one might say, "My afternoon was a nightmare," meaning "I had a difficult afternoon." Metaphors are interesting from a linguistic standpoint because they are, technically, lies. But what tips us off that a metaphor-lie is to be taken in some way other than as literal truth? Few people other than those who lack basic reading skills would think that I fell asleep in the afternoon and had a nightmare. Yet linguists are not entirely certain what, in a metaphor, cues us that it is not a mere lie, but a kind of truth. Every metaphor has the form $X = Y$, in which X and Y are completely different things and the $=$ stands for a verb of being, such as *is*. Y can be called the Source, and X the Target. From the Source, we mentally take some quality that applies to X. So in "My afternoon was a nightmare" we take some qualities of "nightmare"—unpleasant, terrifying, perhaps difficult to understand—and apply them to "my afternoon." We probably decide that I had a lot of work to do, or maybe an irate student in my office, or perhaps I had to give someone really bad news. We probably don't decide that I forgot to wear pants, or fell for a very long time, as would also happen in a nightmare. For some reason, almost everyone is capable of identifying which elements of the Source apply to the Target.

A metaphor could be considered a stronger class of symbol. A symbol says "X symbolizes or represents Y," but a metaphor says, "X is Y." If the candle is a symbol of enlightenment, you might say, "This candle symbolizes enlightenment," which implies "But it's still a candle." In ritual, often, however, you actually make an equation that is metaphorical: "This candle is enlightenment." A certain Buddhist ritual makes this distinction obvious: symbolically, the sutras or holy writings are teachings that guide readers to enlightenment. Ritually, they're often used to stand in for enlightenment itself, so much so that some schools of Buddhism simply chant the titles of particular sutras over and over. The symbol becomes a metaphor when the distinction between signifier and signified becomes a verb of being. A metaphor is therefore in some sense more fundamental and powerful than a symbol; a metaphor is a supersymbol. A symbol and its signifier are always a bit distant from one another, but a metaphor folds them together into one unit.

While there are many theories, Lakoff suggests that metaphors are not simply a figure of speech used to pretty up poetry and fiction but are fundamental to the way we think in language. For example, think about the way you make an adverb in English: you take an adjective like *happy*, and you attach the suffix -*ly* to it, so it comes out (with a few incidental spelling changes) as *happily*. That -ly certainly doesn't look like a metaphor, but in Anglo-Saxon, the adverb-making suffix was -*lice*, meaning "with/in a body." So *happily* originally meant "with a happy body." So one who "happily sang" was one who "sang in a happy body." It makes metaphoric sense, but it lost its metaphoric meaning and became just a sound to put after adjectives to make them adverbs. If you happen to know Spanish, you know the similar suffix to make an adjective into an adverb in Spanish is -*mente*, which originally meant "with a mind." Almost every word in our language can be seen as a metaphor, if you trace it back far enough.

Metaphor doesn't stop at the word level, but continues right up into our most complex uses of language. Lakoff suggests that we "live by" certain metaphors.[130] In other words, metaphors, like codes, organize symbols. For instance, we tend to think "up" is "more" and "down" is "less." When we create more heat in a room, we "turn it up." When we reduce the sound coming out of a speaker, we "turn it down." But the equations *up* = *more* and *down* = *less* are not literally true. In fact, we're not moving anything up or down when we turn up or down the heat, or the volume on our stereo! In fact, we have another metaphor that interacts with that one, *clockwise* = *up* = *more*. This metaphor has its origin in primitive electronics, and a

---

130.   George Lakoff and Mark Johnson, *Metaphors We Live By*. Chicago: University of Chicago Press, 2003.

largely arbitrary decision to standardize dials according to clocks, which mimicked the movements of the sun. This decision was relatively recent in the terms of language, but so deeply is this metaphor ingrained that when I "turn on" my computer, I push a button! And you "turn on" the lights by flipping a switch (upward, I might add). And you "turn on" a special friend by . . . well. Nothing much to do with dials, switches, or electronics.

Such a study of metaphor might seem appropriate to dusty old linguists (although not all of us are so old, thank you), but why does it matter in real life? Lakoff suggests that we often have preconceptions based on these metaphors, preconceptions that can lead us astray. For example, he points out that Republicans and Democrats have different underlying metaphors about government that prevent them from speaking to each other effectively. Republicans, he suggests, conceive of government as a stern father who provides necessary discipline, while Democrats regard government as a caring parent who sees to a child's needs.[131] Obviously, if a Democrat tries to reason from his or her underlying metaphor to a Republican, the Republican will reject that argument on the basis of his or her metaphor. And no communication can occur.

Metaphors We Do Magic By

In my own life I've made an effort to notice, either mundanely or magically, what sorts of metaphors people use so that I can tailor my communication to their mental framework. My mundane method is simply empathy—I imagine what they might be feeling and why they might be feeling it. My magical method is only slightly more involved. I relax myself with the fourfold breath or some other similar exercise and imagine a black mirror or empty space. When an object or image arises, I seek to link it metaphorically to what the person is saying or writing in order to understand what the underlying metaphors might be. Obvi-

---

131.   George Lakoff, *Moral Politics: How Liberals and Conservatives Think*. Chicago: University of Chicago Press, 2002.

ously, George Lakoff isn't particularly interested in the magical uses of his theory, which is why I get to write my own book.

The metaphors that dominate our lives select our perceptions for us, which means that we organize our perceptions through the metaphoric stories we tell ourselves. We might see someone standing in a shadow and, if we have an underlying metaphor of *world = hazard*, might perceive him or her as a mugger or rapist. Of course, the individual could just be waiting for a taxi, from another perspective. For a Democrat who deeply holds the *government = caring parent* metaphor, it's sometimes hard not to see Republicans as cold and greedy. For a Republican holding the *government = disciplinarian* metaphor, it's hard not to see Democrats as indulgent and permissive. If we hold the dominant metaphor, as most scientists do, that *world = matter*,[132] then we will always interpret our observations in terms of matter. Even if we witness something outré or odd, we'll say there must be a "reasonable explanation." The mystic might have a metaphor like *world = game* or *world = illusion*. Those metaphors might lead to behavior that the materialist would find almost insane, but that from the perspective of the mystic makes perfect sense—Rumi spinning in the streets, for example, singing praises to the Beloved. And the magician might deeply and unconsciously (or consciously) hold metaphors like *world = interaction of spirits*, which will lead to observations that are shamanic and animistic in nature. Or magicians might hold to *reality = information*, which will lead to observations and experiences that are consistent with that magical theory.

One of the interesting, or insidious, things about these metaphors is that they often don't seem metaphoric at all. For example, when we say "She's a thief" we're actually not stating a fact but creating a metaphor. "She" is the target and "thief" is the source, and we're supposed to take some element of "thief" and apply it to "she." Of course, there are very few characteristics of the word *thief*, and therefore it's pretty easy to do this

---

132.   Specifically, this is a synecdoche, a type of metaphor in which the part stands for the whole, such as "the bar" standing for the entire system of law, or "hands" referring to entire sailors. Matter is just a part of the world, but here it stands for the whole thing.

task, which is why it passes as a literal truth rather than a metaphor. But think about what happens when you label someone as a "thief"—you discount all of that person's other qualities. No one steals for twenty-four hours of every day. A thief may have a family. You could just as easily say "She's a mother," and mean the same person but give a completely different set of attributes to the target. But once we make such a metaphoric assumption, we have experiences that match it. When someone commits a crime, people who knew him or her often say, "But he or she was such a kind person." Observers find it hard to fit the new information into their old metaphors of "X is a friend."

Alfred Korzybski, the founder of general semantics,[133] actually went so far as to suggest that one avoid the use of the being verb, especially when used as a copula, or a word linking two ideas (in other words, an equals sign).[134] We can avoid such constructions. For example, we can replace all forms of the verb *to be* (*am, is, are, was, were, be, being, been*) that equate two different things with phrases like "appears to me as" and "has some of the characteristics of." Or you could turn nouns into verbs: "Sue is a thief" can become "Sue stole money from work." Notice that this route also, incidentally, changes a judgment into an observation. If you say, "Sue's a thief," the first question people have probably wouldn't be "Why is she a thief?" but if you say she stole money from work, people might wonder why. Not using metaphors in this unconscious or mindless way opens up the possibility of reasoning and questioning.

However, I don't mean to imply that all metaphors subvert clear thinking and worm into our unconscious minds like insidious aliens. On the contrary, metaphors serve a useful purpose, and without them we'd have no language at all, other than perhaps grunting and point-

---

133. While general semantics itself is largely a pseudoscience, the ideas of GS have informed a large number of actual linguists, philosophers, and psychologists, and are therefore of value. Incidentally, semantics is, to every other linguist, the study of word meanings; GS would fall into the category of pragmatics, or language-in-use, to most linguists.

134. Alfred Korzybski, *Science and Sanity: An Introduction to Non-Aristotelian Systems and General Semantics.* Fort Worth, TX: Institute of General Semantics, 1995.

ing and a few words for important objects and actions. And without metaphor, we would certainly have no magic. All magic, no matter how different its practices, hinges upon a set of basic metaphors. For example, a ceremonial magician draws a sigil with the aid of a magic square, reads an invocation to a specific planetary angel, all during the appropriate planetary hour, to achieve some effect. A witch might anoint a candle of a particular color and pray as it burns down. A Hoodoo practitioner gathers natural and not-so-natural materials, binds them into a square of felt, and hides this "trick" somewhere on his or her body or home. All of these practices seem diverse, but they all share the principle of metaphor. The ceremonial magician selects the planetary hour and square according to a metaphor linking his or her desire and the planets. The Hoodoo practitioner and the witch choose particular colors and substances for the same reason: they have a metaphoric relationship to the desire. Anthropologists call this the *principle of sympathy*—the belief that similar objects can affect one another.

The principle of sympathy, and its cousin the principle of contagion (objects once in contact remain in magical contact, so a single hair can affect a person's whole body), could be lumped together as the principle of metaphor, with contagion being a textbook example of synecdoche. One thing, the magical symbol, stands for another thing, the magical signified. The color blue stands for healing for the witch, but money for the ceremonial magician. What they share, however, is that they stand as metaphors for ideas. The only difference, then, between different systems of magic—high or low, folk or religious—has more to do with the aesthetic decision of what sorts of metaphors to use, and less to do with goals. After all, the witch could just as easily burn a white candle to commune with his or her gods, as a green candle for money.

The Aesthetic Element of Magic

Because our choice of magical metaphors is an aesthetic decision, to understand magical metaphor requires understanding aesthetics. Aesthetics, the study of what people find appealing to the senses, is a sub-branch of the philosophical field of axiology, or the study of value. It's always been a sticky issue, because philosophers realized, early on, that what some people find pleasant others find unpleasant. Many philosophers simply threw their hands up, declaring with Cicero "about matters of taste, there can be no argument."[135] But many others recognized that ethics, the philosophy dealing with right behavior, was a subset of axiology. And there are some principles that hold generally in terms of taste: we appreciate the symmetrical or nearly symmetrical; we like proportions based upon the golden rectangle; we tend to prefer completion to incompletion. Even these principles of taste, however, have been violated for artistic effect; for example, many composers have used discord to good effect. Any theory of aesthetics worth its salt, then, has to address both the diversity of taste among humans as well as the fact that, at one time or another, every single aesthetic rule has been violated and regarded as "beautiful" or at least "interesting" by some artist.

In magic, not practicing formal philosophy, we can get away with a rule of thumb, which can be summed up as "I don't know much about art, but I know what I like." More eruditely: "The aesthetic value of anything is a function of its effect upon oneself at a particular time or place." I like anchovies because I have a pleasant series of associations with them, as well as appreciating strong flavors in general. I like punk rock because I'm pleased by its energy and rhythm. I like nature because I feel a sense of awe and calm in the midst of it. Someone else may like country music because he or she finds the lyrics amusing. Of course, this sort of personal aesthetics seems to mean that there can be no aesthetic error. But there can be: an aesthetic error would be to pretend to like something that does not please you. You could certainly learn to like or try to like something, but pretending to like something—lying to yourself about it—is an aesthetic error.

Another aesthetic error is to dismiss all aesthetic questions with a sweeping "Well, if you like it, it's right for you." While on one level that's true, on another it dismisses the possibility of aesthetic innovation. After all, if everything is equal aesthetically, why bother to create

---

135.   "De gustibus non disputandum est." I like to throw out this bit of Latin in the
        middle of conversations about the Sox and the Cubs. It really confuses the Sox fans.

new art or experiment? Decorative art forms, like wallpaper and popular music, fine in their place, become the foundations of all art if one relies entirely upon "I like it so it's good for me." To think and to grow, we also need aesthetic challenges. Magic, if done properly, provides us with those challenges—as does good art, if done well. One of those most important challenges, particularly in our postmodern era, is to recognize that traditions exist for a reason: they have worked over a period of time, appealing to a large number of people. So, yes, if you have a compelling aesthetic reason, it's not wrong to use a feather instead of an athame. But in doing so, a wise experimenter will recognize that the athame and the feather are different objects with different histories and semiotic links.

If liking or disliking something were a simple on-off switch, we could get away with "If it works for you, use it." But there are many ways something can "work" for someone. Let's take an imaginary case study. Amber has been studying ritual magic, and she has reached the stage in which she makes a wand to represent her will. Not belonging to a specific tradition, she's a bit at sea. In the Golden Dawn tradition, that wand is an elaborate and cumbersome lotus-tipped affair, while in the Key of Solomon it's a fairly simple branch inscribed with symbols and collected at a certain time. Some books say it should be of elder (which doesn't grow around her, unless you count box elder), some of oak, and some of ash. One even says yew. She asks around and gets the usual answer: "Find something that appeals to you." Finally, she sees a wand made out of copper with semiprecious stones—agate and quartz, mostly—worked into it. Relieved, she buys it—after all, she thinks it's pretty.

In other words, the wand "works" for her. But Amber's made a pretty glaring magical error here. It has nothing to do with buying her magical tool rather than making it. It has to do with her mixing up the metaphor. In literature, we call that a mixed or clashing metaphor, such as "The stream was as clear as glass and babbled merrily." Glass doesn't babble much, so the metaphor doesn't work. In getting the one-size-fits-all advice of "find something that appeals to you," Amber is fooled into thinking that all metaphors are the same. But the wand has a specific metaphoric role: it represents her power and authority, and it's simultaneously a pointer and extension of her fingers, and therefore of her ability to manipulate the world. If she had used the Golden Dawn instructions, she'd have a wand tipped with a lotus and covered with colors in the shades of the zodiac, representing the spiritual nature of her will as it manifests through the stars that govern, symbolically, her fate. Even if she had used a bare branch of oak, it would represent her implacable will (since oak is a hard wood) and also connect her symbolically to the lightning bolt and to thunder. If she had used ash, she would tap into Norse myths about the first man, Ask, who was formed from an ash tree, as well as diverse other symbols. But copper is a metal of Venus in ritual magic, and therefore hardly seems appropriate to symbolize will. Venus is the planet of pleasure and peace, not directed will. Quartz has a large number of associations, mostly to do with dreams, dwarves, and—lately—the energy paradigm.

Her copper wand is appealing, but not ideal for her purposes. It doesn't represent a carefully considered symbolic decision, but a decision of taste. Now, there might be some readers who point out that in at least one ritual magic system, that of Thelema, will and love are explicitly linked concepts, and so a copper wand, representing love, might not be entirely inappropriate in that context. Exactly. Amber could have made the same decision, but chosen, on the basis of sound metaphoric analysis or intuition, to equate the ideas of love and will in her rituals. In that case, her copper wand would be perfectly appropriate. Being pretty and being appropriate for a specific magical role aren't the same thing.

The Logic of Metaphor

To understand or even create a magical system, we need to understand how each part fits in metaphorically with the other parts. What parts reference other parts, and how? The wand is the will, metaphorically—so then what's the athame? The altar is the universe—but then what's the circle? The advantage of a magical tradition is that at least some of that thinking has already been done, but it still may require you to fit it together. The thing to remember above all is that magic and magical symbolism do not obey the logic of mathematics or science, but what the poet Hart Crane called "the logic of metaphor."[136] The altar may represent the universe in one sense, but the circle may represent it in another sense. Perhaps the altar, you realize, is the universe of physical laws (after all, it is composed of right angles and solid material) while the circle is the universe of nonphysical laws (it, after all, hangs in the air intangible, and is composed of a single unbroken line). Perhaps for you the athame also represents will, but a more aggressive kind of will—the will of war, rather than the will of peace. Chaos magicians sometimes like to experiment by doing magic in, for example, dodecahedrons rather than circles. Fine: but then what might that dodecahedron represent?[137]

The metaphors of magic are like the language we use every day. Anyone who says any particular string of words is wrong in all situations is clearly rather small-minded from a linguistic standpoint. Similarly, someone who says that a copper wand could never be appropriate is rather small-minded from a magical perspective. But similarly, someone who says that any words can be used in any situation babbles incomprehensibly, just as someone who says "Whatever I like, works" babbles magically. The symbols of our spells and magical working must be chosen as carefully as our words, to fit the situation and time. And while taste governs both the selection of what we say in certain situations and what sorts of symbols we use in magic, taste must in turn be governed by a strong sense of purpose.

Magical Systems of Metaphors

Metaphor doesn't just rule our choice of magical tools; metaphor strikes to the root of our magical systems themselves. Every magical system has a ruling metaphor, or a series of them, that selects the codes by which we interpret the symbols. For example, in the above scenario, because Amber was a ritual magician, she interpreted the copper pipe as a metal of Venus. But

---

136.   Hart Crane, "A Letter to Harriet Monroe." *O My Land, My Friends: The Selected Letters of Hart Crane.* Langdon Hammer and Brom Weber, eds. New York: Four Walls Eight Windows, 1997, 278–279.

137.   Maybe twelve interlocking pentagrams representing humanity in the twelve astrological signs or houses. Or maybe, as Plato suggests, it represents the substance of space itself.

if she had been from a different magical tradition, she may not have. If she were a New Ager, for example, she might see the copper pipe as a conductor of energy. For a ritual magician, the overarching metaphor that governs the selection of interpretive codes in ritual magic is "as above, so below." Everything in the heavens has a corresponding substance or representative on Earth, and vice versa. So the planet Venus has a metal, animal, tree, and so on. The overarching New Age metaphor is "all reality is energy," and so we see things in terms of how they interact with energy, and try to discover magical roles from that. A materialist might object, "Yeah, but neither of those metaphors is true." That's right: because no metaphor is true! By definition, a metaphor is always literally untrue. And the materialist sees the world in terms of the synecdoche already discussed: "All reality is matter."

What is the overarching metaphor or metaphors of your magical system? And what sort of codes does that select for you in your interpretation of reality? Let's take some examples just to see how it plays out. Let me preface this bit by affirming that I'm not judging any magical systems, nor is it possible for me to be authoritative. I'll speak only of magical systems I've had some personal experience with, and describe the metaphors that seem to me to rule the systems. Ovens differ; adjust cooking times accordingly. Here are some common overarching metaphors in magic:

The world is made of energy

This metaphor holds that reality, usual physical reality, is all made of energy. This energy, unlike—say—kinetic or electrical energy, can be controlled by one's thoughts and intentions. Magic that functions under this metaphor focuses on detecting, moving, and changing this energy. Sometimes, physical objects are said to have energy that vibrates at a certain frequency. This metaphor is popular because it's fairly easy to imagine energy moving through our bodies, and furthermore it gives a scientific gleam to the surface of magic, which appeals to those with an investment in the scientific method. A magician using this metaphor is more likely to interpret phenomena based on codes of amplitude, vibration, and frequency. Energy will "vibrate" at a "certain frequency" to achieve various aims. Color and sound might therefore figure heavily in magical operations.

As above, so below

This metaphor occurs in many magic systems but is particularly important in ceremonial magic, in which objects in the physical world correspond to ideas, conceived of as existing on a higher plane of existence or reality. An amethyst represents ideas of kingship, generosity, and soberness, all ideas that fall under the control of the planet Jupiter in traditional astrology. Plants, stones, and various other things are said to be identifiable by means of signatures that proclaim their correspondences; these signatures include color, taste, shape, and so forth. To a magician devoted to this metaphor, all or many symbols are reflections of numinous reality. Such a magician may have an appreciation of coincidence. Magic involving objects, graphic symbols, and the ritual manipulation thereof, will figure heavily.

The universe is alive

This metaphor is the foundation of the animist perspective, in which everything has a spirit that can communicate with us. Magic, here, involves developing communication and friendship with these spirits, or compelling them to obey. Usually, the goal of communication is achieved through trance and altered states of consciousness, in which the spirit of a place or idea is given a form and name and treated as if alive. An animist interprets his or her experiences according to codes that govern social interaction. Therefore, animist ceremonies often involve symbolic gift-giving, or conversation and communion.

The universe is, or is controlled by, God

This theistic metaphor allows us to change the world by appealing to God. Magic involving prayer and worship falls into this category. Often there are certain requirements—a life dedicated to a particular type of holiness, for example. A religious magician may disdain symbols of personal power, instead interpreting events as divinely directed. Magic may involve recourse to religious figures of the past and symbols of holiness.

These few metaphors are a great oversimplification. In reality, they all interact in any magical system, and each of them contains other metaphors that we could unpack. For example, "as above, so below" also contains unstated metaphors like "above = better; below = worse," and "sky = above; earth = below."[138]

The point is not to make a full outline of all of these metaphors, but to show that we use them to select and interpret our magical experiences. Someone who says "Everything is made of energy" may experience "negative energy" in a place, while a magician who holds "Everything is alive" as his or her overarching metaphor might perceive a malign spirit. Most importantly, someone who doesn't believe in magic at all, and has a metaphor such as "Reality is entirely material," will never see anything there at all. Even a scientist trained in objective observation will see nothing there, even if he or she feels uneasy for no clear reason, because the materialist metaphor does not admit emotion into the realm of things to be observed about reality.

So our overarching metaphors affect our magic and even our ability to admit its possibility. But we do not simply walk around with a collection of overarching metaphors bouncing around. We are creatures of pattern, and so we try to organize them. We link our metaphors together into stories. The stories or myths are made of metaphors that, along with codes, organize our experiences.

Symbols, Codes, and Metaphors

An example may help clarify the various levels at which symbols, codes, and metaphors interact. Christians believe in a story that says that humans were once perfect, fell from grace, and are struggling to regain that grace through the help of Jesus Christ, who will one day declare an end to the process. This story contains more metaphors than it does words! It contains metaphors like "good is up, bad is down" (we "fell" from grace), "time is a line" (it has a beginning and an end), "sin is an enemy" (against which we "struggle"), and so on, and so on. These metaphors determine codes. "Time is a line," for example, dictates codes that chop time into

---

138. Yes, this, too, is a metaphor. It is only true insofar as we are in a particular place—in orbit, or even during transcontinental flights, much of the sky is "below" with the earth.

chunks—second, minute, day, week—with beginnings and ends—midnight, weekend. It also offers codes that interpret things like lying in bed staring at the ceiling as "wasting" time, because there's only so much of it. The story of Christ selects which metaphors are most important. With the help of codes, such as definitions of "hour" and "minute," "good" and "evil," these metaphors guide the believer's behavior in day-to-day life.

Metaphor of Ritual

It would be tedious to break down every metaphor involved in ritual. In ritual, we recognize the candle as a metaphor for, say, enlightenment, and so on. Or we may have a set of symbols: the wand symbolizes fire; the cup, water; the dagger, air; the disk, earth. We may rarely regard the pentacle as a *metaphor for* earth, merely as its symbol. But we organize those four objects along lines of the overarching "there are four elements to reality" metaphor. And we use them according to codes about what those elements mean (we don't pick our teeth with the dagger, for example).

The attempt to find the overarching structure of ritual has occupied anthropologists for a century. Victor Turner[139] has argued that at least some rituals—particularly rites of passage that mark the move from one social status to another—have a three-part structure: a separation from the normal world, a liminal or in-between state, and a reintegration with the normal world. Turner is particularly concerned with the liminal state and what goes on there, but as a useful structure for rituals from an occult perspective, Turner's analysis is a bit thin. It reminds me of Aristotle's famous insistence that every piece of drama has a beginning, a middle, and an end. While in its time and place it's a useful analytical observation, in actually creating ritual it's not much help. Turner didn't miss his mark; his goal was never to create an outline for writing rituals but to describe and define existing rituals.

---

139. Victor Turner, *The Ritual Process: Structure and Anti-Structure*. Ithaca, NY: Cornell University Press, 1977.

The important link between myth and ritual can give us some guidelines for identifying the stories that organize our ritual. A myth is nothing other than a cultural story. Although the word *myth* has come to mean "not true" to contemporary readers, a myth is simply a way of organizing metaphors for an entire culture. While we might tell ourselves a story like "people who work hard get what they want," and select overarching metaphors based on that story, a myth provides a much more complex and powerful story. For example, the myth of Icarus—Icarus is the son of a craftsman, Daedalus, who is trapped on an island. Daedalus creates a pair of wings for himself and his son out of wax and feathers. They fly off the island, but Icarus flies too close to the sun, despite his father's warnings, and his wings melt. He plunges into the sea. This cultural story gives us metaphors about authority, trust, obedience, danger, freedom, and so on. It isn't just an organizing myth for one person, but an entire culture.

Many myths lead to ritual. For example, Christian communion is the ritual commemoration of a mythological action: Jesus's sharing of wine and bread with his disciples.[140] Other myths that have become rituals include the Christian marriage ceremony, in which the myth of Adam and Eve is usually recounted. Yet magical rituals seem not to be recounting a myth. For example, in the famous Lesser Banishing Ritual of the Pentagram, the magician identifies himself or herself as the center of the universe by defining the points of the Tree of Life on his or her own body, then circumambulates and draws a pentagram in each quarter, which he or she activates with a different divine name, then invokes four archangels. The magician finishes by performing the same ritual action that began the ritual. How does this recount a specific myth? It doesn't. But it recounts a general myth that shapes all, or most, of our magical rituals.

Joseph Campbell argued that all myths are actually manifestations of one large monomyth, the Journey of the Hero. I suggest that most of our rituals have at least some elements of this myth, especially our magi-

---

140.   I do not mean to imply that this event didn't occur by calling it a myth. I only
        mean to imply that it has been repeated as a story by our entire culture.

cal rituals. If we're conscious of the way in which this myth shapes our rituals, we can use it to construct more symbolically effective ceremonies. One formulation of the monomyth has six stages:

1. The hero feels a call to adventure.
2. Answering it, the hero confronts a threshold guardian.
3. The hero has the aid of a mentor.
4. The hero descends into a liminal, dreamlike world.
5. The hero surpasses the mentor and achieves the elixir, a magical artifact or accomplishment.
6. The hero returns to the world from which he or she started, but changed.[141]

The mentor may be any guide, sometimes a former hero or divine figure, or even an animal. The elixir can be almost anything, from a magical object to an abstract idea, such as the sacred marriage, or a reconciliation with a deity or father figure.

We can see how this Ur-myth organizes rituals like the Lesser Banishing Ritual of the Pentagram. The magician starts out, like the hero, feeling the call and identifying himself or herself and separating from the common run of humanity, by pointing out the points of the Tree of Life on the body. Then the hero moves around a path, giving a password or sign at each quarter. The names the magician calls on are significant: in the east, the magician calls upon YHVH, the four-lettered name of God, symbolically identifying God with the rising sun. In the south, the magician calls upon Adonai, "my Lord," identifying the sun in its strength with the ruling power of deity. In the west, the direction of completion, the magician calls upon Eheieh, "I am," aspiring to identify the span of his or her life with that of the sun and therefore the divine. In the north, the quarter of darkness and midnight, the magician calls upon Agla, a notariqon of *atah givor l'olam adonai*, meaning "Thou art great forever,

---

141. Joseph Campbell, *The Hero with a Thousand Faces*. Princeton, NJ: Princeton University Press, 1972.

my Lord," reaffirming the power of God even in the darkest times.[142] The magician returns to the center, now in a liminal space, and calls upon the mentors in the form of archangels. He or she finishes by going back to the beginning and repeating the first ritual action.

From this perspective, the Lesser Banishing Ritual of the Pentagram is a ritual enactment of a myth about going on a journey and coming home again. So are many other rituals. One need only think of how many rituals involve movement toward a goal. In wedding ceremonies there is no reason not to have the bride and groom already waiting, but instead the bride is taken on a procession to the groom by her mentor, her father; she is the initiate who comes away with the elixir, a sacred marriage. In the graduation ceremony, which might seem completely secular, there is a procession of graduates. They are called to adventure. They walk to the stage and are met by a mentor, usually the university president or some other important administrative individual, who gives them a diploma (the elixir) and shakes their hand. At the end, they return to the ordinary world, but now with letters after their names. Such rituals are pervasive because the myth of the journey is such a powerful story.

One wouldn't think there is much in common between the Lesser Banishing Ritual of the Pentagram, with its careful aerial diagrams and chants in Hebrew, and traditional shamanic practices, but both borrow from a similar story. In the shamanic journey, the shaman feels the call to adventure—usually a need, such as healing. He or she enters trance and experiences travel to another place, often visualized as underground. Spirit helpers, often in the shape of animals, act as mentors, and help the shaman achieve the elixir—sometimes a missing piece of a soul, or particular healing knowledge. When the shaman returns, he or she does so changed by the experience, having the power to heal or otherwise deal with the complex situation.[143]

---

142. Israel Regardie, *The Tree of Life: An Illustrated Study in Magic*. Chic Cicero and Sandra Tabatha Cicero, eds. St. Paul, MN: Llewellyn, 2000. This book contains a discussion of the esoteric symbolism of the words of power used in the LBRP.

143. Michael Harner, *The Way of the Shaman*. San Francisco: Harper, 1990.

Many rituals include a test or threshold guardian that must be passed. In marriage, that test is the ritual question "If anyone knows any reason these two should not be married, let him speak now." In graduation, of course, the tests have all already been taken. And in the Lesser Banishing Ritual of the Pentagram, as befits a protective ritual, there is no test or threshold guardian. But one always lurks in potential. In the shamanic journey, many shamans report experiencing an attack or contest somewhere on the journey.

The purpose of recognizing this Ur-myth is to give us a handle for constructing ritual actions. It also illustrates that, ultimately, the ritual of the kitchen witch and the ritual of the ceremonial magician are calling upon the same story. Just as Spanish, English, and Mandarin are different ways to speak, none of them better than the others, so is lighting a candle on the stove as good as a four-hour ceremony. But that doesn't necessarily mean the four-hour ceremony doesn't have its place; for some of us, ritual magic works better because of our own underlying stories and codes. In constructing ritual actions, we can deliberately call upon this myth by first reading several examples of the genre.[144] After becoming more consciously familiar with the metaphors being used, ask yourself some questions when constructing a ritual:

- *Why am I doing this ritual? What's my call to adventure?* The answer to this might be a practical magical goal, or something more diffuse, but you should have some idea how you want to be different when it's done. What code are you shifting, in other words.

- *From where am I traveling, and where am I going to?* You might walk in a circle, or across a path, or just mentally travel somewhere.

- *Who, if anybody, will test me, and how?* In one Wiccan initiation ceremony, the initiate is blindfolded, led to the circle, and stopped

---

144.   I recommend digging up a good translation of *The Odyssey* (I like the Fitzgerald translation), as well as the story of Inanna and her descent into the underworld, the story of the Buddha, and the story of Thor and the giants, among many others. In fact, getting a couple of anthologies of myths, ideally the originals in translation, couldn't hurt.

by someone resting a sword-point on his or her breast. A startling test indeed! Of course, you may also test yourself, or ritually recount a test already taken.

- *Who will be my mentor?* You might invoke a deity or angel, or have an animal spirit or some other guide. In many American folk magic traditions, one calls upon a saint during the operation.

- *What form might the elixir take?* Several options include the sacred marriage (you ritually marry a divine figure or yourself), the elixir (which might be a substance, a talisman, or some other physical, magical object), knowledge (a magic word, perhaps, or something similar), reconciliation or forgiveness, or an apotheosis (i.e., becoming divine). Alternately, you may not be entirely sure what the elixir will be—sometimes, in evocations, for example, you're not quite sure what the spirit will offer.

- *How shall I return?* This step is usually pretty easy. You simply come back the way you came, repeating the beginning.

Not all of these need to be in the same order. You may want the mentor to show up earlier or later, or even leave it out if you have a good reason. The trick is to have a reason, however.

Unlike the restructuring of codes I talked about earlier, rituals built on the mythological structure work on a deeper level. Instead of destroying a code to create a new one around a particular symbol, you're working within the overarching story to make room for the new code. If done in a proper state of mind, this can be effective, and can be mixed with the ecstatic breaking of codes talked about earlier. If you try to create a code that doesn't fit the stories of our culture, you'll have a hard time maintaining it, but if you work deliberately within one of our most pervasive and important stories—the story of the journey from one reality to another—you can ease the new code into place. Or, from another perspective, you can move into a new reality in which that code exists.

Mindfulness

What is the "proper state of mind" I spoke of above? A ritual performed perfunctorily will accomplish little. A shamanic journey requires a trance, so it stands to reason that other rituals may require something trancelike as well. In fact, ritual should be performed in a state of hyperawareness. A ritual, properly performed, requires a state of mind that is both clear and calm. You are not analyzing when performing a ritual, nor are you making symbolic associations. You are simply performing the ritual completely in the present. This state of mindfulness may be difficult to attain at first. I find that the best way to achieve it is to take a few moments preparing the ritual tools, regarding each of them with all the available senses as much as possible. For example, I might take up the wand and remind myself that it symbolizes my control over the element of fire, while feeling its texture, seeing its color and shape, and so on. I might light the incense and say or think, "This incense is my prayers," while smelling it, seeing the swirls in the smoke, and so on. The key is to involve all senses and be perfectly mindful, as much as possible, of the now and here of the ritual space. If you hear sounds outside the circle, you should regard them as inconsequential. For this reason, it helps to have a fairly neat room to work in, so you are not distracted by trash and messiness outside the circle. The point is to be present in the ritual in the physical sense—by connecting to everything physically, you will automatically connect to it metaphorically and symbolically.

An example will make what I mean by mindfulness clearer. Take the simple act of lighting a candle. One way to do it is to say "I want love" and light a candle. This'll have little or no effect. Another way is to carefully say "Okay, the candle represents will, and the light represents change, and the color pink represents love," which is all necessary preparation work. But the problem is, you're still not paying attention to the candle when doing this. Your mind is in the signifieds, not the signifier, and magic works by manipulating signifiers to change signifieds. Instead, you choose materials based on significance beforehand, and when you're using them, you say the incantation—slowly—visualizing each phrase. You feel the texture of the match. You smell the scent of the candle. You let your entire focus narrow on the candle, not what it signifies, but the candle itself. You light the match. You feel the sting of sulfur in your nostrils. You hold the light to the flame and watch it catch. You feel its heat. You smell the scent of the oil. And so on. You do the ritual, in other words, completely conscious of the actions themselves, not what they signify. Your mind—if you did the appropriate preparatory work—already knows what they signify.

Rituals occur in the physical world, but bridge that physical world with the highest level of abstractions: the stories that organize our metaphors themselves. Language does not begin with the word, but with the story, and magic does not begin with spirits and gods, but with the physical world. Even the so-called highest form of magic, theurgy or the invocation of deities, operates ultimately among the symbols of the physical world, manipulating them to re-create the myths where the gods dwell.

Theurgy

The term *theurgy* comes from two Greek roots, the word for "god" and the word for "work." Theurgy, therefore, is "god-work," and any religious ritual is, by its nature, a sort of god-work. Theurgy usually refers to a specific traditional practice in Neoplatonic philosophy that arose mostly after the rise of Christianity. The practice of Neoplatonic theurgy has two branches, exemplified by their teachers. Plotinus advocated quiet meditation about the nature of the gods: for example, one could meditate on the extent of the universe and then mentally abolish all limits.[145] Iamblichus, a student of Plotinus, suggested that for many people, this practice would be too difficult. He suggested that one employ ritual, then, to reach from the physical world—in Neoplatonism, the lowest of all worlds—to the highest world of ideas. His world of ideas is what I call myth: stories that organize our metaphors. So, for example, there is an ideal person to whom we compare ourselves constantly, and this comparison is the basis for morality.

Iamblichus was largely responsible for the current Western mystery tradition. His ideas filtered down and through Christianity. Mostly, Iamblichus advocated ritual of a specific type, in which tokens of the powers of the gods—physical objects—were manipulated in order to act out archetypal or mythological stories. So the traditional sacrifice could be per-

---

145.   Plotinus, *The Enneads*. Stephen MacKenna, trans. Burdett, NY: Larson
        Publications, 2004.

ceived as a story of apotheosis—say, Hercules on his pyre. The theurgist used the physical ritual to entrain his or her mind with the mythological ideas expressed by the ritual actions. Unfortunately, we lack information regarding what a Hellenic theurgic ritual might look like.[146] But we can reconstruct these rituals from things we see in magical practices outside of the Neoplatonic tradition. One example, theophagy, operates in the world of myth and metaphors. Theophagy is the ritualized eating of a god, either symbolically or mystically. It's a pervasive ritual, and it seems to have sprung up not from a common source (what we academic types call an "analogue") but independently in many places. It probably arose from another common ritual—sacrifice. In sacrifice, an object, often a food substance, is ritually destroyed and given over to the god in question. Burning is a common method, and animals—being valuable—were frequently sacrificed. It's a small step from burning an animal to having a cookout, and many sacrifices became just that. After the participants partake of some of the foods, the sacrifice becomes a communion ritual, in which gods and humans eat together. The fact that not all sacrifices involved communion may indicate that communion was added later. For example, an ancient Greek offering to a hero is burned entirely and so is a sin offering.[147] In both cases, eating the food is considered inappropriate. Still, communion isn't theophagy—the food belongs to the gods and the people together, but isn't identified with either.

Theophagy occurs when the worshiper explicitly identifies the food as the god, or at least as symbolic of the god. For example, in Catholic communion, the host is identified with Christ: "This is my body." In other communions, there is a varying degree of such identification. At one communion I attended, the minister offered bread and wine with the explanation that it commemorated the Last Supper, but was a symbol not of the deity's identity, but of the community that gathered in the name of that deity. Thus, we ate an abstract idea rather than a god. Other theophagic

---

146.   Iamblichus, *De Mysteriis.* Emma C. Clarke, et al, trans. Atlanta: Society of Biblical Literature, 2003.

147.   Walter Burkert, *Greek Religion.* John Raffan, trans. Cambridge, MA: Harvard University Press, 1985.

rituals include a Yoruba ritual adapted and described by Jan Fries in his book *Visual Magick*. In this ritual, the priest prays over a cup of fluid and invokes his or her gods into it, then drinks it, taking those gods within.[148]

Unlike some forms of practical magic, designed to break down unhelpful codes, these rituals work within established codes to create new metaphorical connections. The code of eating is a particularly powerful one. In literature, whenever characters eat, it means that they are having some sort of community together. One can predict how well that community will work out by how well the fictional meal proceeds. Eating also is an act of aggression as well as an act of becoming and attaining. When we eat food, it becomes part of us. It becomes something we own eternally. Kissing, oral sex, smiling, sticking out the tongue—all are connected ultimately to the idea of eating and becoming. Eating also breaks down the boundaries between inside and outside. When we eat, what was outside becomes inside. In this respect, it works within the metaphor "outside is other, inside is self," to incorporate the ultimate Other into the Self.

The ritual practice itself varies. In many cultures, theophagy is as simple as asking the deity to enter the food to be consumed. In others, there are lengthy incantations. In British traditional Witchcraft, a form of pagan practice different from Wicca, the bread and wine are "sained" or consecrated to the god and goddess respectively. They are consumed and made part of the worshiper. Depending on the ritual used, this "housle" may be a communion or a full-blown theophagy.[149] What every ritual has in common, however, is that the substance to be consumed is identified, verbally or symbolically, with the deity to be consumed. The practitioner eats it in a ritual, mindful manner.

Theophagy interacts on all levels—symbol, code, metaphor, and myth. The symbol of the food is manipulated to correspond to the code of eating, which invokes ideas of becoming and attaining. The code encourages the creation of the metaphor "I am the god" out of the meta-

---

148.   Jan Fries, *Visual Magick: A Manual of Freestyle Shamanism*. Oxford, UK: Mandrake, 1992.

149.   Robin Artisson, *The Witching Way of the Hollow Hill: The Gramarye of the Folk Who Dwell Below the Mound*. [No location]: Veritas Numquam Perit, 2006.

phor "This food is the god," and—if the god's story has some element of apotheosis, some bridge between the human and the divine such as Christ or Dionysus—that metaphor taps into that story. The worshiper takes on some quality of the deity, undergoes a minor apotheosis. In practical magic, the chain runs the other way: the code is modified to change the distribution of symbols under it. But these two operations are not so different, because the worshiper can easily use the apotheosis to rearrange the codes that are now under him or her.

It's sometimes difficult to tell the difference between a code and, for example, a metaphor, or a metaphor and a myth. In practice, the lines between these ways of organizing symbols blur together. We can reduce the rather complex structure I've discussed in this chapter into three levels: the level of symbol, where X stands for Y; the level of code and metaphor, which tells us how to interpret our symbols; and the level of myth and story, which tells us what those interpretations mean. The useful thing to keep in mind for the practicing magician is that all levels describe ways of organizing and dealing with information, and that the world we perceive and try to manipulate with magic is nothing but a story that matter tells the mind. We can change the story, talk back to matter, through myth.

TEN

Self-Talk:
The Janus of Words

Language is the gateway between body and mind, matter and idea, but a gateway swings two ways. Janus, the Roman god of doorways, has two faces, one that looks behind and one that looks ahead. He both provides and bars entry, as a door does. Language, just like that door, can open up a gateway into the most sublime mysteries of magic, thaumaturgy, and theurgy. But also like that door, it can slam shut on our ability to think clearly or accept our abilities to change our lives.

Language serves as a map. Just like a map, it describes territory, but imperfectly. There cannot be a perfect map, because a perfect map must be the same size as the thing it maps. Moreover, it must be composed of the same stuff. And such a map, by definition, isn't a map: it's a duplicate. A map, no matter how complex, must abstract the territory in the same way that language abstracts our thoughts about reality. On a map, a small triangle might represent a mountain, and a series of triangles may represent a mountain range, even though each individual peak is shaped differently, and not one of them is really a triangle, pyramid, or cone. Similarly, the word *dog* might represent any number of animals—in one conversation, it might represent a black lab puppy; in another, it might represent a fully grown husky or a chihuahua. You might say, well, there is at least really a species of animal called a "dog," or more accurately (using a more precise map designed for this particular purpose), *Canis lupus familiaris.* Sure, but imagine a situation in which we see a particularly odd-looking cat walk by a window, and I say, "Did you see that dog?" and you, thinking that I must have mistaken the cat for a dog, say "yes." I've applied a completely incorrect label to an event having nothing to do with it, but nonetheless properly communicated.

Not only does language imperfectly reflect reality, in many cases it doesn't reflect reality at all, and that includes the higher realities of which we speak in magic. One way around this problem is the use of jargon. For example, we don't have terms in English for the abstract weirdness of subatomic particles, so we invent new ones—we talk about charm, strange, up, down, top, and bottom quarks, for example. In the occult, we talk about parts of the soul, and often fall back on Hebrew—we speak of the ruakh (the intellectual mind), the nefesh (the animal soul), the neshemah (the intuition), and the khiah (the life-force). A jargon is like a specialized map to more accurately explore a certain territory. Another way of getting around the imprecision of language is to use something preverbal, to fall back on symbols. In the Golden Dawn, for example, and in orders that descended from it, strange equations sometimes appear, like $2=1$, or $2=0$. These represent certain states of mind or mystical realizations that are difficult to describe in words. For example, $2=1$ describes the awareness that all our dichotomies, all our beliefs about opposites like male/female, light/dark, good/evil, really collapse when looked at closely. On the other hand, $2=0$ represents the realization that, not only do they collapse into one thing, they really cancel each other out, leaving a sort of pregnant silence.

Language and Duality

One of the reasons we need symbols to represent these experiences of nonduality is that language itself, by its very nature, reaffirms duality with every word. Each word is a signifier representing a signified. If a signifier exists without pointing to some signified, we regard it as meaningless.

Take the stop sign, for example: for a stop sign to be effective, we need both the sign and a driver who understands the symbol's meaning. Similarly, if I say "creampuff," that is a signifier pointing to an arbitrary class of desserts, which are the signified. But if I say "korasum," that is a signifier that points to no signified. It's gibberish, and therefore has no semantic content (although as I've already discussed, it could have pragmatic content depending on the tone of voice with which I say it). All semantic meaning is built on this sort of opposition. Moreover, grammar, or syntactic meaning, is also built on binary oppositions. Each phrase has two parts, a head and a complement. The complement completes the head, so for a prepositional phrase, "in the house," *in* is the head and *the house* the complement. For the phrase to be complete or syntactically meaningful, it must have both parts. One phrase can stand in place of the head or complement in another phrase; this modularity makes language infinitely productive. I can make an infinite number of possible sentences, just by plugging in phrases. But if the ultimate reality is, as the mystic tells us, really unified, language cannot possibly reflect that experience because it is essentially binary.

Or is it? Jacques Derrida points out that when closely examined, our binary oppositions contradict themselves.[150] Light is found in darkness, male is found in female, and vice versa. We create meaning not by distinguishing between binary differences, but by creating them. It's possible that human consciousness is itself binary, especially since the syntactic structure of language is binary on its deepest, most abstract levels—each phrase splits into two parts, and only two parts, the head and the complement. Moreover, our brains are binary—we let the left brain handle logic and the right brain intuition.[151] But even if our consciousness is binary,

---

150.   It's impossible to cite just one work for this idea, since it forms the core of Derrida's deconstruction, but if you would like a clear(ish) example of the method, you can find it in Jacques Derrida, *On Grammatology*. Gayatri Chakravorty Spivak, trans. Baltimore: Johns Hopkins University Press, 1976.

151.   Here's a perfect example of what Derrida is talking about, by the way, since if you closely examine the pattern of brain activity during various activities, you find that even in "left brain" thinking activities, our right brain is still active, and vice versa. But largely, our minds divide up various thinking tasks into two categories, logical and impressionistic.

the ultimate consciousness of which it is a part is not. We know this because we can examine our binaries in reality and watch them collapse—
for example, life and death seem fundamentally opposed categories. But
scientists struggle still to find adequate definitions of life and death. Fire
does some of the things we say that life does—propagates itself, breathes,
eats, leaves behind waste—but it's not alive. More pointedly, viruses cannot reproduce on their own and do not metabolize, both of which are
required to be considered alive; yet they're also not quite dead, as they
do transfer genetic information and evolve, which are characteristics of
life. Where to draw the line is a question that we cannot answer, because
in reality, life and death aren't binary oppositions at all, but parts of the
same process.

The underlying substantial consciousness of reality is not binary, but
unitary. We know this from observing that its manifestation, reality, is
unitary.[152] Thousands of things exist, but they all work together. I realized
this when I became more conscious about the food I eat. For example,
when I eat lots of junk food, I feel sluggish and headachy. But when I eat
well—fresh food that I prepare myself—I feel much better. I also began
to contemplate at what point the food becomes me in the process of eating, and I couldn't pinpoint a moment. If it's when the parts of the food
become parts of my body, that occurs even before I've tasted the food as
odor molecules attach to receptors in my olfactory nerves. Admittedly,
that's a temporary attachment, but so is the attachment of, for example,
the proteins in the lunch I just had to the cells of my body. Eventually,
those proteins will be replaced with others; the process of life is a process
of constant change.

When eating, I'll often perform a kind of grace, but unlike Christian
grace it doesn't involve words. I imagine the origin of each of the compo-
nents of the food as I eat it, and think about what had to happen for that

---

152.   One could also say its neither binary nor unitary, but multifarious. Still, all atoms
       of the universe, however countless, are all unified in a single universe. I want to
       emphasize that I'm not making an argument for monotheism, necessarily—this
       statement can be true whether there is one god, many gods, or even no gods (at
       least, if you define *god* in a certain way).

food to be available to me. A single sandwich requires fields of wheat, days of rain and sun, farmers of diverse backgrounds, truckers and trains and boats, yards of livestock, oceans of fish, entire interlocking ecologies. The sandwich I eat for lunch is a fundamental and necessary component of the universe I know. Perhaps a different farmer could have grown the wheat for the bread—but if so, this would not be quite the sandwich I have now. I am forever involved in both the good and the bad when I eat a piece of food. If the animal was treated poorly, I am involved in that poor treatment—not necessarily morally culpable, but at least involved. If the animal was treated well, I am involved in that. I participate in the world; I participate as the world.

There's no duality between Self and Other, but we make one in language, because otherwise communication would be impossible, and the universe yearns for the beauty that communication engenders. Imagine if we did not abstract, if every thing we saw had its own name, its own noun. So each tree had a name, and each animal, not just each species, and my arm was called something different from your arm, and so on. We'd have an infinite number of words, and communication would be impossible. We must abstract; it's our prison. But it's also the key that opens the door, because through abstraction we can communicate and through communication I can experience you as a you. So I hold this cup of coffee and smell it and drink it as if it were separate from me, but I know that the way I think about it is conditioned by my dual mind. On another level of reality, the coffee, I, my workspace, my apartment, my city, my country, my world are all atoms, which on another level of reality are all composed of twists of probability, which on another level of reality are all flowing and ebbing seas of information. But at that level of reality, language fails us, and we run up against the ineffable.

When William James wrote *The Varieties of Religious Experiences*, he identified several commonalities of religious experiences the world over. One of these was the ineffability of the experience—in most cases, the experience could not be described.[153] This ineffability seems mysterious,

---

153. William James, *The Varieties of Religious Experiences*. New York: Modern Library, 1999 [1902].

since we have little problem describing any idea we choose in language. But all those ideas and experiences rely on a duality that the mystical experience—and the magical experience, I might add—transcend. A student recently asked me, "When a mystic has the experience of nonduality, does he return to the ordinary world, or just live in that nonduality?" I had to think for a second, because while I could answer the question, I knew that each answer was incomplete. So finally I said, "Your question assumes a duality between the ordinary world and the experience of nonduality that isn't there." It's an unsatisfactory answer; it isn't an answer. But it's the best one can do when describing the numinous.

I could have explained that the mystic must fall back into language, just as the fish must fall back into water, but is changed by the experience of nonduality so that he or she participates more carefully in language. And sometimes the mystic may even fail to see a person as part of the whole that he or she knows the individual to be, and may treat the person like an it. That happens. We seem so disappointed when it happens to our spiritual leaders and icons, too—if the Pope wears Prada, we think he's become a materialist. If the Zen master gets caught drunk, we assume he was a fraud all along. But all this arises from the assumption that there is a perfect and nonperfect, and that our spiritual leaders must be perfect. In reality, there is all one perfect nonperfection, and we all participate in it not as separate observers, but as players.

I've also heard the explanation that after the experience of nonduality, there is no duality to fall back into, and so the mystic remains perfect. It is others' perceptions that are imperfect, because they are trapped in duality. When a fully enlightened Zen master gets drunk, he or she does it to teach us something. When an adept yells at someone in traffic (as I tend to do, especially driving in one particular suburb of Chicago), he or she is expressing compassion in an unusual way.

I prefer the first of the above two explanations, because the second makes me suspicious, but neither of them is completely true or completely false. In reality, the question can't mean anything, because it asks a question that presumes the answer is possible when it's not. Both of the above are lies because they are in words, and the experience of nonduality is an experience beyond the ability of words to communicate. We are lifted up, in our experience, out of our petty fears and hopes to look over the temporal landscape of our lives for a moment, and we come back thinking, "So that's all okay then." But we can't really say why it's okay, only that we know beyond the ability to express that it is. The limit of language is the limit of duality.

We use language to limit ourselves in another, less esoteric way. Unless you're actually striving to have the Vision of No Difference, the inability of language to express it probably doesn't much impact your life. But for most of us, language presents another obstacle in our day-to-day functioning. Cognitive psychologists speak of the ongoing dialogue we have in our heads as "self-talk." There can be positive self-talk, and negative self-talk. Our moods and feelings and even actions are usually based on this self-talk, much more so than on outside stimulus. For example, there's a famous Zen story of a monk who is traveling by foot across country. He loses the road in the dark and finds himself stumbling through trees and broken stones and tall weeds. Finally, exhausted and parched with thirst he collapses, praying desperately for water and rest. His hand comes to fall on a cup, filled with water, and he drinks thirstily and then sleeps, grateful for the drink. When he awakes in the morning light he sees that what he thought was a cup filled with pure water is a broken human skull, filled with maggots and worms and brackish green sludge. He vomits, and in vomiting, suddenly realizes that he was not sick until the moment he realized what he had drunk; if he had remained ignorant, he never would have been ill.

It is what we tell ourselves about the things we see that make us feel emotions. We see brightly colored litter and think "That's a shame that someone littered. People shouldn't throw away their wrappers!" when what we *could* think is "That's a nicely colored piece of paper." Of course, it isn't good to litter and what we could best do is pick it up and throw it away, but the point is we feel upset if we think about what people should do, and we feel okay if we just appreciate it for what it is. Sometimes we are perfectly justified to feel certain emotions and tell ourselves certain things—it would be inhuman not to witness a tragedy and think "That was terrible!" But much more often we feel emotions based on negative self-talk that shares almost no resemblance to reality at all. It's as if we are navigating by completely random, even maliciously incorrect, maps.

Negative self-talk leads to feelings of anxiety, powerlessness, and depression. For example, you might have some unpleasant task—like sending out resumes, say—and every time you are confronted with the task you may feel anxiety or a desire to procrastinate. If you introspect carefully, you may find that your internal monologue changes to something like "That's going to be a lot of work. It won't help anyway" and so on. Psychologists suggest several ways to deal with this anxiety-provoking self-talk. Some students, for example, feel strong anxiety during tests. Psychologists suggest that students who feel test anxiety confront negative thoughts by mentally shouting "Stop!" at them and then replacing them with a more positive thought. A student might find himself or herself thinking "I should have studied more. I'm going to fail!" At which point, he or she might mentally shout "Stop! I studied for six hours and reviewed all week. I know enough to pass this test." Similarly, negative thoughts can be replaced by writing them down and responding in writing. Something about the process of writing helps us remain objective about thoughts that, unspoken and unwritten, might seem overwhelming. A depressive's thought "No one loves me" could be replaced, then, with something like "Several people love me, including my wife and kids." Often, negative self-talk looks silly or embarrassing when written out; sometimes, merely writing down your internal dialogue is enough to change it.

Methods of Mindfulness

Magically, we cannot change our self-talk until we can recognize it. The ability to recognize our thoughts as they arise requires conscious development; we're not necessarily born with introspective skills. If you cannot trace back your unpleasant feelings to the thoughts that cause them, it may be hard to change them. Therefore, I strongly stress introspection in magic. There are several ways to do so—writing things out, for example, is often effective. But a meditative practice called *vipassana* is useful, not just for the study of magic, but in many other ways. Attempts to use vi-

passana meditation in prisons in India and the United States have proven
successful, dramatically cutting down on prison violence and recidivism.

Vipassana is originally a Buddhist technique, but it need not come
with Buddhist doctrine to be effective. Anyone of any religion can do
vipassana, and it is easy to learn, unlike many other religio-magical techniques. The first step is to sit in a comfortable position with the spine
straight; lying down is not recommended unless you must do so for
health reasons. If you recline while doing such meditation, the relaxation
may lead you to fall asleep. The next step is to pay attention to your
breath. Don't worry about changing your breath or controlling it. If it's
quick, just observe that it's quick. If it's slow, observe that it's slow. It
might even stop for a while; just observe. When thoughts arise, as they
inevitably will, just observe them. Don't judge them or label them good
or bad. Just observe that you are thinking and bring your mind back to
your breath. Notice, also, where tension is in your body and what sorts of
ambient sounds are in your environment. Don't worry about controlling
any of these things. You'll naturally relax, but even if you don't, do not
worry about it. Do this for ten or twenty minutes; it's a good idea to do it
every day if you can. Without any effort on your part, you'll find yourself
much more aware of the things that are occurring in your mind.

What I present above is a nonsectarian version of vipassana. A Buddhist teacher may disagree with the way I present it, pointing out that
the first step should actually be the cultivation of certain virtues. I agree
that, in a Buddhist context, that is the way vipassana should be done, but
I am not presenting it in a Buddhist context. If you wish to learn a more
specifically Buddhist version, I encourage you to seek out and attend
one of several classes available all over the country at Theravada Buddhist centers. Usually those classes are free, or request a reasonably small
donation, and most Theravada Buddhist teachers do not require you to
convert or even join their center to take classes and get the benefits of the
dharma. The dharma has a lot of good, solid, common sense that anyone
can benefit from (and quite a bit of uncommon sense, too).

When we speak to ourselves with negative self-talk, we have emotions that psychologists call "disturbed." Such disturbed emotions might
include anything from the grinding self-loathing of depression to terrifying

anxiety to mild grumpiness. Emotions can be strongly disturbed or slightly disturbed, and even very slight disturbances in our emotional states can affect our magic. Even sane and healthy people sometimes have disturbed emotions about things important to them. Imagine that you want money, but you tell yourself things like "I never have money" or "I should work harder" or "If I could only come up with a good idea, I could make millions." These are all examples of self-talk that can lead to disturbed emotions, and if you perform a spell for money, you might find that on some deep level you don't believe it will work. If your incantation for money is drowned out by incantations of self-doubt, you won't manifest money. But by being aware of our internal incantations, we can figure out what kinds of spells we're casting on ourselves and work to replace such disordered thinking with a clearer, more open, more joyful internal dialogue.

The first step, as I've said before, is watching what we say to ourselves. Certain patterns of self-talk are particularly likely to quash a magician's belief in his or her own power and ability to change. I call these patterns of language "antimagic words." You need never say them aloud for them to have an effect on your mind, emotions, and magic. In fact, if you do write them down, they sometimes lose their power. But before I talk about how to counter antimagic words, let me explain how to detect them.

Even if you haven't had much success in vipassana meditation, you've probably at least quieted enough to hear the inner monologue. If so, then you know that your inner monologue is always ongoing, and we usually don't even listen actively—that means the things we say go directly into our deep mind, causing changes that bubble to the surface. It helps to catch these antimagic words before they have their antimagical effects. One way to do that is to notice when you *have* a disturbed emotion and ask yourself three questions:

1. What objective event in the world or in my mind triggered that emotion? (Trigger)

2. What did I feel about that? (Effect)

3. What did I say to myself about that trigger that made me feel that way? (Cause)

Notice that it's not the trigger in the world that causes the effect; it's the self-talk. For example, imagine that you're looking for a job, and one of your good friends gets a job that you wanted. You might feel betrayed, angry, jealous, annoyed—especially if you tell yourself things like "I should have gotten that job! I'm a loser! I'll never get a job." But you might feel happy, proud, and pleased if you tell yourself things like "What helps my friend helps me. I can ask him for a recommendation if there's another opening later. The fact he got a job in what I'm looking for proves that it can be done!" I'm not describing mere positive thinking; sometimes negative thinking is perfectly accurate. I'm suggesting that replacing negative thoughts can lead to a more complex, balanced, and therefore magical perspective on the world.

You'll probably eventually come up with your own list of antimagic words, but I'll list some common patterns, and some that have been identified by psychologists.

Antimagic Words

Should, ought, must

When we say *should*, either "I should" or "they should," we're pretending there's an objective standard regarding what we should or shouldn't do. Even if we believe our ethical rules are objective, it is irrational to expect that everyone in the world would obey them, or even be aware of what they are. One of the great thinkers in cognitive behavioral therapy is Albert Ellis,[154] who ranks this as a central disordered thought-pattern. He recommends replacing all "shoulds" with preferences: so instead of thinking "He shouldn't talk so loudly on his cell phone in public!" we think "I'd like it if he wouldn't talk so loudly on his cell phone in public." The first thought demands that the world conform to your own preferences—something that not even the most powerful of adepti can expect—while the second leaves you open to all manner of possibilities, including asking

---

154.   Albert Ellis, *Handbook of Rational-Emotive Therapy.* New York: Springer
       Publishing, 1977. Ellis is a materialist and does not regard magical thinking
       highly, but there are valuable insights to be gained in his work.

the cell-phone user to tone it down, or just ignoring him. It's harder to ignore someone who breaks the Law of Should. But it's pretty easy to ignore someone who is just violating a preference.

Am, is, are, was, were, be, being, been

The field of general semantics, an exploration of how language affects thought, is famous for forbidding the use of verbs of being, as I've already discussed. In reality, GS simply suggests that verbs of being often encode assumptions about the world that aren't true. For example, we often label ourselves and other people, but no one can really be reduced to a label. I taught a GED class part time, and students often told me "I'm really bad at math," even after doing a series of rather difficult problems. The label had outlived the truth. I helped them replace those thoughts with new ones, such as "I used to have difficulty in doing some math problems, but I find many of those same problems easier now."

Never, always

Cognitive behavioral therapists are fond of pointing out that no one can really predict the future, so that when we self-talk about our future we're often wrong. Of course, many practitioners of magic think they can predict the future, but even so, no one can predict with perfect accuracy what will always be true or never be true. When we tell ourselves "I'll never be able to play the piano," we've made a self-fulfilling prophecy, but not a real prediction. If we say "I'll always be alone," we base that on limited evidence from the past. Even if the tarot or Yi Jing says we'll be alone for the foreseeable future, that doesn't mean always. "Never" and "always" not only rob us of our future, they leech our desire to perform magic. If I believe I'll always be alone, why do a love spell? It just won't work anyway, because I'll always be alone. The easy way to fix these antimagic words is to replace them with present tense. "I'm alone right now. I might meet someone tomorrow" or "I don't play the piano very well yet, so I'll practice more." These two antimagic words can also work against you in the past tense. Psychologists call this a *negative filter*. For example, if you wake up some morning to discover your hot water heater broke and you have to take a cold shower, you might think "This sort of thing always happens to me!" completely ignoring the fact that every day you've woken up for the last few years, it's worked fine. Or you might screw up putting together a piece of furniture and think "I never do anything right." Never? Ever? Anything? That seems unlikely; like most of us, you probably do some things right and some things wrong, and sometimes have to redo things you got wrong until you get them right.

I, you

Psychologists don't recognize these, necessarily, as disordered thoughts, but a careless use of these pronouns in magic can be self-defeating. For one thing, these are the blaming pronouns; any time you blame a "you" for one of your emotions, you know you're thinking irrationally. Your emotions are a function of your thoughts, not someone else's actions. Even the most horrid actions one can imagine need not crush someone's spirit if he or she can control his or her thoughts. Magically, there's also the question of what "I" am and what "you" are. People are made up of multiple parts and layers, all interacting complexly, and what I was yesterday I am not today. I can sometimes feel embarrassed about things I said or did five years ago or more! That's irrational; the person who said those things or did those things was a different person, with different ideas, different beliefs, even a different body. Similarly, one can hold a grudge against a "you" for decades, never recognizing that people change and the grudge may no longer be valid or reasonable (if it ever was in the first place; I've rarely seen grudges that were).

I feel

A sneaky one, this one! Identifying your feelings and expressing them is important and valuable. We can benefit from expressing our feelings honestly both to ourselves and to others. But when looking for the thoughts that make you feel a certain way, it's a mistake to identify other feelings as those thoughts. Qabalists speak of a four-part soul. The lower two parts, the nefesh and the ruakh, are involved in emotion and thought respectively. If we think with our nefesh, we're in trouble. So for example, someone might feel blue and think "I'm blue because I feel so depressed!" That doesn't get to the root of the self-talk. It just masks it with another emotion. Instead, try "I'm blue and depressed because I'm thinking I'll never amount to anything." Then you can see that it's the "never" antimagic word causing the depression. Similarly, people sometimes use their emotions as proof of events; people might feel guilty and so assume they did something wrong. Or someone might feel jealous and assume that his or her lover is cheating. Of course, in magic, we sometimes do have feelings whose origin we can't identify, and they might very well be premonitions. In that case, I recommend careful vipassana to trace back the origins of the self-talk. If you find that it seems to end in a brick wall, that when you trace it back the emotion comes from nowhere, then it's possible it comes from another part of the soul, the neshemah, the intuition. But it's wise to be very careful to distinguish between emotions coming from the intuition and emotions coming from the animal soul of the nefesh. Mixing them up can have humiliating results.

Can't

We can't do very few things, relatively speaking, that aren't simply physically impossible (and some of those, I suspect, we might be able to do somehow anyway). For example, if I pick up a guitar and try to play it, I'll discover that I don't know how yet. But to say "I can't play the guitar" is to imply that no matter how hard I try, I'll never master it. Similarly, if we say "I can't sing" or "I can't speak Spanish" or "I can't drive far from home" or whatever other limit we put on ourselves, we're actually lying. Even if you don't know a single word of Spanish, you can learn it if you wish. I replace *can't* with *can't yet*, or better still, *don't yet know how to*.

No, not

Many people have written about *no* and *not*, making the claim that our subconscious mind doesn't understand negatives, and so one should be careful to do magic only for positive things: for example, "health" rather than "not to get sick." There's no research that shows our subconscious can't understand negatives; quite the contrary is true. The fact that there is always a way to negate a verb in every language on Earth indicates that negation is firmly ingrained in our deep minds, where the structures of our underlying grammar lurk. What I'm pointing out here is my experience that thinking in negative terms often limits possibility, while the same idea couched in positive terms increases possibility. For example, if I say to a child, as most of us do, "Don't talk to strangers," I'm laying down a hard, fast rule. It's important to do so for children, of course. But many children keep that rule in the back of their minds long after they become adults; they become fearful of social interaction. Now that they are adults, they could replace the negative with a positive: "Interact carefully with strangers." Also, we sometimes compound the negative with labels or predictions: "I won't go to Europe because I don't have the money" we think, and continue to think, long after we have gotten the raise that would provide the money.

The problem here is that *not* is a pretty vague word in English: it means both "not ever" and "not yet." Bahasa Indonesia, one of the languages spoken on the islands of Indonesia, has several words for *not*. For "not ever," speakers of Bahasa Indonesia use *tidak* or *tak*, and for "not yet" they use *belum*. *Tidak* is used with things that are plainly impossible or clearly untrue: "Did you go to Australia last year?" might be answered with "tidak," meaning "absolutely not." But "Did you eat lunch?" might be answered with "belum," because one could eat lunch in the future. Interestingly, questions like "Have you been to the moon?" could be answered "belum," even though the speaker has no intention of going there, because the language recognizes the possibility! It's useful for magicians to develop a *belum*-attitude.

There's another problem with *no* as an answer to a question; it shuts down creativity. Imagine your child asks you "Can I go to the park?" and you don't have time to go and watch her. If you say "no," you've solved the problem by shutting down possibility. But imagine what would happen if you said "Yes, if you can come up with an adult we both know who would be willing to go with you" or "I'm busy right now, but we could go Saturday instead of going to the mall like we'd planned." Similarly, in magic, *no* sometimes limits opportunities for growth. Say we have a visit from a "spirit" in a dream, and we can trace back everything that spirit said to something we wish were true, but probably isn't. We could ask ourselves "Was that a real spirit?" and answer it pretty confidently "no." But that shuts down possibility. Maybe it wasn't a real spirit, but we could also ask "What can I learn from the experience anyway?" One thing you could learn is what you really, really want subconsciously. Try eliminating *no* for one week, and see what happens.

These antimagic words aren't enemies to be railed against, nor are they evidence of deeply disordered minds or moral culpability. If you find yourself "shoulding" a lot, you might like to try replacing those *should*s with preferences, to see what happens. But I don't want to suggest that you *should* watch what you think and keep a close eye on yourself, and if you use one of these words punish yourself and berate yourself. Gods forbid. There's enough punishment in our culture without doing it to yourself. There might even be perfectly good reasons to say *should* or *never*. Still, being more conscious of the words we use and the effects they have both in our mundane lives and in our magic can't hurt.

I've discussed vipassana as a way of doing this, but other methods exist as well. For example, Aleister Crowley suggests carrying about a razor and giving oneself a good slash with it whenever one uses the word *I* for a set period of time. Talk about self-punishment! Still, the exercise can be adopted for those of us who aren't psychotic. One thing I find useful is to carry a rubber band around my left wrist and, every time I use a word I'm trying to become more conscious about (like *should*—I *should* all over the place if I'm not careful), I snap it. It doesn't hurt, but it's a wake-up jolt that makes me aware that I've used a word unconsciously. By training our body to expect a physical reaction to a verbal expression, we teach our conscious mind to be aware of what it's saying to itself. Incidentally, the other advantage of this method over Crowley's is that one can do it in public without being taken to the hospital, and there's no risk of infection.

Ineffability

So much for how to overcome antimagic words that limit our emotional freedom and magical confidence. What about that other issue concerning words that I discussed earlier, the fact that words assume a dualistic world that is, in its deepest reality, unified beyond unity? How can one overcome the obstacle of speaking about unity in a communication system founded on duality?

Ineffability, or the inability to put an experience into words, characterizes much of the mystical experience. Many religions contain ideas such as that in the *Tao Te Ching*: "The Tao that can be understood cannot be the primal, or cosmic, Tao, just as an idea that can be expressed in words cannot be the infinite idea."[155]

Zen teachers frequently dissolve language by being contradictory. For example, a student asks a (fairly dumb) question: "Does a dog have Buddha nature?" According to the doctrine of Buddhism, yes, a dog, as well as anything else, has Buddha nature. But the student in this story is trying to trip up the teacher by getting the teacher to bite a bullet and admit to something kind of absurd. We have a bit fonder attitude toward dogs in the contemporary West; an equivalent example in our codes might be "Does a pig have Buddha nature?" The "correct" answer in language is "yes, because . . ." and then an explanation for how our conceptions about things are not as fundamental as Buddha nature and so on. Instead, however, the teacher in this story answers "mu," which is an archaic Chinese syllable that means something like "nope" and also sounds like a dog's bark. This answer forces the student to move beyond language and realize the answer at a deeper level than language. Other Zen teachers have historically answered students by shouting, pointing, slapping, or behaving oddly—all preverbal responses.

Language relies on the binary opposition of ideas. Something is large because it is not small, or hot because it is not cold. The mystical experience, however, operates on the most fundamental binary opposition of all: Self and Other. It breaks down the difference between you and reality, and breaking down this binary opposition breaks down, it seems, all others. For one precious moment, you find yourself in a world where there are no words to explain your experiences. All you have are pure experiences, and you discover that pure experience can be enough, even without words.

---

155.   Dwight Goddard and Henri Borel, trans. *Tao Te Ching*. Whitefish, MT: Kessinger, 1919. Online at http://www.sacred-texts.com/tao/ltw/index.htm (accessed 16 May 2008).

The door that bars the way can become the door that opens and admits access to the mystical state of mind, a consciousness of unity. The mystical state is a state of mind that occurs when the verbal apparatus is completely stymied. Unlike the state of mind encouraged by vipassana, which can be called "mindfulness," the mystical state of mind is a result of a different style of meditation, called *samatha* in Buddhism. *Samatha* literally means "stopping." It's a meditation that uses intense concentration to move beyond thought into pure mindless bliss, sometimes called *samadhi*. The way to do this is through single-minded concentration on one thing.

Samadhi is not easy to attain, but one can attain varying degrees of it. In Hindu meditation, there are three steps to attaining samadhi: first, *dharana* is the exclusive focus on one idea or image. Sometimes, it's exclusive focus on one part of the body, or a mantra. In any event, constant focus on a single thing is harder than it sounds. Simple shapes warp and twist, simple sounds become garbled, body sensations become painful or itchy. But sticking through these mutations and gently bringing the mind back, again and again, to dharana on a single object will eventually lead to *dhyana*, pure identification with the object of concentration. Prolonged experience of dhyana can lead, eventually, to samadhi, in which the mind itself melts and the personal ego dissolves into the underlying consciousness.

The yogic methods of the East can take a while, sometimes years, to arrive at the state of wordlessness or samadhi. For this reason, magicians in the West have created other methods that work faster (although perhaps not as safely or as surely). One such method was described, sort of, by the English magician and contemporary of Crowley's, A. O. Spare. I say "sort of" because Spare was easily the most abstruse occult writer to come out of the early twentieth century.[156] But Spare's paintings, on the other hand, act as keys to his writing, and one can elucidate his meanings by examining both. It appears that Spare suggested a system of meditation he called "neither/neither." In neither/neither, the mind comes to rest on an

---

156. Yes, that includes Waite.

idea—this is simple contemplation. The magician then extrapolates that idea out into its opposite. Since we have a tendency to think in dualities, that isn't difficult. If you contemplate light, you extrapolate light into its opposite, darkness. Then, Spare suggests, combine the two ideas and recognize that they're poles on a spectrum, not dualities at all. We don't have light and not-light, but just light/not-light as one conceptual unit. Now, the mind desires duality, so we have a natural tendency to seek an opposite for any idea—Spare seems to suggest we encourage the mind, at this point in its contemplation, to do so. Take the complex you've created of light/not-light and ask "What is neither light nor not-light?" In other words, what is the opposite of light/not-light? The mind will balk for a moment; that moment can be an opening into samadhi.[157]

Chaos magicians in the early 1990s took Spare's idea of vacuity and ran with it, renaming it "gnosis" and claiming that they could achieve it through orgasm. Other methods of achieving gnosis include intense pain, exhaustion, and drugs. Anything, in other words, that shuts down the verbal part of the mind is regarded as leading to gnosis. These methods of gnosis are another way of achieving samadhi, and chaos magicians regard this state of consciousness as essential to magic.

If reality is linguistic, then achieving a state of consciousness before language provides greater leverage against the network of meanings that make up reality. In a state of samadhi, I can act free from preconceptions (which by definition must be verbal) and doubts (results of negative self-talk). If I repeat an affirmation in a usual state of consciousness, it comes with other ideas—each word carries with it strings of linguistic and sociolinguistic meaning that might obscure the ultimate goal. But if I reduce a desire to a prelinguistic symbol, a meaningless scribble or an anagram without semantic content, then I can plant that idea underneath where language dwells in the deep mind. The deeper you plant a seed in the deep mind, the more likely it is to sprout into a full plant in the linguistic world.

---

157. The clearest explanation of Spare's method from his own hand is probably in A. O. Spare, *The Zoetic Grimoire of Zos*. London: Fulgur, 1998. See http://www .hermetic.com/spare/grimoire_of_zos.html (accessed 29 April 2008).

One cannot work entirely in samadhi, however. Such a state is not conducive to life in the real world; those who spend all their time in such a state of consciousness are clinically insane, withdrawn, or autistic. Even chaos magicians working in states of gnosis start with a verbal expression of desire and work toward preverbal symbols. Similarly, the method of defixio starts with a verbal expression of desire and ends with a visceral, bodily action of throwing that desire in a well. There is a back-and-forth, a sine wave, between the verbal and preverbal, between reality and our conceptions about reality. We create an idea in verbal terms, express it in symbolic format, plant it in some preverbal way, and it returns to the conceptual word of linguistic reality. You could couch this in purely psychological terms: we modify our ideas about the world by getting underneath their verbal expression to the physical reality abstracted by words. Or you could couch it in more controversial, magical terms: we constantly bridge the verbal and the preverbal, ultimate reality and con-sensual reality, as a shaman stands with a foot in both worlds.

Once you do arrive there in the place without words, you are lifted up above the temporal landscape of your life, as if by the top of your head, and all meaning becomes all other meaning, all symbols are laid out and you see that they spread over the vastness of the space of a single mathematical point. You can achieve this by deliberately collapsing every binary, and finding the X in the Y and the Y in the X. Or you can just focus on the point between two binary oppositions, between a signifier and its signified. Try to measure the space between a symbol and what it means. Or try to forget how to talk, as if you are awakening from amne-sia. By whatever method, when you arrive at the place where there are no words, you will come back with a great handful of elixir of your own, and your hands will be empty.

Language is not just the way we do magic or order a pizza. It's also the way we connect to each other. It is not my place to say how people should live, but I have learned, as I have studied language and magic over the years, that our language means nothing unless we have someone to speak it to. I see people speaking at each other, yelling at each other, even laughing at each other, but I rarely see people speaking to each other. We have this tool of language, and sometimes perhaps we will choose to use it to inflict hurt on other people, or take out our frustrations, or even engage in argument. But even if we choose to do that, let's not forget that we can use it for other means, too: we can use it to make magic, both by changing reality and by truly, honestly communicating with the people around us. The roots of such communication delve into silence and the place without words, and the leaves unfold into our complex reality. Language is our doorway to ultimate reality, with a dirty window through which we peer tentatively. No matter how much we clean that window, we can never experience reality fully until we open the door, step through, and plunge into the ineffable.

APPENDIX ONE

Liber Numerorum:
A Dictionary of
English Gematria

The following dictionary is arranged according to the sequential, 1–26 ordering of the English alphabet. Words selected for this dictionary include words regarded as important in magic and religion, with several more common words included. The vocabulary of Basic English, a beginning English vocabulary of the language's most common words, was used as the seed of this dictionary. It was supplemented with words included in Crowley's *Sepher Sephiroth*, as well other terms chosen from diverse sources. Mostly, proper names of spirits, gods, and deities have been eschewed, with the exception of some Thelemic concepts that might be interesting to those trying to create an English Qabalah to interpret the *Book of the Law*.

7
  bad
  be

9
  I

10
  bag

11
  bed

12
  bee

13
  had
  he

14
  dead

15
  face
  if

17
  acid
  back
  ice

18
  head

19
  and
  do
  egg
  idea
  Ra

20
  able
  cake

21
  band
  edge

22
  go
  lead

23
  end

24
  act
  blade
  cat
  ear
  leaf
  leg
  sad

25
  all
  far
  sea

26
  card
  dog
  flag
  god

27
  ball
  base
  care
  fat
  hand
  off
  red

28
  air
  dear
  feel
  man
  need
  read

29
  black
  hat
  no
  page
  see

30
  arch
  baby
  bread
  day
  deep
  eagle
  fact
  fear
  hang
  make
  map
  peace

31
  bath
  bell
  bit
  chief
  coal
  damage
  debt
  fall
  hard
  land
  male
  meal
  old
  safe

32
  arm
  get
  hear
  high
  pig

33
  bird
  birth
  cheap
  comb
  ill
  name
  neck

seed
the

34
chance
chin
cold
dark
free
hate
heat
ink
kick

35
ant
chain
chalk
clean
eye
feeble
knee
pen
rice

36
agree
bite
bone
come
crack
field
hair
have
law
nail
oil

37
brake
bulb
flame
fold
keep
let
like

lip
place
rod
shade
side
take
teach
up

38
balance
boat
boil
change
death
farm
fire
gold
kind
late
near
road
same
sand

39
angel
angle
art
belief
clear
coat
fix
flat
may
meat
net
pin
rat

40
any
blue
board
cord
cup

food
hole
line
mind
pain
scale
table
toe

41
awake
bent
box
camera
cow
good
help
key
king
lock
mine
rub
sail
wide

42
boy
cart
female
fish
gun
Hadit
new
pay
rain
seem
self
send
tail
war

43
book
brick
but
false

fly
frame
give
goat
left
mark
meet
than
tin

44

brain
clock
cook
degree
hope
office
rate
ray
shake
space
talk
week

45

basin
bridge
cheese
east
effect
knife
match
milk
much
needle
range
say
seat
spade
tall
tax
use

46

body
branch
cry
drain
draw
even
girl
guide
how
mix
pipe
shame
who

47

cork
dry
force
judge
lift
medical
middle
react
shoe
then
time
walk

48

blood
build
crime
fool
join
live
long
plane
ring
sex
sock
son
trade
tree
wall

wax
wet

49

cause
danger
garden
grain
green
hook
laugh
not
servant
sign
that
way
year
yes

50

animal
apple
circle
ever
fight
fork
grip
learn
low
offer
open
shelf
snake
when
wind

51

before
demon
detail
full
great
Mars
metal
pot

price
silk
soap
such
thick
thin
top
wash
wave
wine

52

blow
boot
door
earth
form
heart
last
loud
mass
now
salt
ship
some
stage
tire
well

53

drop
look
machine
nose
ready
run
sheep
skin
till
wait
wheel
wing

54

breath
chemical

cough
engine
health
linen
love
note
plate
play
roof
sun
voice

55

burn
chest
cloud
grey
horn
jewel
move
nut
part
sky
song
warm
watch
wire

56

attack
because
down
drink
equal
foot
fowl
friend
iron
level
light
out
oven
paper
past
rule

shock
slip
there
this
thread
tired
whip
why
will
wise

57

army
moon
put
roll
sleep
small
stem
while
wood

58

basket
cloth
design
drive
father
feeling
glass
hammer
kiss
night
please
science
smile
star
steam
thing

59

about
amuse
brass
breathe
copy

credit
cruel
delicate
finger
island
manager
pencil
size
solid
view
where

60

canvas
desire
jump
knot
list
orange
order
over
paint
second
smash
soft
step
stiff
with
word

61

church
early
glove
mist
news
paste
pull
quick
room
smell
steel
trick
value
you

62

bucket
disease
doubt
flight
general
harbor
hearing
hour
noise
rest
right
sense
sharp
stick
think
train
under

63

color
cover
grow
know
limit
plant
public
record
smoke
witch

64

bright
dust
jelly
mercy
nerve
Nuit
poor
push
swim
test
thou
thumb
tight

tray
true
unit

65

angry
broken
dress
grass
horse
loss
music
special
state
taste
white
wool

66

event
family
floor
happy
loose
only
other
pump
sugar
woman

67

alchemy
exchange
slope
sudden
touch
water
west
work

68

berry
boiling
brush
house
language

market
married
root
screw
shut
ticket
waste

69

crush
curve
elastic
leather
reward
rough
slow
stamp
verse
worm

70

certain
enough
insect
month
pocket
secret
stop
very

71

snow
soup

72

brown
first
liquid
money
quiet
quite
reason
river
round
school
sort

still
sweet
town
weight
world

73

common
copper
crown
front
kettle
kingdom
living
muscle
nation
normal
number
prose
regret
sound
stone
turn

74

beauty
between
bitter
bottle
error
fruit
increase
point
shirt
simple
sneeze

75

across
distance
electric
every
fertile
humor
north
owner

Ra-Hoor
write

76

addition
dirty
example
fiction
receipt
sponge

77

account
glory
group
mouth
parallel
power
print
skirt
store
wound
wrong

78

building
decision
little
start
tooth

79

develop
flower
healthy
material
mother
plough
polish
spoon
stitch
stomach

80

answer
behavior
burst

learning
letter
short
weather

81
powder
square
Venus

82
measure
minute
produce
regular
throat
tongue
vessel
young

83
monkey
south
spring
wisdom

84
amount
daughter
profit
strange
umbrella

85
hollow
library
reaction
separate
silver

86
brother
butter
curtain
motion
respect
triangle

87
company
cotton
dependent
different
natural
person
potato
punish
sticky
street

88
agreement
complex
poison
window

89
complete
cushion
memory
narrow
religion
summer
unity
winter

90
button
comfort
morning
sister
smooth
tendency
thunder

91
future
growth
prison
private
theory
twist

92
education
opinion

picture
porter
rhythm
yellow

93
physical
Saturn
stretch
strong
trouble

94
discuss
harmony
payment
relation

95
attempt
discover
impulse
pentagram
process

96
knowledge
society
whistle

97
beautiful
control
direction
pleasure
possible
present
story
sulfur
through
violent

98
station
stocking
together

99
argument
current
disgust
Jupiter
servant
thought

100
hospital
ornament
writing

101
division
system

102
selection
straight

103
automatic
committee
condition
mercury

104
existence
experience
substance

105
quality
request

106
destroy
serious

107
military
mountain

108
business
important
journey

109
necessary

110
interest
purpose

111
amusement
witchcraft

112
connection
victory (the 7th Sephi-
rah)

113
protest
universe

114
history
secretary

115
opposite

116
country

117
expansion
position
statement

118
attention
conscious

119
foundation (the 9th
Sephirah)

120
discovery
question

121
attraction
scissors

122
yesterday

123
comparison
severity (the 5th Sephi-
rah)

125
support
surprise

127
adjustment

131
development

133
government
property

134
responsible

135
trousers

136
suggestion

137
authority
tomorrow

139
competition
punishment

141
transport

145
structure

150
understanding

151
Jesus Christ

153
instrument

155
advertisement

The Hebrew Alphabet

Traditional	Handwritten	Name	Sound	Meaning	Tarot
א	X	alef	ʻ	ox	0–The Fool
ב	‍ב	bet	b, v	house	I–The Magician
ג	‍ג	gimel	g, gh	camel	II–The Priestess
ד	‍ד	dalet	d, dh	door	III–The Empress
ה	‍ה	heh	h	window	IV–The Emperor
ו	‍ו	waw	w, v, o, u	nail	V–The Hierophant
ז	‍ז	zayin	z	sword	VI–The Lovers
ח	‍ח	khet	kh	fence	VII–The Chariot
ט	‍ט	tet	t	serpent	VIII–Strength
י	‍י	yud	y	hand	IX–The Hermit
כ ך	‍כ ‍ך	kaf	k, kh	palm of hand	X–The Wheel
ל	‍ל	lamed	l	whip, goad	XI–Justice
מם	‍מ ‍ם	mem	m	water	XII–The Hanged Man
נן	‍נ ‍ן	nun	n	fish	XIII–Death
ס	‍ס	samekh	s	prop, peg	XIV–Temperance

Traditional	Handwritten	Name	Sound	Meaning	Tarot
ע	ע	'ayin	'	eye	XV–The Devil
ףפ	ף פ	peh	p	mouth	XVI–The Tower
ץצ	ץ צ	tzaddai	tz	fishhook	XVII–The Star
ק	ק	qof	q	back of head	XVIII–The Moon
ר	ר	resh	r	head	XIX–The Sun
ש	ש	shin	sh, s	tooth	XX–Judgement
ת	ת	taw	t	mark, cross	XXI–The World

APPENDIX THREE

Suggested Correspondences between the Tarot and the English Alphabet

Letter	Tarot
A, a	0–The Fool
B, b	I–The Magician
C, c	II–The Priestess
D, d	III–The Empress
E, e	Swords
F, f	IV–The Emperor
G, g	V–The Hierophant
H, h	VI–The Lovers
I, i	Wands
J, j	VII–The Chariot
K, k	VIII–Strength
L, l	IX–The Hermit
M, m	X–The Wheel
N, n	XI–Justice
O, o	Disks
P, p	XII–The Hanged Man
Q, q	XIII–Death
R, r	XIV–Temperance
S, s	XV–The Devil
T, t	XVI–The Tower
U, u	Cups

Letter	Tarot
V, v	XVII–The Star
W, w	XVIII–The Moon
X, x	XIX–The Sun
Y, y	XX–Judgement
Z, z	XXI–The World

APPENDIX FOUR

Applications

Books on magic, whether they focus on theory or practice, still cannot do the magic for you. You need to practice magic to do magic—it's nearly tautological. But tautologies can't help being true, and books on magic cannot deny that it's the reader who must do the magic. We can be frustrated by this nature of occult texts. I remember reading one well-regarded occult book, and thinking, "Well, I could sum that up in a couple of sentences." True—but the book still required thought and practice. I can also be excited by that prospect: when I pick up an occult book, I don't know if I'm going to get instruction or theory, but I know that either way it'll have to take shape under my hand, become something new that makes sense to me.

And what makes sense to me isn't what might make sense to someone else. My early rituals were formulas taken from the old hoary occult tomes; they worked better than my improvisations at that level. But at the same time, I realized I'd eventually have to move beyond those traditional rituals just as I moved beyond the formulaic obeying of recipes in cooking. Just as in cooking, we eventually learn that recipes are guides and we may, and must, innovate; we learn in magic that rituals, exercises, and even magical textbooks and books of theory are just incentives to practice.

In this book I wondered whether to include exercises in the chapters, at the ends of chapters, or here at the end of the book. I eventually settled on this last option for three reasons. First, including exercises in the chapters implies that they are the meat of the book, when really I feel that the ideas are the contribution this book makes to occult study. Second, including them at the end makes them easy to find and refer back to when the book is finished; they act as a sort of précis of the whole book, rather than a series of roadblocks to reading and comprehending the separate chapters. Third, including these exercises at the end of the book gives me a chance to move beyond mere précis, as well, and offer a parting dose of—I hope—thought-provoking ideas.

What follow are simply some notions—not complete rituals or step-by-step exercises, which I believe are often of limited value. The notions are designed to be adopted, adapted, and transformed by readers into exercises and rituals of their own origin and use. In all instances, the aesthetic needs of the reader must guide the form these exercises ultimately take. Therefore, readers must do some work, which might frustrate some. On the other hand, magic isn't called the Great Work for nothing. I'd be less than honest if I suggested that you could get the benefits of magic (or, for that matter, of anything) if you didn't actually do it.

One easy way to transform what follows into rituals is to apply the notions to already-existing rituals that you currently do. You can, for example, rework your usual banishing rituals into a new, symbolic form. Or perhaps you can try to translate your healing rituals from concepts of qi or prana into models of communication and metaphor, or vice versa. If you don't do any rituals, and this book is your introduction to magic, then apply them to ideas you already have about magic. How do they change, for example, your view of magical energy? How do they change your idea of prayer, or your approach to sigil construction? How do they address your hopes and fears about magic?

Overall, if these ideas don't inspire you to have some fun, if they seem like a syllabus or to-do sheet, then please disregard them. Alternatively, you might try to consider them in another way: a mandate to experiment, but not a requirement. Yes, to gain benefit from magic, you must work at it—but you needn't follow someone else's slavish method. Rigor is fine and useful, but not as useful, ultimately, as enjoyment. Life need not be hard and painful if approached playfully and mindfully, and neither does magic.

Chapter One
The Theory of Symbols: The Practice of Magic

- Try identifying one troubling thought every day, and drawing a semiotic web for it, in order to replace it with a more "rational" thought. Try doing this for one week, and notice if your thinking changes.

- Use a sigil mandala to solve a problem that has resisted your earlier magical efforts. Rather than forgetting the magical operation, use one of the other methods described in this chapter: cultivating the "need-not-be/does-not-matter" attitude, substituting desire, or acting in accord.

- Create your own layouts for divination, by drawing one card from a tarot deck or one rune, then drawing a semiotic map around it. Draw an additional card or rune for each node of that semiotic web, with the intention of shedding light on your associations with the original rune. Continue until you feel done.

- Create a semiotic web for an entity you wish to invoke or evoke. Consider getting a blank book and drawing a semiotic web for each of the entities you frequently use, so you can keep them all in one place. The webs themselves may come to act as sigils for contacting the intelligences involved.

Chapter Two
Language: The Bridge of Mind and Matter

- Try to be mindful, throughout the day, perhaps at particular times, of the physical sensation of language. Pay attention to where your teeth, lips, tongue, and other parts of your mouth are as you speak words or carry on a conversation. You may notice a heightened sense of the miracle of language, as you realize how much we coordinate just to carry on a conversation.

- Practice altering your breath to relax and to change consciousness. Use the fourfold breath throughout the day, whenever you feel stressed, as a way to calm yourself. Breathe in for a count of four, hold for a count of two, out for a count of four, and hold again for a count of two. If you get in this habit, you may find yourself doing it unconsciously when in a stressful situation, causing you to immediately relax.

- Make a list of sounds, perhaps a few a day, and meditate on them with the aim of figuring out their magical usage. Alternately, or additionally, consider the matter logically—is /a/ more airy than /e/, or more earthy? Try to create a chart of correspondences between sounds and magical models—the elements, the planets, or some combination. Make sure your model has room to be fluid and adaptable. You can use these correspondences in rituals, perhaps to construct your own barbarous words.

Chapter Three
Incantation: The Poetry of Power

- Make a note of performative utterances in your day-to-day life. Once you become aware of them, you may notice them popping up everywhere. Consider, as well, the borderline cases—for example, advertising isn't performative, but it does perform something; we're changed on a subtle level by the things we hear and see.

- Decide on what your own felicity conditions are for magical incantation. What does it mean to speak an incantation correctly? What does it mean to be qualified to speak an incantation, in your mind? What does it mean to construct an incantation correctly or incorrectly? In your opinion, define what an incantation needs to be effective. This exercise could make a handy entry in your magical journal, so that you can go back later and revise your ideas about incantation as you gain more experience using them. Eventually, you'll create your own criteria for constructing and using incantations.

- Construct your own incantations for simple needs, such as getting a parking space or speeding up paperwork through a bureaucracy. Include an invocation or address to a spiritual power, a complex and perhaps paralogical metaphor, and repetition.

- Create an incantation based on Taliesin's incantation, identifying yourself with the things, metaphorically, that you wish you were. Cast it in the present tense: "I am a fierce lion, an eagle on a mountain, an ear of corn . . . " Speak it in ritual as a promise to yourself to become your ideal self (but beware—it works).

Chapter Four
Sigils, Glyphs, and Characters: The Alphabets of Magic

- As an attempt to appreciate our alphabet, try learning and writing in another alphabet. You needn't learn the language that belongs to that alphabet (although that'd be fun, too), but try to write English in the Russian alphabet, or the Hebrew alphabet—or try to learn how to look up and write Chinese characters, and see if you can learn a few simple phrases. For some systems, such as syllabaries, you may have to cheat—my name in Japanese, for example, would have to be something like Paturiku Dunu. But I could write it with only six characters.

- Devise your own magical alphabet. Either use automatic writing, or just draw symbols that appeal to you for each of the letters. Alternately, you could change another alphabet—such as the Egyptian writing system—to make it more suitable for writing English. You can use this new writing system as a way of drawing your mental attention to the text you are writing.

- Try writing down a simple, casual desire on a piece of paper and exposing of it ritually, either through the *derive* described in this chapter, or by some other means. You'll be surprised at how well this works.

- You could create a defixio book. Carefully choose paper, bind it together yourself, give it an attractive cover, and dedicate it ritually so that anything written in it will come true. Only write in it in a ritual state of mind, and only include things that you want to happen.

- Keep track of the sigils you use to devise your own alphabet of desire, a vocabulary of symbols that describes your usual desires and magical aims. Obviously, such a system might be useful in magic or for divination, but it can also act as an unorthodox but creative way of keeping a magical diary. You can use your alphabet of desire as a mirror for introspection, detecting patterns and rhythms in the symbols and their meanings.

Chapter Five
From Babel to Enochian: The Search for the Primal Language

- Write a short statement of intent suitable for invoking your higher genius at the beginning of rituals. Try translating it into Enochian.
- Alternately, use it as a list of vocabulary to start creating your own language. You can scry the vocabulary or simply make it up. Alternately, you can apply some simple rules to an existing language to derive a new one—for example, you could decide to use Latin but not conjugate verbs or decline nouns. The result, depending on which form of nouns and verbs you decide to make standard, will create something that looks like Italian or Spanish.

Chapter Six
Speaking in Tongues: Glossolalia and Barbarous Words of Invocation

- Try using glossolalia in your rituals or prayers. Once you get the knack of speaking glossolalia, it becomes easy to turn it on and off at will. Start by clearing your mind as much as possible. Then open your mouth and let syllables form without conscious control. When you can speak at a normal speaking speed, with normal inflection, you will have achieved skill in glossolalia.

- See where you can integrate glossolalia into your magic. For example, I find it very useful in evocation, and often augment or replace the usual traditional evocations with glossolalia. I also find it useful in stressful situations as well as more traditional rituals. Can you construct a ritual conducted entirely in glossolalia?

- Consider the issue of borrowing from other cultures. What are some guidelines you can accept for yourself to make sure that you do it respectfully?

Chapter Seven
The Qabalah: The Grammar of Number

- Add up the values of your name and the names of people important to you, either in English or Hebrew—or both. Are there any relationships between those values?

- Try analyzing the names of spirits that you encounter in order to better understand their nature. For example, if a spirit seems to have a name involving violence and war, and claims to be a spirit of Venus, you would be reasonable to doubt that spirit's veracity.

- Identify numbers that are important to you, and use them to test other numbers, such as the value of your magical or mundane name.

- Use temurah or tziruf to create words of power from phrases and other words. Use those words of power in ritual to quickly symbolize complex ideas.

- Try finding a hidden link between two randomly chosen numbers, using either English or Hebrew gematria. Keep track of these investigations in a journal, keeping in mind that the real purpose is to develop the flexibility of the mind, not to uncover some eldrich secrets.

Chapter Eight
Mantras: Formulas of Power

- Choose a mantra. Keep it running in the back of your mind as much as you can as you go about your day. Notice whether or not it helps you maintain a particular state of mind. Some results might be surprising—for example, as your mind clears, you may discover tensions you've never noticed before. You may conclude that the mantra makes you tense, when in reality it just uncovers tensions you were previously unconscious of.

- Develop a mantra for each of the four (or five) elements, or borrow a traditional one. In ritual, meditate on each element while repeating your mantra a set number of times (108 is a good number). When you need to call upon that element use its mantra—for example, if you want to clear your mind, call upon air with its mantra.

- Create a formula of an important occult truth, so that you can call upon it in a single word during ritual. For example, if the idea that everything is one is important to your magical practice, you might create a formula that asserts that truth. EIO, for example, abbreviates "everything is one" and can also be analyzed as a glyph of a crown turned sideways, or as the sun rising behind mountains.

- Make a magical formula based on the tables of correspondences in appendix 2 or 3. Use the tarot correspondences of the Hebrew or English alphabets to make a word of power for a particular aim. Activate it by repeating it a number of times in the appropriate state of mind (i.e., while visualizing the outcome intently), and use it when appropriate to trigger its effects.

Chapter Nine
Magical Narrative: Metaphor, Myth, Ritual, and Theurgy

- Identify the metaphors that define your opinion of magic. Look for statements with the word *is* in them, especially ones that seem obviously true, such as "All is one" and "Everything is energy." What assumptions do those metaphors make that might not apply if you chose other metaphors instead? What advantages do they offer?

- Apply the "Journey of the Hero" structure to ritual. First, analyze rituals with which you are familiar, seeing how and if they fit into this structure. Then, try using it to design rituals, as described in the chapter.

- Create a theurgic ritual to connect you to your chosen view of the divine. Make it simple enough to perform daily and do so for an extended period of time (such as three months). Note any changes in your life as a result.

Chapter Ten
Self-Talk: The Janus of Words

- What dualities do you assume about the world that limit your experience of it—such as male/female, or smart/stupid? In what ways can you break down these binaries and experience them afresh, without making the assumption of duality?

- Identify some of the habits of negative self-talk that you have, if any. Try to replace negative self-talk with more realistic statements. For example, if you routinely tell yourself that you can't do something, replace that thought each time it occurs with the thought "I don't know how to do this yet, but I could learn to."

- Choose an antimagic word, such as *should* or *never*, and count the number of times you say it aloud or to yourself in a day. Keep track in a small notebook, and continue the exercise for three days. Notice how you feel as you use the word less and less frequently.

Glossary

abjad: A method of writing in which consonants are written, but vowels are frequently left out. Very common in Semitic languages.

alliteration: A poetic device involving the repetition of initial sounds of words.

alphabet: A system of writing in which each separate sound is given its own symbol.

alveolar: A sound involving stopping or restricting the airflow at the alveolar ridge, such as /t/ and /s/.

alveolar ridge: A hard ridge of tissue just behind the upper teeth.

approximant: A sound made by restricting the airflow slightly, such as /w/ and /y/.

assonance: A poetic device involving the repetition of vowel sounds.

axiology: The field of philosophy concerned with moral and aesthetic value.

charactres: The nonlinguistic symbols appearing on defixiones.

chemognosis: The use of drugs to achieve an altered state of consciousness for the purposes of magic.

code: A set of assumptions about symbols that aid interpretation.

consonance: A poetic device involving the repetition of consonant sounds.

consonant: A sound that involves the obstruction or stopping of the airflow, such as /f/, /p/, and /w/.

daven: A Jewish prayer, often involving a swaying motion.

defixio (*pl.* defixiones): A traditional magical operation that involves writing desires on a lead plate and throwing them into a well or other hole in the earth.

dental: A sound involving obstruction or stopping of the airflow near or on the teeth, such as the /th/ in *those.*

derive: A technique of mental exercise or exploration involving an aimless drifting around a locale.

Enochian: A magical "language" involving the names of angels and methods to invoke them. Invented by John Dee and Edward Kelley in the sixteenth century.

evocations: A magical operation involving summoning or contacting a spirit outside of one's sense of self.

felicity condition: The set of situations or requirements for a speech act to be regarded as effective.

formula: A magical word containing an entire idea or magical teaching.

fricative: A sound involving the obstruction of the airflow to the point of turbulence, characterized by hissing, such as /s/ and /f/.

gematria: A method of analyzing words in Hebrew, and sometimes other languages, on the basis of their numerical values.

general semantics: A philosophy developed by Alfred Korzybski that advocates the careful regulation of language in order to think more clearly and effectively.

glottal: A sound that involves the obstruction or stopping of the airflow in the glottis, such as /h/ or the catch in the throat in *uh-oh*.

Goetia: A type of magic involving the summoning of demons; a grimoire of that name.

Hexcraft: An American folk-magic tradition based on German, Native American, and Christian magical practices.

high vowels: Vowels that involve a wide open mouth, rather than a relatively closed mouth, such as /a/ and /o/.

Hoodoo: An American folk-magic tradition based on African, Native American, and Christian magical practices.

ideographic writing: A method of writing involving symbols that stand for ideas rather than sounds.

ideolect: A personal language, or the personal version of a language.

illocutionary speech: An utterance that in itself also constitutes an action, such as "I now pronounce you husband and wife."

International Phonetic Alphabet (IPA): An artificial alphabet designed to depict every possible speech sound unambiguously and accurately.

isopsephia: A mystical method of interpreting Greek involving reducing words to their numerical equivalence.

labial: A sound involving the obstruction or stopping of the airflow at the lips.

liminal: A state between two other states.

linguistics: The systematic and scientific study of language.

low vowels: Vowels made with the mouth relatively closed, rather than wide open, such as /i/ and /e/.

mala: A string of beads used to count prayers in Hinduism and Buddhism.

mantra: A word of mystical significance, usually repeated to achieve a spiritual or magical goal.

metaphor: A figure of speech in which one thing (the target) is equated to another thing (the source), with the intention of transferring characteristics of the source to the target.

metaphor, antilogical: *See* metaphor, paralogical.

metaphor, paralogical: A metaphor in which the characteristics of the source are not easily mapped onto the target.

monomyth: A single story, of which all other myths are simply parts or versions.

nasal: A sound, either consonant or vowel, that involves diverting some of the airflow through the nose, such as /m/ or /n/.

nefesh: The animal part of the soul in the Qabalah.

neophyte: In some magical traditions, a new initiate.

notariqon: A method of qabalistic analysis that involves using the initial letters of words to create an acronym.

numen (*pl.* **numines**): A Roman god, often imagined as an impersonal force or power.

onomatopoeia: A poetic device in which the sound of the word depicts its meaning, such as *bang* and *meow*.

orthography: The system of writing of a particular language; not all languages have orthographies. *See also* alphabet, ideographic writing, and syllabary.

parataxis: The practice of joining phrases and clauses with a conjunction like *and*. Common in oral poetry.

performative: An utterance that performs an act, rather than simply reports it. Performative actions are illocutionary.

perlocutionary: An utterance that reports, but does not commit, an act.

phatic: Communication concerned with making connections, rather than conveying information. "Good morning" is a phatic communication.

phonetic: The study of speech sounds.

pragmatics: The study of language in use and the meaning of context.

presymbolic communication: Forms of communication that do not involve language, such as crying, laughing, growling, and so on.

Qabalah: A mystical system, originally Jewish but now often used in other systems of magic, that uses the analysis of numbers and words, as well as a complex cosmology, to achieve union with God.

relexification: The practice of replacing a word with another, often made-up, word.

rhyme: A poetic device in which the vowel sound and last consonant sounds of a word's final syllables are the same as another word's.

Rule Zero: A personal rule: if anything—ritual elaboration, necessary materials, or whatever—prevents you from actually performing magic, throw it away.

samadhi: A state of consciousness in which one experiences a profound mental silence.

samatha: The practice of slowing or stopping the thoughts.

self-talk: Internal utterances that shape a person's expectations, self-image, and mood.

semantic satiation: The phenomenon of a word losing its meaning due to repetition or overfamiliarity.

semantics: The study of meaning (not to be confused with general semantics).

semiotic: The formal study of signs and symbols.

sigil: A magical symbol, usually one invented by the magician himself or herself, for a specific purpose.

sorko: A specific type of Songhai sorcerer, skilled in incantation.

stop: A sound in which the airflow is completely cut off, such as /p/ and /k/.

subvocalize: To speak silently to oneself, making minute movements of the tongue and mouth, as if speaking aloud.

surrealism: An artistic movement of the early twentieth century, involving the spontaneous creation of art.

syllabary: A type of writing in which each symbol represents a single syllable, rather than a sound or idea.

synecdoche: A metaphor in which a part stands in for the whole.

syntax: The study of the ways in which words arrange themselves into grammatical utterances.

temurah: A method of qabalistic analysis in which letters are rearranged to create new words, much like anagrams.

thaumaturgy: Practical magic.

theophagy: The mystical act of eating a deity, symbolically or otherwise.

theurgy: Magical practice involving communication or unity with gods.

tziruf: A form of qabalistic analysis in which letters are replaced systematically in order to yield new words.

unvoiced: A sound in which the vocal cords do not vibrate, such as /p/ and /s/.

velar: A sound involving the restriction or stopping of the airflow in the velum, the place where the hard and soft palate meet.

Verfremdungseffekt: The "alienation effect," a phenomenon in which something familiar is made strange by artistic or other means.

vipassana: Insight or mindfulness meditation.

voice qualification: Changes to the voice that do not change phonemes, but may convey pragmatic meaning. For example, crying, whispering, and so forth.

voiced: A sound in which the vocal cords vibrate, such as /b/ and /z/.

vowel: A sustainable sound involving no restriction of the airflow.

Bibliography

The American Heritage Dictionary of the English Language. Boston: Houghton Mifflin, 2000. Index of Semitic Roots.

Artisson, Robin. *The Witching Way of the Hollow Hill: The Gramarye of the Folk Who Dwell Below the Mound*. [No location]: Veritas Numquam Perit, 2006.

Austin, J. L. *How to Do Things with Words: Second Edition*. Cambridge, MA: Harvard University Press, 2005.

Barrett, Francis. *The Magus: A Complete System of Occult Philosophy*. York Beach, ME: Samuel Weiser, 2000.

Barry, Kieren. *The Greek Qabalah: Alphabetic Mysticism and Numerology in the Ancient World*. York Beach, ME: Samuel Weiser, 1999.

Beck, Judith. *Cognitive Therapy: Basics and Beyond*. New York: Guilford Press, 1995.

Bernstein, Henrietta. *Cabalah Primer*. Marina del Rey, CA: De Vorss, 1984.

Betz, Hans Dieter. *The Greek Magical Papyri in Translation*. Chicago: University of Chicago Press, 1997.

Bloomfeld, Maurice, trans. *Hymns of the Atharva Veda. Sacred Books of the East, Vol. 42*. Oxford: Oxford University Press, 1897. Online at http://www.sacred-texts.com/hin/sbe42/av140.htm (accessed 4 November 2007).

Buber, Martin. *I and Thou*. Walter Kaufmann, trans. New York: Simon & Schuster, 1970.

Burkert, Walter. *Greek Religion*. John Raffan, trans. Cambridge, MA: Harvard University Press, 1985.

Buzan, Tony. *The Mind Map Book: How to Use Radiant Thinking to Maximize Your Brain's Untapped Potential*. New York: Plume, 1996.

Campbell, Joseph. *The Hero with a Thousand Faces*. Princeton, NJ: Princeton University Press, 1972.

Carmichael, Alexander. *Carmina Gadelica: Hymns and Incantations Collected in the Highlands and Islands of Scotland in the Last Century*. Edinburgh, UK: Floris, 1992.

Carroll, Peter J. *Liber Kaos*. York Beach, ME: Samuel Weiser, 1992.

———. *Liber Null & Psychonaut*. York Beach, ME: Samuel Weiser, 1991.

Catford, J. C. *A Practical Introduction to Phonetics*. Oxford: Claredon Press, 1998.

Christenson, Larry. *Answering Your Questions About Speaking in Tongues*. Minneapolis: Bethany House, 2005 [1968].

Coward, Harold G., and David J. Goa. *Mantra: Hearing the Divine in India and America*. New York: Columbia University Press, 2004.

Crane, Hart. "A Letter to Harriet Monroe." *O My Land, My Friends: The Selected Letters of Hart Crane*. Langdon Hammer and Brom Weber, eds. New York: Four Walls Eight Windows, 1997.

Crowley, Aleister. *777 & Other Qabalistic Writings*. York Beach, ME: Weiser, 1986.

——. "Liber Samekh: Theurgia Goetia Summa Congressus Cum Daemone." In *Magick: Liber Aba : Book 4*. Boston: Weiser, 1998. Online at http://www.hermetic.com/crowley/libers/lib800.html (accessed 22 April 2008).

——. *Magick Without Tears*. Scottsdale, AZ: New Falcon, 1991.

Derrida, Jacques. *On Grammatology*. Gayatri Chakravorty Spivak, trans. Baltimore: Johns Hopkins University Press, 1976.

Dukes, Ramsey. *S.S.O.T.B.M.E. Revised: An Essay on Magic*. London: The Mouse That Spins, 2002 (third revised edition).

Dunn, Patrick. *Postmodern Magic: The Art of Magic in the Information Age*. Woodbury, MN: Llewellyn, 2005.

DuQuette, Lon Milo. *The Magick of Aleister Crowley: A Handbook of the Rituals of Thelema*. Boston: Weiser, 2003.

Easwaran, Eknath. *Meditation: A Simple Eight-Point Program for Translating Spiritual Ideals into Daily Life*. Tomales, CA: Nilgiri Press, 1991.

Easwaran, Eknath, trans. *The Upanishads*. Tomales, CA: Nilgiri Press, 1987.

Ellis, Albert. *Handbook of Rational-Emotive Therapy*. New York: Springer Publishing, 1977.

Etkes, Immanuel. *The Gaon of Vilna: The Man and His Image*. Jeffrey M. Green, trans. Berkeley, CA: University of California Press, 2002.

Frater U.·. D.·., *Practical Sigil Magic: Creating Personal Symbols for Success*. St. Paul, MN: Llewellyn, 1990.

Fries, Jan. *Visual Magic: A Manual of Freestyle Shamanism*. Oxford, UK: Mandrake, 1992.

"Glossolalia in Contemporary Linguistic Study." Metareligion. http://www.meta-religion.com/Linguistics/Glossolalia/contemporary_linguistic_study.htm (accessed 22 April 2008).

Goddard, Dwight, and Henri Borel, trans. *Tao Te Ching*. Whitefish, MT: Kessinger, 1919. Online at http://www.sacred-texts.com/tao/ltw/index.htm (accessed 16 May 2008).

Godwin, David. *Godwin's Cabalistic Encyclopedia: A Complete Guide to Cabalistic Magick*. St. Paul, MN: Llewellyn, 1989.

——. *Light in Extension: Greek Magic from Homer to Modern Times*. St. Paul, MN: Llewellyn, 1992.

Grasso, Stephen. "Beneath the Pavement, the Beast." In *Generation Hex*. Jason Louv, ed. New York: Disinformation, 2006.

Griffith, F. Ll., and Herbert Thompson. *The Demotic Magical Papyrus of London and Leiden*. New York: Dover, 1974 [1904]. Online at http://www.sacred-texts.com/egy/dmp/dmp19.htm (accessed 22 April 2008).

Hafele, J. C., and R. E. Keating. "Around-the-World Atomic Clocks: Predicted Relativistic Time Gains." *Science* 177 (1972).

Hale-Evans, Ron. *Mind Performance Hacks: Tips & Tools for Overclocking Your Brain*. Sebastopol, CA: O'Reilly, 2006.

Harner, Michael. *The Way of the Shaman*. San Francisco: Harper, 1990.

Hayakawa, S. I. *Language in Thought and Action*. New York: Harcourt Brace, 1990 [1939].

Herodotus. Book II, chapter 2. Perseus Digital Library Project. A. D. Godley, ed. Tufts University. Online at http://www.perseus.tufts.edu/GreekScience/hdtbk2.html (accessed 22 April 2008).

Hoffman, John George. *Pow-Wows; or, Long Lost Friend*. [No location: self-published], 1820. Online at http://www.sacred-texts.com/ame/pow/index.htm (accessed 21 April 2008).

Iamblichus. *De Mysteriis*. Emma C. Clarke, et al., trans. Atlanta: Society of Biblical Literature, 2003.

James, William. *The Varieties of Religious Experiences*. New York: Modern Library, 1999 (1902).

Jarrett, R. H. *It Works*. Camarillo, CA: DeVorss & Company, 1976.

Klauser, Henriette Anne. *Write It Down, Make It Happen: Knowing What You Want—and Getting It!* New York: Fireside, 2000.

Korzybski, Alfred. *Science and Sanity: An Introduction to Non-Aristotelian Systems and General Semantics*. Fort Worth, TX: Institute of General Semantics, 1995.

Kraig, Donald Michael. *Modern Magick: Eleven Lessons in the High Magickal Arts*. St. Paul, MN: Llewellyn, 1988.

Krapp, George P., and Elliot V. K. Dobbie. *The Exeter Book*. New York: Columbia University Press, 1936.

Lakoff, George. *Moral Politics: How Liberals and Conservatives Think*. Chicago: University of Chicago Press, 2002.

Lakoff, George, and Mark Johnson. *Metaphors We Live By*. Chicago: Chicago University Press, 1980.

Lord, Albert B. *The Singer of Tales*. Cambridge, MA: Harvard University Press, 2000.

Luck, Georg. *Arcana Mundi: Magic and the Occult in the Greek and Roman Worlds*. Baltimore: Johns Hopkins University Press, 1985.

Magnus, Margaret. "Magical Letter Page." http://www.conknet.com/~mmagnus/ (accessed 29 April 2008).

Mathers, S. L. MacGregor. *The Kabbalah Unveiled*. York Beach, ME: Weiser, 1992.

Nema. *Maat Magick: A Guide to Self-Initiation*. York Beach, ME: Weiser, 1995.

Newton, Isaac, trans. "The Emerald Tablet of Hermes." Internet Sacred Texts Archives. http://www.sacred-texts.com/alc/emerald.htm (accessed 18 April 2008).

Ong, Walter. *Orality and Literacy: The Technologizing of the Word*. New York: Routledge, 1982.

Plato. *Phaedrus*. Benjamin Jowett, trans. New York: C. Scribner's Sons, 1871. Online at http://www.sacred-texts.com/cla/plato/phaedrus .htm. (accessed 21 April 2008).

Plotinus. *The Enneads*. Stephen MacKenna, trans. Burdett, New York: Larson Publications, 2004.

Reddy, M. J. "The Conduit Metaphor—A Case of Frame Conflict in Our Language about Language." In *Metaphor and Thought*. A. Ortony, ed. Cambridge: Cambridge University Press, 1979.

Regardie, Israel. *Foundations of Practical Magic*. Wellingborough, UK: The Aquarian Press, 1979.

———. *The Golden Dawn*. St. Paul, MN: Llewellyn, 1986.

———. *The Tree of Life: An Illustrated Study in Magic*. Chic Cicero and Sandra Tabatha Cicero, eds. St. Paul, MN: Llewellyn, 2000.

Ruhlen, Merritt. *The Origin of Language: Tracing the Evolution of the Mother Tongue*. New York: Wiley, 1994.

Sarangerel. *Chosen by the Spirits: Following Your Shamanic Calling*. Rochester, VT: Destiny Books, 2001.

Smith, Huston. *The World's Religions: Our Great Wisdom Traditions*. San Francisco: Harper, 1991 [1958].

Spare, A. O. *The Book of Pleasure (Self-Love): The Psychology of Ecstasy*. Oxford, UK: I-H-O Books, 2005.

———. *The Zoetic Grimoire of Zos*. London: Fulgur, 1998. http://www .hermetic.com/spare/grimoire_of_zos.html (accessed 29 April 2008).

"Speaking in Tongues." Religious Tolerance. http://www.religioustoler- ance.org/tongues1.htm (accessed November 4, 2007).

Stoller, Paul, and Cheryl Olkes. *In Sorcery's Shadow: A Memoir of Apprenticeship among the Songhay of Niger*. Chicago: University of Chicago Press, 1989.

Taliesin. "I Am Taliesin. I Sing Perfect Metre." Ifor Williams, trans., 1999. http://www.cs.rice.edu/~ssiyer/minstrels/poems/175.html (accessed 21 April 2008). Also available in a print version in the *Mabinogion*.

Turner, Victor. *The Ritual Process: Structure and Anti-Structure*. Ithaca, NY: Cornell University Press, 1977.

Tyson, Donald. *Enochian Magic for Beginners: The Original System of Angel Magic*. Woodbury, MN: Llewellyn, 2005.

Whitcomb, Bill. *The Magician's Reflection: A Complete Guide to Creating Personal Magical Symbols and Systems*. St. Paul, MN: Llewellyn, 1999.

Yelle, Robert A. *Explaining Mantras: Ritual, Rhetoric, and the Dream of a Natural Language in Hindu Tantra*. New York: Routledge, 2003.

Index

 **Free Magazine**

Read unique
articles by Llewellyn
authors, recommendations by experts,
and information on new releases. To receive a free copy of
Llewellyn's consumer magazine, New Worlds of Mind &
Spirit, simply call 1-877-NEW-WRLD or visit our website
at www.llewellyn.com and click on New Worlds.

LLEWELLYN ORDERING INFORMATION

Order Online:
Visit our website at www.llewellyn.com, select your books, and order them on
our secure server.

Order by Phone:
- Call toll-free within the U.S. at 1-877-NEW-WRLD
  (1-877-639-9753). Call toll-free within Canada at
  1-866-NEW-WRLD (1-866-639-9753)
- We accept VISA, MasterCard, and American Express

Order by Mail:
Send the full price of your order (MN residents add 7% sales tax) in
U.S. funds, plus postage & handling to:

> Llewellyn Worldwide
> 2143 Wooddale Drive, Dept. 978-0-7387-1360-1
> Woodbury, MN 55125-2989, U.S.A.

Postage & Handling:
Standard (U.S., Mexico, & Canada). If your order is:
$24.99 and under, add $3.00
$25.00 and over, FREE STANDARD SHIPPING

AK, HI, PR: $15.00 for one book plus $1.00 for
each additional book.

International Orders (airmail only):
$16.00 for one book plus $3.00 for each additional book

Orders are processed within 2 business days.
Please allow for normal shipping time. Postage and handling rates subject to change.

Postmodern Magic
The Art of Magic in the Information Age

PATRICK DUNN

Fresh ideas for the modern mage are at the heart of this thought-provoking guide to magic theory. Approaching magical practice from an information paradigm, Patrick Dunn provides a unique and contemporary perspective on an ancient practice.

Imagination, psychology, and authority—the most basic techniques of magic—are introduced first. From there, Dunn teaches all about symbol systems, magical artifacts, sigils, spirits, elementals, languages, and magical journeys, and explains their significance in magical practice. There are also exercises for developing magic skills, along with techniques for creating talismans, glamours, servitors, divination decks, modern defixios, and your own astral temple. Dunn also offers tips on aura detection, divination, occult networking, and conducting your own magic research.

978-0-7387-0663-4

264 pages $14.95

Magic of Qabalah
Visions of the Tree of Life

Kala Trobe

This introduction to the Golden Dawn system of Qabalah covers the usual ground in an unusual way. It uses creative visualizations and analysis of mythologies and tarot symbolism to bring the reader into a direct, personal experience of this universal system. Use the exercises for specific purposes as diverse as physical/spiritual courage (Geburah), integration (Binah), and magickal foundation building (Malkuth).

The introduction provides a condensed history of the Qabalah, along with a quick trip up the Tree of Life to familiarize the novice with the system, plus information on its metaphysical context and use of tarot attributions.

Ten chapters follow, one for each Sephirah—containing an exploration of its traits and contemporary application, a brief description of the Path by which one might mentally arrive at the desired destination, and information on the God names, angels, and symbols. Each chapter culminates in a guided creative visualization.

978-0-7387-0002-1
312 pages

$14.95

Enochian Magic for Beginners
The Original System of Angel Magic

Donald Tyson

The most remarkable artifact in the entire history of spirit communication is the legacy of the Enochian angels, who presented themselves to the famed Elizabethan mathematician Dr. John Dee through his seer, the alchemist Edward Kelley, between the years 1582 and 1589. Enochian magic is a method for summoning and commanding angelic beings and demons, although the angels gave Dee strict instructions never to use the magick for evoking evil spirits. Now, *Enochian Magic for Beginners* provides this system in its complete and original form.

Newcomers to Enochian magic will not find a clearer or more comprehensive overview. Experienced Enochian scholars will be pleasantly surprised by how many gaps in the communications have finally been filled in. Donald Tyson gives all of the essential magical teachings of the angels along with the necessary symbols, sigils, and letter squares required to put these teachings into practice. More importantly, he explains how these sigils and squares were derived and what they signify.

978-1-56718-747-2
408 pages $16.95

The Golden Dawn

The Original Account of the Teachings,
Rites & Ceremonies of the Hermetic Order as
Revealed by Israel Regardie

Originally published in four bulky volumes of some 1,200 pages, this complete 6th revised and enlarged edition is compiled in one volume! It includes additional notes—by Regardie, Cris Monnastre, and others—and an index of more than 100 pages! All of the original pagination is retained in marginal notations for reference.

Also included are Initiation Ceremonies, important rituals for consecration and invocation, methods of meditation and magical working based on the Enochian Tablets, studies in the Tarot, and the system of Qabalistic Correspondences that unite the world's religions and magical traditions into a comprehensive and practical whole.

This volume is designed as a study and practice curriculum suited to both group and private practice. The 6th edition of *The Golden Dawn* is a complete reference encyclopedia of Western Magick.

978-0-87542-663-1
848 pages $34.95

The Tree of Life

An Illustrated Study in Magic

ISRAEL REGARDIE
EDITED AND ANNOTATED BY CHIC
CICERO AND SANDRA TABATHA CICERO

In 1932, when magic was a "forbidden subject," Israel Regardie wrote *The Tree of Life* at the age of 24. He believed that magic was a precise scientific discipline as well as a highly spiritual way of life, and he took on the enormous task of making it accessible to a wide audience of eager spiritual seekers. The result was this book, which adroitly presents a massive amount of diverse material in a remarkably unified whole.

From the day it was first published, The Tree of Life has remained in high demand by ceremonial magicians for its skillful combination of ancient wisdom and modern magical experience. It was Regardie's primary desire to point out the principles of magic that cut across all boundaries of time, religion, and culture—those fundamental principles common to all magic, regardless of any specific tradition or spiritual path.

978-1-56718-132-6
552 pages

$19.95

Modern Sex Magick
Secrets of Erotic Spirituality

Donald Michael Kraig
(Contributions by Linda Falorio, Nema, Tara, and Lola Babalon)

Deep within you is a center of power so potent and strong it defies imagination. Now you can learn to control and direct it when it's at its most intense and explosive moment—during sexual arousal. *Modern Sex Magick* provides easy and precise exercises that prepare you to use the magical energy raised during sexual activity, and then it shows you how to work with that energy to create positive changes in your life.

This is the first book to clearly reveal the secrets of Western sex magick without relying on Tantric theory. It explores the latest scientific discoveries in the field of human sexuality. This unique mixture of science and magick produces a simple fact: practicing these techniques will help you increase and extend your sexual pleasure! You will uncover depths of ecstasy experienced by only a few, and the results can enhance and deepen your relationships. Four powerful women sex magicians also contributed articles to this book.

978-1-56718-394-8
400 pages
$19.95